The Design Experience

The Design Experience

The Role of Design and Designers
in the Twenty-First Century

Mike Press and Rachel Cooper

Routledge
Taylor & Francis Group

LONDON AND NEW YORK

First published 2003 by Ashgate Publishing

2 Park Square, Milton Park, Abingdon, Oxon OX14 4RN
711 Third Avenue, New York, NY 10017, USA

Routledge is an imprint of the Taylor & Francis Group, an informa business

First issued in paperback 2016

British Library Cataloguing in Publication Data
Press, Mike
  – The design experience: the role of design and designers in
  the twenty-first century.
  1. Design. 2. Design, Industrial.
  I. Title. II. Cooper, Rachel, 1953–
  658.5'752

Library of Congress Cataloging-in-Publication Data
    The design experience: the role of design and designers in
  the twenty-first century/Mike Press and Rachel Cooper.
     p. cm.
  Includes bibliographical references.
  ISBN 978–0–566–07891–0
    1. Design, Industrial. I. Cooper, Rachel. II. Title.
  TS171.P72   2002
  745.2—dc21   2001046267

ISBN 978-0-566-07891-0 (hbk)
ISBN 978-1-138-27315-3 (pbk)

Typeset in Stone Serif by Wileman Design

Transfered to Digital Printing in 2012

Contents

List of boxes

List of tables

List of figures

Acknowledgements

As with our previous work, in developing the content and argument of this book we owe much to the many students, academic colleagues, designers and industrialists with whom we have worked. This has provided us with a rich tapestry of material for examples and case studies and also, unbeknown to them, our developing theories of the future of design and designers.

There are many sources of inspiration that have driven the ideas within this book. Firstly is the inspiration initiated by Noman Potter, whose book '*What is a Designer*', is still as valuable a contribution today as it was in 1966 when it was originally published. A visit to New York in 1995 involved discussions with Tucker Viemeister, Eric Chan and Wendy Brawer. Their perceptions, energy, radical insights and demonstration of design practices that are rooted in social responsibility and active citizenship proved essential in forming an early focus and direction for this book. Another key inspiration from the United States is the Design Management Institute and its President Earl Powell. The Institute's engagement with 'experience' as a research issue within corporate branding and industrial design, through both its conferences and *Design Management Journal*, has generated a wealth of ideas that we have drawn from.

On this side of the Atlantic, our involvement with the European Academy of Design and the *Design Journal* has provided us with a constant connection to the wealth of research, critical insights and methodological advances being made throughout all design disciplines. Through conversations, collaborations and conferences we have learned much from our research colleagues. Some deserve special mention for insights and approaches we have drawn on: Margaret Bruce, Katie Bunnell, Jack Ingram, Ray Holland, Bob Jerrard, Birgit Jevnaker, Julian Malins and Lisbeth Svengren.

Both individually and jointly we have conducted research projects with the Engineering and Physical Sciences Research Council, the Design Council and the Crafts Council. We are grateful for the opportunities provided by all these organisations to explore issues and test ideas, and for the encouragement and support provided by their staff. In particular we would like to thank Stephen Burroughs, Andrew Summers, Alison Huxley and Kim Davids, Vince Osgood, Jaqui Williams, Phil Burnell and Peter Hedges.

Our colleagues at Sheffield Hallam University's Art and Design Research Centre and the University of Salford's Design and Innovation Research Unit have been a constant source of inspiration and support. In a number of cases their insights have directly found their way into these pages either through collaboration or discussion. So thanks to Caroline Davey, Tom Fisher, Kate Shepherd, Jim Roddis, Chris Rust, Anne Tomes, Karen Yair, Andrew Wooton and especially Jo Heeley who has been an invaluable collaborator with us both for several years.

On the publishing side, we are particularly indebted to Suzie Duke at Ashgate who has pushed and cajoled us along the way, to our desk editor Ellen Keeling, and to Pauline Brooke who has with patience provided secretarial support.

This book simply would not have been written without the support of our partners – Hazel White and Cary Cooper – and the understanding patience of Rachel's daughters Sarah and Laura. Calum Press was born the day after the book's manuscript was completed. This book is dedicated to him for helping to speed the project along during its latter stages, and for providing the best experience of all.

Figure 2.16 on page 60 is reprinted from *Journal of Product Innovation Management*, Vol. 11, Cooper, R. G., 'Third Generation New Product Processes', pp. 3–14, copyright 1994, with permission from Elsevier Science.

The JBL car audio case study in Chapter 2 is reproduced courtesy of the *Design Management Journal* (volume 7, number 4, Fall 1996), a publication of:
The Design Management Institute
29 Temple Place
Boston, MA 02111
Phone: 617-338-6380
Fax: 617-338-6570
dmistaff@dmi.org
www.dmi.org

Introduction

The task is no longer to design for a universal audience, or national groups, or market segments, or even the ideological abstraction known as 'the consumer'. Despite the continuing role of mass-production in many societies, the task is to design for the individual placed in his or her immediate context. Our products should support the individual in the effort to become an active participant in culture, searching for locally significant coherence and connection. Products should be personal pathways in the otherwise confusing ecology of culture.

Richard Buchanan, Professor of Design, Carnegie Mellon University[1]

GREEN, UNIVERSAL AND DIGITAL

Operating from her cramped office in New York's Lower East Side, Wendy Brawer's Modern World Design combines the functions of a design consultancy, networking hub, information centre and educational think-tank on environmental design. In 1991 Wendy began work on a simple yet revolutionary idea which aimed to change the way people viewed and used New York. Her Green Apple Map (Figure 0.1) challenged residents and visitors to 'experience our city a whole new way!' The city's street plan was mapped, with initially 200 positive features in the urban ecology, including cycle paths, community gardens, greenmarkets and

Figure 0.1   Green Apple Map
Wendy Brawer and Green Maps
Source: Wendy Brawer, *Modern World Design*

ecologically designed buildings, together with some of the more rotten parts of the Green Apple.

Maps are powerful tools, shaping our view of the space around us and charting new possibilities for exploration. Wendy Brawer's Green Apple Map is a particularly compelling example of how maps can change viewpoints and spur people to action. Through a website (www.greenmap.org) and tireless networking by e-mail and conferences, Wendy has seen her idea taken up worldwide by allowing her mapping icons and design methods to be used freely by others. As the 1990s drew to a close, over 100 Green Map projects were under way in 30 countries, with maps already published for Toronto, Barcelona, Liverpool, Tororo in Uganda and 20 other cities. The New York map is now in its fourth edition and is accompanied by an interactive web-based version, and the Green Map System has received a National Design Award from the President's Council on Sustainable Development. Evidence suggests that Green Maps, now available for more than 75 cities, towns and regions, have provided a spur to environmental school projects, raised trade for eco-businesses and increased visits to urban nature trails, community gardens and other eco-projects. In short, these maps are indeed beginning to change our experience of city life.

Picture a woman walking down the street. She is a stooped figure, holding a walking stick in her right hand; her unkempt grey hair falls over her thick glasses. The woman, who appears to be well into her 80s, is hard of hearing, and her stumbling and uncertain gait show that she clearly has difficulties in walking. This woman is in fact a late 20-something designer from Raymond Loewy's New York office. In 1980, Patricia Moore embarked on a three-year experiment disguised as an 85-year-old, travelling around North America to experience life as a senior citizen. Bandages around her knees restricted her leg movement; sellotape wrapped around her fingers beneath her gloves simulated arthritis. She had impaired her hearing and vision and dressed in the clothing we associate with an old woman. The prejudice and discrimination she faced astonished her, as did the overall inability of the designed environment to cope with her particular needs.

Patricia Moore's pioneering research plunged the youthful design world into the experience of being an older person and as a consequence gave rise to the Universal Design movement which aims to improve the accessibility and adaptability of products and environments. At a time when populations throughout the industrialised world are ageing rapidly, with life expectancy rising, the birthrate slowing down and most consumer spending power already in the hands of those aged over 50, design professionals have to find new ways of seeing the world through the eyes of others, involving older people in the process of design and improving their experience of the designed world. The Good Grips range of kitchen tools, developed by Smart Design, is one example of applied Universal Design, providing a wide selection of utensils from vegetable peelers to kettles that combine elegance, durability and usability for all consumers, regardless of age. Such products are making the experience of preparing food easier and more enjoyable for both the arthritic and the able-bodied.

In a feature on her work in *Crafts* magazine in 1990, Jane Harris described herself as 'making cloth that becomes clothes that are also sculptures'. Regarded as one of the leading and most innovative UK textile designers of her generation, Jane produced delicately flowing and sculpted forms in cloth that expressed and embodied her patiently acquired craft skill and knowledge through working with constructed textiles by knitting, weaving and embroidery. Her work was exhibited in craft galleries and exhibitions throughout the world.

Figure 0.2   Digital textiles by Jane Harris

A decade later, Jane Harris still creates intricately flowing and sculpted forms that exploit the interactive movement between body and cloth, but no longer with loom and yarn. Using mouse, screen, scanner and an array of software packages, she crafts her virtual textiles to add realism to digital imaging (Figure 0.2). From her doctoral research, Jane is developing new techniques for creating realistic movement in textiles that can be applied in special effects for cinema and video. She is one of an increasing number of designers who move seamlessly between hand making and digital techniques, and in the process give form to the emergent craft of the new media. She demonstrates how the very experience of designing is undergoing a radical shift.

BEYOND THE TWENTIETH CENTURY

Things were so much simpler in the old days – way back in 1990. At the dawn of the twentieth century's closing decade, there was every reason to believe that the designer 1980s was merely the prelude to a golden age of design in which 'the profession' would find its rightful place in the powerhouse of industry and commerce. In London you could hardly move for thrusting young design consultants in yellow spectacles, wielding metal briefcases. Their salaries were spiralling up on the thermals of the consumer boom. The multi-billion-pound consultancy industry had just been celebrated in London's new Design Museum, founded by Sir Terence Conran, who at the time presided over the Storehouse design-led retail empire.

The newly launched *Design Management Journal*, published by the US-based Design Management Institute, provided evidence that design was at last being taken seriously in business schools and in the corridors of corporate power. And of course in government too. The UK's prime minister in 1990 was a great champion of design, convinced that it was part of the UK economy's competitive salvation. Business managers were deluged with books, brochures and videos with titles such as 'Win by Design', 'Winning Ways', 'Competing by Design', 'Design: the Competitive Edge'. In the UK Mrs Thatcher presided over design's glory days.

Two years later much had already changed. Mrs Thatcher was gone, and so too were many designers, as the design consultancy industry collapsed dramatically, more than halving in size, with the onset of recession. Conran had long been ousted as head of Storehouse, which by 1992 had sold off his original Habitat chain to Sweden's IKEA.

Other changes were under way in the early 1990s that would have a major impact on design. In 1992 many of the UK's art colleges and polytechnics, which provided degree-level education in design, were being transformed into 'new' universities as part of a series of educational reforms that involved a massive increase in student numbers. Just at the time when the design professions were being subjected to a recessional pruning, so the new universities were producing record numbers of graduates in design disciplines. This called into question the vocational rationale of design education and its future direction. Accompanying this came new pressures and incentives for design education to develop research activities and thus define the nature of scholarship in their disciplines.

In 1990 an event occurred that attracted next to no attention at the time. At the European Particle Physics Laboratory a UK computer scientist, Tim Berners-Lee, developed a new computer networking program. He named it the World Wide Web.

DEVELOPING A NEW AGENDA

In 1995 we wrote a book called *The Design Agenda: a guide to successful design management*.[2] It was written for managers and business students, aiming both to demonstrate the value of well-managed design and to provide methods that could be applied by companies large and small in placing design on the corporate agenda and harnessing its competitive power. Researched and written in the first half of the 1990s, *The Design Agenda* drew largely on the fast-developing field of design management research in both the UK and the USA.

Writing the book was driven by a strong personal commitment held by both of us that design was underused and undervalued by UK industry especially, and what was needed was some convincing evidence and evangelising for our captains of industry. Design management therefore provided the key to getting design taken seriously.

We still stand by this, but by the late 1990s it was clear that something else was needed as well – design graduates who have an acute sense of changing times, a sense of self-definition and direction, who take initiative, who can 'see the world through other people's eyes' and can take a principled, responsible position in a complex and dangerous world. We also recognised that our focus on issues of management and business needed to be broadened to include other perspectives from the social sciences that were exploring the cultural and social significance of design.

The Design Experience is a book about the changing nature of design – and in particular the changing roles of designers – at the start of the third millennium. It is written primarily for students of design to help them make some sense of the turbulent currents of change around them and to find a sense of place in their world. It will also be of interest to students of business, cultural studies and others who have an interest in what designers do and how they should view design's place in our culture and economy.

We have written this book for three main reasons: first, because self-definition has never been a particular strength of the design community and, indeed, as we will argue later, there is much evidence that what designers say they do often runs counter to what they actually do; second, as a consequence of this, because designers too often constrain their ambitions and aspirations, thereby limiting their potential contribution to society; and third, because the world is changing at an ever-increasing rate. Understanding change, dealing with it and developing strategies to gain a sense of personal direction are essential for all of us. *The Design Experience* aims to provide a bridge between the literatures of design management, design theory and cultural studies and in the process develop a perspective of design that is more inclusive, balanced, relevant and empowering for the designers of tomorrow.

This book is much like Wendy Brawer's Green Apple Map. We identify various features on the landscape of contemporary design – different perspectives and examples. How you use this, and the routes you travel in your own personal design experience, are up to you. Much of the book represents starting-points for further reading and consideration, and for this reason we have included a glossary. But of course, like Wendy, we have been selective in what we have included – we want you to experience design in a wholly new way.

WHAT IS A DESIGNER?

Over thirty years ago, the late Norman Potter wrote *What is a designer: things, places, messages*, and to this day, no better exploration to this question has been written. Norman Potter concludes his challenging and radical book with these words:

> Design is thus simultaneously a realm of values and a matter of engrossingly particular decisions, many of which are highly technical. There is a threshold up to which we can quantify, and this is often enough the task for a professional: less an equation of meaning than one of ordered evidence. Beyond this threshold, design is strictly a cultural option. It always has been. We humble ourselves, we sharpen our wits, and we offer, at the very least, our moments of lucidity. Our concern is always 'the place of value in a world of facts', but there is no role waiting for us, there is merely the chance of making one out of the sheer courage of our perceptions. In the same way, if you want to link hands with the spirit of the modern movement, it won't come to meet you; you must go out and make it your own.[3]

However much our world has changed, and will change in the future, these words still hold true. Design is a value-driven activity. In creating change, designers impose values upon the world – values of their own or those of their client. To be a designer is a cultural option: designers create culture, create experience and meaning for people. And finally, designers make their own futures – this is their most crucial creation. Design education provides possibilities, challenges, skills and understanding, and, with these, they make their lives.

A designer is a maker. This definition works on a number of different levels. First, and most fundamentally, the activities and skills of making lie at the very heart of design. 'Craft' may have evolved culturally as a term that has become intellectually divorced from the pursuit of beauty (art) and purpose (design), but as a definition for the skills and knowledge that put things together, and make things work by using hand and brain in tandem, craft is an essential part of design.[4]

Second, the designer makes meaning possible. Crafting a design solution is merely the first part of a design process which is continued by users or consumers as part of their lives – or 'everyday consumption work' as Chaney describes it.[5] Every designed product, communication or environment provides human experiences. Wendy Brawer's Green Apple Map provides a new way of experiencing New York. Good Grips' kitchen tools provide an easier cooking experience for those with arthritis, Jane Harris's digital textiles enhance the realism and viewing experience of animated movies. And all experiences, whether in the city, kitchen, cinema or elsewhere, carry meaning and forms of representation. By enabling meaning, the designer is a maker of culture. As we will argue in the following chapter, the designer is a **cultural intermediary**.

Third, the designer makes their own definition of what it is to be a designer and how to use the distinctive skills, knowledge and thinking of design to find a place in the world. This is especially true in today's age of the knowledge economy, flexible employment patterns and fast-changing technology. Creativity, ingenuity and imagination are increasing in value in the new economy that is emerging, and these are qualities that design education encourages above all. At the same time, the old certainties regarding patterns of work and life-long careers are dissolving.

What designers actually do, how they work and earn a livelihood are no longer fixed ideas, if they ever really were. Opportunism, enterprise and flexibility are equally vital qualities that designers must possess. Wendy Brawer exemplifies how coming up with a good design idea is not enough. She brings her entrepreneurial skills and opportunistic use of new communication technologies together to turn this into a worldwide agent of change. Jane Harris shows how skills and knowledge learnt in one field of design can be applied to another related field.

So, designers are a combination of craftmaker, cultural intermediary and opportunistic entrepreneur. And of course they are other things as well. They are skilled researchers, life-long learners, who understand that design – as a very process of change itself – must be informed by changing knowledge. Indeed, design is an expression and embodiment of knowledge. Good Grips kitchen tools express our understanding of the changing ergonomic requirements of people in an ageing society. Part of this understanding comes from quite literally stepping into the shoes of users to research needs, as Patricia Moore did. Furthermore, Good Grips embodies a whole range of research into materials, usability and marketing. Jane Harris's digital textiles embody four years' painstaking doctoral research.

Designers are also adept communicators who can place their work in context and act as champions for it. Research and communication have always lain at the heart of design although they have been seen as somehow tangential to the creative process. Part of the new experience of being a designer is that they are now seen as central activities.

Finally, designers are active citizens. Again, they always have been, but during the Thatcherite glory days, design was seen solely as the engine of added value and competitiveness, and designers were seen as part of the business consultancy industry whose main job was to downsize, re-engineer, rationalise and tart up public utilities before they were sold off. In 1997, Tony Blair's New Labour government signalled a change in this narrow view of design. Alongside growing encouragement for design to contribute to innovation and competitiveness were policy measures to use design to tackle social and environmental problems and contribute to the national culture in more inclusive ways. This rekindles the idea of responsible citizenship in the design professions – to use design as a form of social entrepreneurship concerned with the quality and experience of life for all people.

UNDERSTANDING THE DESIGN EXPERIENCE

The Design Experience explores the contexts, practices and roles of designers as we move into the Third Millennium. It links together two main, fundamental ideas. First, design must be seen increasingly as the process that creates meaningful experiences for people. Creating products, communications or environments is merely a means to this end. Designing for experience involves putting people first, seeing the world through their eyes and feeling with their senses. Second, the experience of being a designer is radically and irrevocably changing. New roles, methods and activities are emerging that place a far greater emphasis on innovative, relevant research linked to creative methods, effective communications and proactive entrepreneurship.

The first chapter, 'Design and consumer culture', presents a cultural perspective of design, drawing on research and analysis predominantly from sociology and cultural studies to examine how consumers create meaning from the experiences enabled through design. 'Design in industry and commerce' (Chapter 2) examines issues of competitiveness, innovation and design management, placing design in its economic and industrial context. 'Designing the experience' (Chapter 3) considers how we should view design as a creator of human experiences and the issues that are likely to affect it in the future. 'Research for design' (Chapter 4) discusses the new methods used by designers to understand users and consumers and explores some of the emerging issues in the new 'research culture' of design. 'Communicating design' (Chapter 5) is concerned with the role of communications in design – both the skill of the designer in interacting with design stakeholders and expressing design decision making using appropriate communication media. Finally, 'The design professions' (Chapter 6) examines the diversity of professional design and considers the recurrent issue of professional recognition. We question whether the idea of 'a profession' is actually limiting in that what was a source of weakness in the past may be a source of strength in redefining the role of tomorrow's designer.

IN SEARCH OF THE RELEVANT

It is a profound and necessary truth that the deep things in science are not found because they are useful; they are found because it was possible to find them.

Robert Oppenheimer, The Manhattan Project

If science is indeed the deep art of the possible, surely design is the deep art of the useful. Designers are prospectors for nuggets of usefulness and relevance in the fast-flowing waters of applied science.

That is the myth that design would like to believe, but unfortunately it was never true, and it is even further from the truth today: designers pursue the possible, when they should be pursuing the useful and relevant. In his pursuit of the possible, Robert Oppenheimer developed the atomic bomb and in our pursuit of the possible we develop cultural irrelevance, unusability, dysfunctionality and, of course, ever-increasing piles of garbage. We are pursuing the wrong thing and are headed in the wrong direction.

In writing *The Design Experience* we have – within the human limits of objectivity – adopted a balanced view of the changing nature of design. However, underlying this book is a view that design has yet to realise its potential as a progressive and responsible agent of change that was promised throughout the twentieth century. If we have a hidden agenda, it is that tomorrow's designers should find ways of recovering design's sense of radical mission to address the urgent problems facing the world. At the start of the new millennium, the problems of poverty, inequality, war and ecological crisis are more acute than they have ever been.

The quote from Richard Buchanan that opened this introduction encapsulates our view of what designers should do. They should look at the world, not as an amorphous, anonymous group of consumers, but as a dazzlingly diverse collection of individuals all trying to find their way – to find meaning and purpose in the world, to discover dignity, tolerance and balanced ways of living. Design is a process that can empower them to do this. Equally, design has the ability to compound the problems of a divisive and dangerous world.

If the new millennium means anything at all, it is a time for designers to take stock, to look at the world around them and ask themselves: of all the possible things I could do with my skills and knowledge, what is relevant and how can I make a positive difference? We hope that this book helps readers to find their own answers.

NOTES

1. R. Buchanan (1994) 'Branzi's dilemma: design in contemporary culture', *Design Issues*, **14**(1), 3–20.
2. R. Cooper and M. Press (1995), *The Design Agenda: a guide to successful design management*, Chichester: John Wiley and Sons.
3. N. Potter (1980), *What is a designer: Things. Places. Messages.* London: Hyphen Books, p. 109.
4. P. Dormer (1997), *The Culture of Craft*, Manchester: Manchester University Press.
5. D. Chaney (1996), *Lifestyles*, London: Routledge, p. 156.

1 Design and consumer culture

Let's start here: 'culture' is everything we don't have to do. We have to eat, but we don't have to have 'cuisines', Big Macs or Tournedos Rossini. We have to cover ourselves against the weather, but we don't have to be concerned as we are about whether we put on Levi's or Yves Saint-Laurent. We have to move about the face of the globe, but we don't have to dance. I call the 'have-to' activities functional and the 'don't have tos' stylistic. By 'stylistic' I mean that the main basis on which we make choices between them is in terms of their stylistic differences.

Brian Eno[1]

WHAT'S THE MEANING OF LIFE?

In former times we derived the meaning for our existence from God. Religion provided a framework for human behaviour, defined our place in the overall scheme of things, and provided individual and collective aspirations. God's power and our relationship to it was expressed symbolically through the scriptures and the rituals of the Church.

In the industrialised world at the very start of the third millennium, God would appear no longer to provide the same sense of social coherence and individual purpose. So how do we derive meaning and gain a sense of identity in a complex and confusing world? Most of us go shopping.

Consumption provides meaning, or at least legitimises the lack of meaning, in the secular modern world. Through consuming we meet individual needs, construct our identities and confirm our membership of social groups. Increasingly we define ourselves in terms of our styles of consumption and the values about our lives that they express – our *lifestyle* – rather than the job we do. Ours is a culture of acquisition, possession and consumer experience. One hundred years ago an average household could count probably around 500 objects in their home – utensils, furniture and so on. Today a typical home bulges with over 3,000 bits of stuff – and that's just the hardware, in addition to which we must consider the programs within our PCs and the multiplying channels on our cable TVs. Acquiring all this stuff is now our number one leisure activity. The average adult spends six hours each week shopping. By way of contrast, the average parent spends forty minutes each week playing with their children.

To consume involves far more than just to shop and possess; it provides a range of experiences gained through our relationship with material culture: we eat out, see a band, watch a video, surf the net, go cycling. The designed products, communications and environments of our consumer culture – the tableware, set designs, VCRs, web browsers and sports goods – are the media that provide these experiences. Together, these experiences help to define our culture, and indeed to define ourselves – they provide us with meaning.

This chapter will examine the cultural context of design. It will begin by exploring the concept of *culture*, then examine various accounts and perspectives of *consumer culture*. The notion of *lifestyle* is vital for understanding the differences and diversity of today's world. Using examples, we will show how design gives form to those differences. We will present a view of design as a cultural production and consumption system – the engine of cultural experiences. This is not to say that professional designers are the sole creators of these experiences – far from it. The point is that design should be seen as both a specialised professional practice and as a creative means of consuming: for example, designers design items of clothing while consumers design how they go together and how they are used on different occasions.

UNDERSTANDING CULTURE

You enter the bathroom and are confronted by a low stool, plastic bowl and small hand towel. What do you do? How should you behave? What does all this mean? This is a bathroom in Japan, and you are desperately trying to understand Japanese *culture*.

People's behaviour, rituals and values vary from country to country and in our multicultural and socially diverse world, within countries as well. The objects used and their configuration reflect and reinforce the expected behaviour of everyday life. When we travel to other countries we are all the time trying to interpret the designed environment to figure out how to eat, how to buy a bus ticket and how to bathe. In short, we are trying to understand the underlying culture.

Understanding culture is clearly essential to the process of design. According to American marketing professor Michael Solomon, 'culture is the lens through which people view products'.[2] It is culture that gives products meaning, that provides the rituals within which they are used and the values that are often reflected in their form and function.

There are many ways of defining and understanding the term culture. Its meaning has evolved historically from 'the tending of natural growth', as in agriculture, to 'a general state or habit of the mind', linked to ideas of human perfection and 'the general body of the arts' where it is associated with 'high' culture.[3] Such conservative definitions of culture have been challenged in recent years by the rise of *cultural studies* as a field of inquiry which draws on anthropology, sociology, linguistics, history, psychology and other disciplines to explore culture as 'the social production and reproduction of sense, meaning and consciousness'.[4] Cultural studies has been greatly influenced by ideas from Marxism, feminism and multiculturalism to become a radical project viewing culture as a terrain upon which different social groups play out power struggles, seek to resist subordination and assert their identities. While we shall be drawing on some perspectives from cultural studies later in this section, at this stage we will settle with a broader definition of culture as *distinctive patterns of social life that reflect shared values, meanings and beliefs expressed in preferred material objects, services and activities*. However, you will notice as our discussion develops that other definitions will be used. For the student of design it is essential to appreciate and interpret the various uses of this term.

We find references to culture in a variety of discussions that concern design. In James Pilditch's account of how innovation and design are harnessed by successful companies, he draws attention to *corporate culture* as the 'soft' shared values that create vision and commitment to excellence through particular styles of management.[5] Dick Hebdige has advanced the idea of youth *sub-culture* in his analysis of punk that explores how the punks of the late 1970s created meaning and identity through fashion and style.[6] Peter Dormer entitles his examination of the values and role of contemporary studio crafts as 'the culture of craft'.[7] There are also explorations of national culture to account for the characteristics of design in particular countries, such as Frederique Huygen's examination of the Britishness of British design.[8]

Box 1.1 summarises some of the key factors that account for the differences between national cultures and determine their constantly changing nature over time. These factors also explain variations in design between cultures. While the figure within Box 1.1 focuses on national culture, it could be adapted to account for other forms of culture.

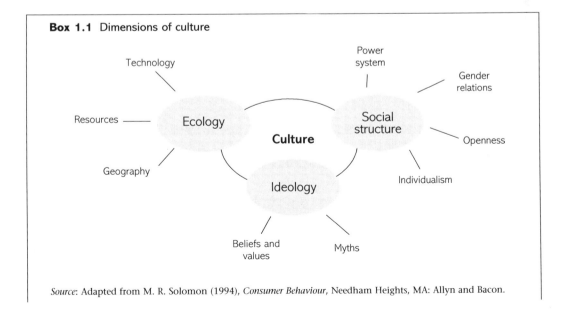

Box 1.1 Dimensions of culture

Source: Adapted from M. R. Solomon (1994), *Consumer Behaviour*, Needham Heights, MA: Allyn and Bacon.

Box 1.1 (concluded)

Ecology refers to how a social system and its culture adapt to their immediate habitat. The system's geography will determine the resources at its disposal and the technology that can be developed within the constraints of those resources. The distinctiveness of Japan's culture, for example, is very much a product of its ecology. The limited space for cultivation on Japan's islands led to a premium on living space and an aesthetic for the miniature and portable that is seen from Bonsai to consumer electronics. A country with virtually no energy reserves of its own, which had to import most of its raw materials, Japan could not industrialise simply by making things cheaper than other countries. Rather, Japan had to add value to its manufactured goods, thus concentrating on product areas which were knowledge based, such as computers and robotics.

Social structure is often a consequence of this ecology. Overcrowded countries, such as Japan and the Netherlands, find different ways of maintaining a well-ordered, cohesive society. Political structures can determine the degree of cultural diversity and are linked to the notion of openness. The distinctiveness of Japanese culture, for example, is a consequence of its insularity for several hundred years. Opposition to a dominant power system is often expressed culturally, as in the youth counterculture of the 1960s that produced new fashions, music and art. Changing gender relations have a major impact on social structures, ways of life, and demands on design. Finally, the more individualism is stressed in society, the more diverse the culture and its material forms. Here we can contrast Japan's collectivist culture with the more individualistic 'American way', with subcultures that express ethnic identity, sexuality, regionalism and a diverse array of lifestyles and consumer preferences.

Ideology refers to the ideas and views that people hold concerning the world around them and their rights and responsibilities within it. These beliefs and values concern conventions and customs of behaviour, ethics and aspirations. It is the different conventions and customs of personal hygiene that make the Japanese bathroom so perplexing to the Western visitor. This shared ideology is expressed literally and symbolically as myths: symbolic narratives that act as a form of self-identity to the culture and as guides to behaviour. Myths are to be found in religion, literature, motion pictures and TV commercials. Through its storytelling a culture defines itself.

CONSUMER CULTURE

Let us now focus specifically on the role of consumption within modern culture, trace its rise historically and consider different conceptual perspectives. As we have already seen, consumption is more than just shopping; it is a way of describing the use of commodities – both material goods and services – to satisfy our desires and needs. On a deeper and more significant level, it is a process that gives meaning to these commodities. The term *consumer culture* refers to how consumption has become a central focus of our social life and cultural values.

From the late 1980s, sociologists began giving serious attention to consumption. Until then their main concern had been the sphere of production – the world of work – as it was generally felt that this was the major determinant of social development.

Driven partly by *feminist* accounts which drew attention to the role of housework, shopping and other 'traditional' female tasks in shaping the attitudes and family structures of society, sociologists started to consider consumption as a vital and little-researched area of social analysis. It was also clear from this time that modern societies were undergoing a radical shift as employment levels in manufacturing were falling, while those in retailing, services and the *cultural industries* were rising.

The growing sociological literature on consumption is of great significance to the field of *design studies*. This is partly because it provides concepts and theories which help us understand how and why people consume – how they create experiences with designed artefacts. However, this literature also points to a new significance for design in economic terms and in the shaping of contemporary culture. Sociologists Scott Lash and John Urry, in their major account of social and economic change, explain how 'we analyse, not so much knowledge- or information-intensivity in production, but design-intensivity and, with the decline of importance of the labour process, the growing importance of the design process'.[9] Another sociologist, David Chaney, concludes his book on lifestyle with a chapter on design which argues that 'the creative energies involved in articulating and sustaining new patterns of social association are in a very profound sense a form of design'.[10] We will explore the ideas of these and other theorists later. Before we do so, it is necessary to place such contemporary analysis in the context of the historical rise of consumption. For a fuller treatment of the history of consumption than we can provide, the reader is referred to Bocock's 'Consumption and lifestyles'.[11]

If we are to see consumption as more than just the meeting of basic needs – Brian Eno's 'have-to' activities – then up until the eighteenth century it was an activity restricted to the aristocracy. With the emergence of new middle classes based on the professions, industry and commerce from the early nineteenth century, consumerism became more widespread. Industrialisation brought new goods and services and new ideas of *fashion*, *style* and *taste* to a wider range of people. We can trace the emergence of the department store and the foundations of modern packaging and advertising to this period.

From the late nineteenth century the working classes began modest participation in consumerism, and this period is associated with the emergence of city centres as spectacles of display, consumption and entertainment. From the early twentieth century we see the rise of mass production, mass media, and suburban housing development, all of which accelerated and diversified consumption. As the next section will explain, this period saw the professionalisation of design, with the new industrial designers giving form to the consumer durables of the 1920s and 1930s.

Mass consumption took hold in the US during the war, and in other industrialised countries during the 1950s and 60s. The rise of the 'affluent worker' in the 1950s created a market for mass-produced durables such as televisions, domestic appliances and cars. This period also saw the development of the new youth subcultures and the definition of 'the teenager' as a marketing opportunity. As affluence continued to increase, Bocock describes a significant shift in the nature of consumption:

As the majority (between two-thirds and three-quarters) of the populations of western capitalist societies became more affluent, the mode of consumption changed from one concerned primarily with basic material provision (which many people still lack in the major capitalist societies as well as in the world as a whole) to a mode concerned more with the status value and symbolic meaning of the commodity purchased. (p. 133)

If this new mode of consumption equates to *consumer culture*, how are we to understand it and what implications can be drawn for design? In his examination of the theories of consumption, Mike Featherstone identifies three main approaches to viewing consumer culture:[12]

- A distinctive new stage in economic development.
- A social process by which people use goods and services to create social bonds or distinctions.
- A creative process in which myth and desire become part of the consumption process to give aesthetic and emotional pleasure.

We could broadly define these as economic, sociological and psychological perspectives, although such disciplinary envelopes are not appropriate to all the accounts within any one category. Below we will briefly examine these perspectives.

Consumer culture as a new stage in economic development

In our previous book *The Design Agenda*, we explored the idea that a move away from mass production and consumption to flexible manufacturing and more diverse patterns of consumption could be viewed as a radical shift in the nature of capitalism which is bound up with ideas of *post-Fordism* and *post-modernism*.[13] Rather than revisit our previous discussion, we will begin by summarising some elements of the detailed account provided by Lash and Urry.[14] In their book *Economies of Signs and Space*, the authors present a theory of global socio-economic change that is far-reaching and radical.

They share with other theorists the view that globalisation is a fundamental characteristic of change. In the first part of the twentieth century, the economy was organised mainly on a national basis to provide mass production and mass consumption, with money, labour power and commodities circulating predominantly within nation-states. The 'disorganised capitalism' of today they describe is international in scope, with investment, people and commodities circulating across the globe. The things we take for granted today – driving a Toyota made in England, foreign holidays, the overseas students with whom we study, our Levis made in the Philippines, bunches of flowers sold on New York streets that are grown in Africa, e-mail exchanges with friends in other countries – reflect a level of globalisation that was unheard of a generation ago.

This process of globalisation, our increased mobility, and the greater level of

production and consumption that this makes possible have a number of consequences. First, commodities lose the meanings formerly given by the symbolism and
myths of their national culture. In their place, the Benetton ads, McDonald's golden
arches and all the other advertising imagery, product styles and brands provide a
seemingly meaningless jungle of *signs*, divorced from any commonly accepted underlying meaning. In the new system of production,

> what is increasingly being produced are not material objects, but signs. These signs are primarily
> of two types. Either they have a primarily cognitive content and thus are post-industrial or infor-
> mational goods. Or they primarily have an aesthetic, in the broadest sense of the aesthetic, content
> and they are primarily post-modern goods.[15]

STOP! The concept of *signs* is very important to our understanding of consumer
culture and you should read the explanation in Box 1.2 before proceeding further.

Box 1.2   Sign language

Our world is full of signs – commonly understood references to an action or to something else
other than itself. Road signs, for example, warn us of hazards ahead, or instruct us how to
negotiate a junction. But signs can be more complex and subtle than this. When a man gives
a rose to a woman he is giving more than just a flower, rather he is presenting the rose as a
sign of his love and passion. Clearly for the sign to work as intended, the woman must share
this same understanding of what is being signified.

Semiotics is the study of signs. It examines how words, photographs, styles and other
design forms can work as a language to communicate a range of ideas, associations and feelings. In semiotics, a sign has two elements – the signifier (its physical form, for example a rose)
and the signified (the mental concept that it refers to, for example undying love).

In our consumer culture, commodities are marketed through advertising using a range of
signs that trigger cultural associations and desires, so that in the end the product becomes a
signifier. Marlboro cigarettes are signifiers for a rugged American masculinity and CK One is
a signifier of youthful sexual desire.

Product styling, advertising design, graphics, branding, architecture and fashion all
become media of communication – signs – for particular qualities, myths and other associations. Colour, for example, is used as a sign: red as a sign of danger, as in the case of the stop
sign, or as a sign of passion in much perfume advertising, and of course the rose. Brands are
developed as strong associations of particular qualities or myths for which the products and
services marketed using them become signs. For example, the Virgin brand is associated with
value for money and youthful entrepreneurialism. The myth of Richard Branson as a dynamic
but honest risk taker is what we're buying into when we fly 'his' airline, drink 'his' vodka, buy
'his' records and travel in his trains.

For Lash and Urry, then, two of the key developments in their new economies of
signs is a greater production of informational, post-industrial or cultural goods – such

as popular music, publishing, cinema and video – and an increase in the *aestheticisation* of most other goods and services. By this they mean a greater aesthetic content in terms of the goods and services being conceived, styled and marketed as signs – or, as they say, 'the design process is progressively more central'.[16]

Associated with these developments are changes in the structure of economies and production, with flexible networks of producers beginning to take the place of the large integrated corporations of the past. The greater mobility of people and investment means that places – cities and regions – now have to package and present themselves as they compete for tourists and investors. Every city now has its own logo and slogan – 'Glasgow's Miles Better', for example – together with its heritage trails, business parks and unique street furniture. In this and other ways 'economic life is itself becoming cultural and aestheticized'.[17]

Because of their reliance on assumed sociological knowledge and terminology, Lash and Urry's book is often inaccessible for students of design studies. However, the Open University's Cultural Studies team provides a clearer account that uses the notion of *cultural economy* to describe and conceptualise the economic significance of consumption and culture. 'Cultural economy' is a very useful term for understanding the changes that have taken place in the economy because of 'the crucial importance it allots to language, representation and meaning – to "culture" – for understanding the conduct of economic life and the construction of economic identities'.[18] The idea of cultural economy comprises the following key elements:

- *Viewing the economy as a cultural phenomenon itself*   We tend to think of 'the economy' as an objective set of components and processes, such as companies, markets, exchange rates, employment levels, and so on. However, the concepts and terms we use to describe these, because they use language, involve meaning and interpretation – and as such are cultural, reflecting values and beliefs. Consider, for example, how the culture of Margaret Thatcher's economy with its emphasis on 'market forces' differs from Tony Blair's 'stakeholder' economy.
- *Viewing corporations in terms of their culture*   The idea of corporate culture reflects how new practices and forms of organisation in companies are used to carry meanings to employees and customers to reinforce certain behaviour, encourage staff and communicate values. For example, The Body Shop has a distinctive 'culture' that includes a commitment to employee training, environmental best practice, high standards of customer service and overall a distinctive culture 'of doing things'.
- *The rise of cultural industries*   Companies involved in the production and distribution of cultural hardware and software – music, film, TV, publishing, audio systems, print and electronic media – are now major industrial players. Cultural industries are now beginning to eclipse traditional manufacturing sectors in their economic and employment significance.
- *The aestheticisation of goods and services*   The argument advanced by Lash and Urry, among others, that a whole variety of goods and services are conceived,

developed and marketed as 'cultural' products using signs to engender meaning and association. Whether it is bank accounts, instant coffee, consumer electronics or cosmetics, the symbolic content of the product and the meanings bound up with it becomes paramount.

- *Increasing importance of cultural intermediaries*   Those working in design, advertising and marketing now play a pivotal role in giving commodities their cultural meanings. They have developed into significant professions and industries in their own right, and as such are significant in economic and employment terms. However, it is their role in the aestheticisation process that is most crucial. We will explore this issue in more detail later in this section.

The perspectives we have considered so far see the significance of consumer culture from a conceptual, academic point of view, but their conclusions are broadly consistent with those from a more pragmatic, managerial standpoint. Tom Peters is an American management consultant who writes in a highly readable 'zesty' style using many examples of products and companies. His journalistic style of writing replaces terms such as 'the aestheticization of production' with 'Yo! Fashion'. Peters's books, such as *Liberation Management*, which appear to account for much of the turnover of airport bookstores, are written in order to provoke and challenge, and as long as we bear this in mind and read with a critical eye, can provide some useful insights.

The key argument in *Liberation Management* is that fashion has permeated everything: *product life cycles* have speeded up with a faster rate of obsolescence, there are many more new product launches 'with a rash of products spewing forth, each aimed at customers' ever-shifting, ever narrower-gauge needs', and customers are seeking new values and new experiences from their goods and services.[19] Peters draws out some critical implications for management in terms of how to structure organisations to 'get closer to the customer', take more risks in developing goods and services and, to use his words, 'get brain-based' in changing their culture. The significance of Peters for our discussion is the importance he places on design, with *Liberation Management* containing a chapter dedicated to 'a special case of wow: an encompassing view of design'.[20]

From a very different starting-point, and using very different research to both Lash and Urry and the Open University team, Tom Peters comes up with a very similar argument – that we are living in a new age of business in which people expect different things from the goods and services they consume. As a consequence design is a far more essential part of the production process than it was in the past. In his view, design is one of the essential software components of 'a product'. In considering what we mean by 'a product', Peters argues that 'there is still something recognisable as a lump', although new information and production technologies, teamworking and research methods have made this lump 'softer'.[21] However, within this soft lump of 'a product' are six software elements that also have to be designed, most of which could be seen as processes concerned with aestheticisation – injecting culture into product (Table 1.1).

Table 1.1   Tom Peters's software elements of a product

Software I	EMBEDDED SMART	Built-in software now found in 'smart cars', buildings and shopping trolleys
Software II	INDUSTRIAL DESIGN	Focused on user-friendliness and differentiation
Software III	SYMBIOSIS WITH THE END-USER	Identifying with and understanding users – a concept that goes beyond market research
Software IV	RETHINKING PROVISION	Radical change in delivery methods and service
Software V	EXTENDING SERVICE	Reformulating the idea of service
Software VI	EXPERIENCE	Seeing the product or service in terms of entertainment or experience

In the spirit of Peters's style of analysis, and building further upon it, Joseph Pine II and James Gilmore are two management consultants who have developed the term *experience economy* to describe the shift towards an economy more focused on the supply of consumer experiences.[22]

Table 1.2 summarises Pine and Gilmore's central idea. They argue that the 'experience economy' is a distinct historical stage of economic development. In the industrial age the main economic function – the central activity of working life – was making goods that people bought according to their demand for particular features. In the age of the service economy most working people are engaged in the delivery of services that are purchased according to the benefits that they offer. Pine and Gilmore argue that we are currently moving towards an economy in which more people will be staging experiences that provide particular sensations, and they cite data from the USA that support the idea that 'experience employment' is growing at a faster rate than manufacturing, services or commodity production.

Table 1.2   Economic phases

Economy	Economic offering	Factors of demand	Economic function	Employment growth – US annual 1959–96 (%)
EXPERIENCE	**Experiences**	**Sensations**	**Stage**	**5.3**
SERVICE	**Services**	**Benefits**	**Deliver**	**2.7**
INDUSTRIAL	**Goods**	**Features**	**Make**	**0.5**
AGRARIAN	**Commodities**	**Characteristics**	**Extract**	**- 0.7**

Source: Adapted from J. Pine and J. H. Gilmore (1999), *The Experience Economy: Work is theatre and every business a stage*, Boston: Harvard Business School Books.

As examples of this growth, they cite the theming of restaurants and bars, such as Planet Hollywood and Hard Rock Café, and the development of theme parks, such as Disneyland, to support their thesis that businesses are becoming theatres within which consumer experiences are staged. Faced with this inexorable rise of the experience economy, manufacturers have to – in their terms – 'ing the thing'. This means conceiving products in terms of how they add value to the activity of using them and the experiences that they create. Out goes producing chairs – in comes the creation of sitting experiences.

We can illustrate their idea of economic change in terms of rice, and how the smart entrepreneur doesn't sell rice, but sells the experience of 'riceing'. To buy one kilo of rice wholesale costs little more than £1. In this case we are buying rice as an undifferentiated commodity which provides a single serving for just a few pence. The trading of commodities was the basis of pre-industrial agrarian economies, which evolved into industrial societies characterised by the application of manufacturing to such commodities, creating marketed, differentiated products. A box of rice in the supermarket is a processed, branded product, and may cost £1.50 for 500 grams, working out at 20 pence or so per serving. But in the age of the service economy, we are less likely to have the time or inclination to cook our own rice and prefer to pay somebody else to do it for us, so the local Chinese takeaway will sell us a single serving of cooked rice for £1 or a restaurant will serve a portion for £2. However, increasingly service is not enough. We don't just want our rice cooked for us and served at the table; we expect it to be part of an experience.

During the writing of this book, we met in central London to discuss progress over lunch. We chose a sushi bar in South Kensington where we sat at a table, next to which a variety of tempting dishes passed by us on a conveyor, to be taken as we pleased. The place was busy, with wok-wielding chefs providing a sense of theatre, as the colourful, exquisitely crafted displays of food glided past us. From the décor, to the design of the menus, selection of tableware, dress and attitude of staff, preparation and presentation of the food, everything had been carefully considered and orchestrated – indeed, designed – to provide a pleasing, surprising and stimulating experience. When we finished, the waiter simply counted the serving bowls on the table and billed us. Sushi is mainly rice, and we had eaten at most 100 grams, although the £20 bill was good value. We left feeling well fed, well served and well entertained. It had been an experience.

But the creation of experiences is not the final stage in Pine and Gilmore's new economy. They suggest that on the horizon is the new *transformation economy*, in which customised experiences change the individual by building upon their aspirations. Some websites and store loyalty card schemes are moving towards this. The on-line Amazon bookstore, for example, will suggest to each customer new books that they may be interested in, given their previous buying habits.[23]

We can view the concept of *experience*, as used by Peters, Pine and Gilmore, as describing four key developments in the design of *consumer culture* ((Table 1.3).

Table 1.3   Design in the age of consumer culture

Design development	Description	Outcome
USER DRIVEN	Product and service development driven by a richer understanding of users	More specific and tailored meaning and association
CYCLE OF USE	All phases in the cycle of a product's use – including packaging, delivery, after-sales service and disposal – considered and co-ordinated	Holistic experience of use
DESIGN CO-ORDINATION	All design elements within a product or service are co-ordinated	Richer multisensual experience
COMPLEXITY	Development of more complex forms of consumption, integrating service, product and communication, such as theme parks	Multisensual, time-based and interactive consumption
CUSTOMISATION	The use of new technologies to maximise opportunities for customisation	Unique-use experiences and 'creative' consumption

Some of these are far from new. The emergence of department stores in the nineteenth century, for example, could be seen as a complex form of consumption in much the same way as today's theme parks are. However, it is the conscious adoption of such design strategies and their mutual reinforcement that is transforming the nature of consumption.

From the perspectives examined above comes a fairly consistent and clear view that the entire system of production and consumption has undergone a profound shift (see Box 1.3). Through concepts such as *cultural economy*, we can see how culture – the creation and interpretation of meaning – permeates the system. Significantly this creates a new role for designers as *cultural intermediaries*, understanding users and creating meaningful forms of consumption for them. These new forms can be seen in terms of *experiences* that integrate different stages of consumption in a multisensual way. We will explore this issue in more detail in Chapter 3. Now we turn to perspectives of consumer culture that consider how consumption can be seen as a social process to create social bonds or distinctions.

Consumer culture as a means of distinction

Like Tom Peters, we aspire to symbiosis with our end-user – you, the reader. If we used a lyric from Fat Boy Slim or The Super Furry Animals to illustrate a point here it would identify with the age group that our publisher is targeting for this product. If we went for The Rolling Stones, it would immediately mark our difference from most of our readership. Piece together a typical Stones listener and their lifestyle – 40-something, shops at Habitat, wears Levis and sensible shoes. At least we didn't mention Elton John!

Box 1.3   Sheffield's new cultural economy

Source:
Author's photo

Sheffield, England's fourth largest city, was once the steel- and cutlery-making centre of the country, surrounded by the coal mines of South Yorkshire. Since the late 1950s, 28,000 cutlery jobs have gone. A total of 20,000 steel jobs was lost during the 1990s, and in that same period South Yorkshire's 36 coal mines were reduced to just two.[24]

The stainless steel domes of the Nigel Coates-designed National Centre for Popular Music are signifiers of the economic changes under way in Sheffield, and indeed throughout industrialised economies. Each year the UK music industry is worth $4 billion to the national economy, with export earnings that exceed those of the UK steel industry.[25] Together with film, television, design, publishing and software, music is part of the cultural industries that recent research suggests represent the second largest source of new employment in the UK, providing 104,000 extra jobs in the five years up to 2001.

The city, once famed for its cutlery and special steels, is today more known for *The Full Monty* and *Gatecrasher at The Republic*. The National Centre for Popular Music lies in the heart of the city's Cultural Industries Quarter, which has attracted film, multimedia and other cultural enterprises to Sheffield. Successful computer games businesses have ensured that 'Made in Sheffield' today applies more to software for Playstation than it does to tableware.

Photograph
courtesy of the
Design Council

Cutting-edge industrial design is also part of the new Sheffield. Richardson, a long-established manufacturer in the cutlery industry, secured Millennium Product status for its Forme range of seamless stainless steel kitchen knives. The company's in-house design team was given a free rein in developing this bold new concept. But the logic of the global economy dictated that the knives were to be manufactured far from Sheffield. According to Marketing Director Mark O'Kelly, 'It took us a long time but we eventually identified a company in Korea through our Hong Kong sourcing operation that was able to manufacture the knives out of French steel at costs that enabled us to market them to our target customers'.[26]

There are two key themes in literature concerning consumer culture. The first is that our choice of goods and services is often made to differentiate ourselves; thus it follows that we judge others by their consumption choices, including their brand of cigarette. The second theme is that while consumption may give us pleasure, it fails to provide satisfaction as it is based on 'a frustrated desire for totality'.[27] While this latter issue is beyond the scope of our discussion, we will focus on consumption as a means of difference and distinction – as a signifier of lifestyle.

The most defiant act is to be distinguished, singled out, marked.
Put our jeans on. The Gap.

Got a life? Get a car to put it in.
The new Renault Mégane Scenic. It talks your language.

In today's culture, difference is everything. Particularly among young people we can identify increasing subcultural differences based on class, gender, ethnicity and sexuality.[28] These differences are expressed through distinctive fashions, musical tastes and other forms of consumption. Clothing in particular, as the most immediate, obvious and intimate signifier of difference, is a crucial form of distinction.[29] The Gap is selling jeans to people who see consumption as a form of expressive, defiant behaviour.

Renault is selling product to an older consumer, but in much the same way – the product contains and expresses our life values: it talks on our behalf. Back in the 1950s the young were the first 'ordinary people' to use consumption as a form of expression, to mark their difference by creating a consumer-driven generation gap, the first-ever teenage consumers. Those very same consumers are today facing retirement and, as we will see in Chapter 3, are taking consumer values of difference into a highly lucrative and very significant *third age* market. Indeed, many shop at The Gap. And four of them play in a band called The Rolling Stones.

In accounting for patterns of consumption – who buys what and why – market researchers tended to concentrate on segmenting the population by social class, and this seemed to work up to the 1980s. Social class remains a fundamental determinant of people's attitudes, tastes and lifestyle, and therefore a marker of distinction. Before considering some of the new segmentation techniques of market research, we must first look at the importance of class.

Table 1.4 shows the definitions of social class used in the UK, and there are similar systems in other countries. While issues of gender, ethnicity and generation now make social class a far less determining factor in people's identity and cultural behaviour, a person's class determines their disposable income and is therefore critical to understanding consumption patterns. Class, and the notion of status which is bound up with it (although not necessarily determined by it), is a form of social distinction which is expressed through consumption.

Table 1.4   Definitions of social class used in the UK

Social class	Description	Occupations
A	Upper and upper-middle class	Higher managerial, administrative and professions
B	Middle class	Middle managerial, administrative and professions
C1	Lower middle class	Supervisory, clerical and administrative
C2	Skilled working class	Skilled manual workers
D	Working class	Semi-skilled and unskilled manual workers
E	Subsistence	State pensioners, casual and lowest grade workers, state benefit recipients, long-term unemployed

One study in particular has mapped out the class-based patterns of consumption. In the 1960s and 1970s French sociologist Pierre Bourdieu carried out a major questionnaire survey of people's tastes and consumer preferences which included music, literature, painting, clothes, furniture and food.[30] He argued that different social classes distinguish themselves by their tastes, through identifying three taste zones that broadly correspond to educational level and social class:

- legitimate taste – preference for works by Bach, Brueghel or Goya, which 'is highest in those fractions of the dominant class that are richest in educational capital';
- middle-brow taste – preference for the minor works of the major arts, such as Gershwin's *Rhapsody in Blue* and paintings by Renoir, and the major works of the minor arts, such as the songs of Jacques Brel, and is found in the lower middle classes and the intellectual fraction of the dominant classes;
- popular taste – preference for light music such as *The Blue Danube* and 'songs totally devoid of artistic ambition or pretension such as ... Petula Clark', found mainly in the working classes.

Bourdieu's observations on food preferences also demonstrate class-based distinctions:

- upper class – here Bourdieu distinguishes between the 'economically dominant fraction' which prefers rich sauces and desserts, and luxury items such as vintage champagne and truffles, and the 'culturally dominant fraction', which prefers *nouvelle cuisine*'s emphasis on aesthetic presentation;
- middle class – preference for *cuisine* displaying knowledge of preparation methods, presentation and nutritional understanding;
- working class – preference for abundance, with strong red meats, robust wine, bread and cheese.

Bourdieu is therefore presenting us with a map of taste and lifestyle, broadly measured by the contours of social class (see Box 1.4). However, he is not saying that

---

Box 1.4   Beyond class – the pukka lifestyle

According to Bourdieu, we are what we eat – our social class determines our taste for food and drink. Today's lifestyles, which cut across class boundaries, are producing hybrid tastes that draw upon both 'conventional' working class culture and connoisseur values, providing new taste codes of distinction. In 1999 when the ailing supermarket chain Sainsbury revamped its stores and identity to reposition itself in the market, the considerable shelf space it used to sell the collected works of the 'very middle class' Delia Smith were turned over to 'Essex lad', TV chef Jamie Oliver.

Oliver's recipes include bacon sarnies and burgers, alongside braised pigeon breasts and stuffed baby chillis. His style and recipes express both the shift towards informality and the importance of emotional experience in eating. By combining 'no-nonsense' working-class sociability with middle-class *cuisine*, he is part of a wider redefinition of a significant middle class lifestyle group. In 2002 it was reported that Jamie Oliver had increased the company's profits by millions. He has helped with 'product development as well as appearing in our TV advertising,' increasing sales 'significantly'. (www.sainsburys.co.uk)

---

patterns of consumption simply reflect a person's class through their level of income. In his book *Distinction*, Bourdieu argues how class differences are constructed through consumption, and indeed taste is an essential marker to assert the difference of one social class from another. He introduces some important concepts for understanding the processes at work.

An individual's consumption patterns are determined by their *habitus*. This term refers to the tastes and preferences a person has for art, food, leisure activities and other cultural goods. A person's habitus is expressed not only through consumption, but through their body – their accent, body language, manners, shape, and so on. Bourdieu argues that each class and class fraction has its own distinctive habitus that contains and expresses a system of taste and lifestyle. Habitus is determined not only by access to economic capital – a social class's level of income – but also by *cultural capital*. This describes the level of education, understanding of art, literature, design and other cultural activities, the ability to produce culture and make cultural distinctions and judgements.

Through his concepts of habitus and cultural capital, together with his examples of how class differences are constructed through consumption, Bourdieu's analysis is essential to this discussion. However, he has been criticised for his largely exclusive focus on social class at the expense of other social distinctions such as gender and age. There is also a methodological criticism based on his use of a questionnaire survey which provides a static view of what is consumed rather than a dynamic understanding of how things are consumed.

On a more prosaic level, from the 1980s market research was suggesting that social class was becoming a poor predictor of consumer preferences and the notion of **lifestyle** developed as a means of understanding and accounting for patterns of consumption. This made sense in the context of a social and cultural shift in advanced societies away from a mass culture, with a shared value system and conventions of living, to a far more diverse set of social values and conventions.

One of the first commentaries on this cultural shift is Alvin Toffler's *Future Shock*, published in 1970 and still a readable and relevant observation on developments in consumer culture.[31] A key theme in Toffler's book is diversity – in the range of products available, in art, in mass culture, in value systems and in the subcults that make up our society. Lifestyle helps us to make sense of the cultural confusion around us: 'In the welter of conflicting moralities, in the confusion occasioned by overchoice, the most powerful, most useful 'super-product' of all is an organising principle for one's life. This is what a lifestyle offers'.[32]

We can think of lifestyle as a 'distinctive mode of living' or as 'the reflection of life values in a preferred style of consumption'. As our society and culture change ever faster and throw up more consumer choice, so the range of lifestyles become more diverse. In lifestyle research, people's attitudes, opinions, beliefs and consumption patterns are clustered to identify broad lifestyle categories, usually given irritating titles such as yuppies – young, upwardly mobile professionals – and dinkies – double income, no kids. Lifestyle groups are often associated with *consumption constellations*, in which sets of products reinforce their symbolic meaning to each other. The 1980s yuppie, for example, is linked to a constellation which includes BMW cars, Rolex watches, the Filofax and Gucci. Products often gain their symbolic value by being positioned in an appropriate constellation through advertising and product styling. Corporate sponsorship can also imbue brands with life values, as in the case of Reebok's support for Amnesty International.

Most lifestyle research is focused on examining a specific consumer group that a company wishes to market its products to. Often such research will take the form of *psychographics*, which segments consumers into motivational groups according to their attitudes on social issues, the environment, purchasing, and so on. The aim of psychographics is to understand why consumers buy certain products and to identify the lifestyle segment that accounts for most customers of a product. It is generally held that 20 per cent of a product's users account for 80 per cent of the volume sold,[33] so identifying heavy users can assist in the better targeting of marketing resources.

A well-documented example is CLM/BBDO's advertising campaign for the International Wool Secretariat.[34] In seeking to market the woolmark label to a pan-European segment, the agency commissioned psychographic research which broke the market down into the motivational categories of 'sustenance-motivated', 'outer-directed' and 'inner-directed'. The research focused in particular on pan-European 'social innovators' at the forefront of the market, aged between 20 and 35. The key motivations for this group were:

1. Desire for emotional experience
2. Polysensuality
3. Risk taking
4. Networking
5. Exploring new mental frontiers

Two of these terms are in themselves significant to the core arguments of *The Design Experience*. *Desire for emotional experience* refers to people having the need 'to feel their body in new and different, intensive ways, the desire for frequent emotional experiences and the enjoyment of doing something which is just a little dangerous or forbidden'.[35] *Polysensuality* refers to the need for consumers to experience through all the senses, expressed through the pleasure of feeling silk against the skin, smelling fresh coffee and the texture of ripe brie. Following this research the agency designed an image-led campaign that was highly sensual, featuring a youthful jumper-clad couple locked in a warm woolly embrace.

The concept of lifestyle can be used in a number of ways to inform design. First we can map changing values, attitudes and social trends – emerging forms of distinction – which can act as a starting-point for further design research and concept development. Second, designers can 'lifestyle' an existing product to adapt it to a range of different niches. Du Gay (1997) has described how the Sony design team adapted the Walkman to a new My First Sony range of products aimed at children. Product styling combined with packaging and visual presentation to provide a distinctive brand identity: 'through the deployment of their particular symbolic expertise, designers made a series of products achieve a new register of meaning'.[36]

Finally, we can use marketing-led strategies, such as the Woolmark example, which aim to design lifestyle into a product through advertising, suggesting distinction through a marketing campaign which may place the product into a consumption constellation, or use other associative signs to imply the product's values (see Box 1.5).

Consumer culture as a creative process

From much of the discussion so far there is an implied view that consumption is a passive act, where we as consumers are manipulated by advertisers, marketers and designers into buying the signs that mark our differences. Bourdieu seems to be saying that taste is learned through the acquisition of cultural capital. Psychographics would appear to be a ruse to sell jumpers in the right way, using the right signs, to people who never thought they needed them. Jean Baudrillard, an influential writer in this field, even refers to an 'indoctrination into systematic and organised consumption'.[37]

Baudrillard's early writings concentrated on the meaning and role of objects and commodities and, like other theorists we have considered, how individuals and groups use the sign value of commodities like a language to mark out differences of taste and status. In his later work Baudrillard argued that commodities and signs had merged completely in the *hyperreality* of the media age. Surface appearance was all that mattered, all that was meaningful. Signs increasingly take on a meaning of their own.

In Baudrillard's view our mass media has become a huge image machine, forever needing and creating new images which are simulations of reality, effectively break-

Box 1.5   Designing for difference – the Apple iMac

Jurassic Park star Jeff Goldblum opened the TV commercial for the Apple iMac by asking why computer companies only ever make their machines in beige. 'That's nuts. Have they been in thinking jail?' We cut to the Bondi Blue version of the iMac and finish with Apple's campaign slogan – 'Think Different'.

From the all-in-one colourful translucent box to G3 processor inside it, and of course its user-friendly Mac Operating System, everything about the iMac and accompanying iBook range of computers was different. Offered in a range of different colours, the iMac was developed by UK industrial designer Jonathan Ive and his team at Apple. Their design brief was to recover Apple's mission to develop computers as creative personal tools, and design with the user experience paramount. Far more than a styling exercise, the iMac and iBook involved materials innovation, a rethink of the computer's internal architecture and simplified wireless connectivity. Above all, it was designed for 'plug in and go' access to the Internet.

The iMac became the fastest selling computer of all time, winning over many of the crucial first-time buyers, denting – albeit slightly – the Windows-PC dominance of the market, and returning Apple to its position as one of the world's largest and most profitable computer manufacturers. Launched with a $100 million advertising campaign that stressed difference, the iMac has spawned a raft of copy-cat products that bring colour and translucence into the otherwise bland beigeness of the computer market.

As a winner of the 1999 D&AD Design Awards in London, the iMac drew praise from Richard Seymour, partner in consultants Seymour Powell and D&AD President: 'We are on the threshold of enormous diversity and customisation in a mass sense. The days of settling for what you are given are gone forever. Consumer choice now means how they want it, not how you are prepared to give it. It is going to have the greatest impact on everyone.'

Innovative industrial design wedded to effective marketing has propelled the PC market into a new phase – one that recognises that the PC is no longer just a functional commodity, but an expression of an individual's taste and personality. The computer is now a fashionable lifestyle product. While marketing can emphasise difference, design is the process that gives it physical form.

'The computer industry is ripe for this,' claims Mark Kimbrough, a principal with the Texas company Design Edge. 'It's finally come of age. I mean, when you look at any computer on the market technologically, they're basically the same. So what's the strategic advantage? It's design.'

ing down the distinction between the real and the imagined. Jean Baudrillard's position is a fatal one. Styles are packaged and sold to us, simply to promote our consumption of them rather than to meet any fundamental need. Media images do not represent reality – because now they *are* reality. All we can do, he argues, is to enjoy the spectacle.

As you read this, what are you thinking? Are you passively accepting everything we write as 'the truth'? We certainly hope that you are not. Writers such as ourselves or Jean Baudrillard, or any of the others whose work we have drawn upon, present ideas for readers to engage with. Some you will reject, others you may *appropriate* and from them develop your own interpretation based on your own particular experience and from that create your own new idea. That is our hope, anyway. As with reading, so with anything else we consume or interact with.

In considering the sophistication of advertising, marketing, design and other means that seek to manipulate consumer choice, we could at first be forgiven for adopting a fatalistic view. However, the inherent creativity of people and their often stubborn rejection of slick marketing has led some writers to present consumerism as a liberating force. The reality, of course, lies somewhere between these two perspectives.

In a well-known and very detailed article, Dick Hebdige has looked at the history of the motor scooter.[38] This product may have been designed and marketed for women, indeed designed specifically to be ridden without difficulty by someone wearing a skirt, but somewhere along the way the product was re-contextualised, re-appropriated and indeed re-genderised by another group. The scooter became synonymous with the mods of the early 1960s who used the Lambretta as a lifestyle fashion accessory, customised by every rider. A whole new *subcult* placed the scooter at the centre stage of their identity. The scooter therefore became something that had not been intended – a machine to be driven by young men in suits, festooned with mirrors and other accessories.

Over a decade later, another youth subculture *appropriated* a male garment as a female fashion item. The story of women's leggings flies in the face of the manipulative, *trickle-down* theory of fashion. Angela McRobbie has explained how leggings first appeared as winter underwear for men in places like Camden Market in London, featuring an elasticated waistband and button fly. In the late 70s, punk girls started buying them, dyeing them black and using them as summer garments. The stall-holders responded by dyeing them first, but there were some inherent design faults – they were cut too low at the waist and the button fly cluttered the line on the front. Soon small firms had redesigned them and were selling them as women's garments. 'By the summers of 1985 and 1986 these were being worn by what seemed the entire female population aged under 30'.[39]

These two examples introduce a crucial aspect concerning design's role in consumption. Design is the process by which a product is *encoded* with symbolic meaning both through product design and advertising design. This encoding aims to point towards a *preferred reading* of the product. The styling and marketing of the scooter, for example, encoded a preferred reading of the product as a feminised form of transport. However, when the product is consumed, its symbolism is *decoded*, is read, in different ways by different subcultures. Alternative readings are therefore possible, so that the scooter became a masculine product. Products can therefore fit into practices of everyday life that their original designers had not anticipated. This creative re-contextualisation of products often requires designers to redesign them for their new reading and use – as in the case of leggings.

This notion of encoding/decoding comes from Stewart Hall's analysis of the reading of television texts, but we can apply it to a range of cultural products.[40]

According to Hall, there are three forms of decoding: dominant, which involves accepting the preferred reading; negotiated, which provides some limited re-interpretation; and oppositional, which is a radical rejection of the preferred reading in favour of an alternative. The scooter and leggings are both vivid oppositional examples, as one may expect of youth subcultures which adopt different value systems and symbolic codes in their patterns of consumption. See also Box 1.6.

Box 1.6   Nokia's global culture of creative consumption

Most products have readings that are negotiated as, through their consumption, they present new possibilities and fit into our changing patterns and practices of life. New information and communication technologies exhibit this process of negotiation. For example, the mobile (cellular) telephone was originally designed and marketed in the early 1990s as a male, status-oriented product for businessmen. However, this technology fell into a world inhabited by students living in temporary accommodation, courier drivers working on the road, affluent housewives and others who could see benefits in mobile telephony. As a consequence this luxury high-tech product was decoded and eventually redesigned and remarketed into a user-friendly device for social interaction and blue-collar efficiency.

Commenting on the consumption of such new communication technologies, Mackay makes the following point:

> Rather than being built into hardware, technologies are shaped, in a very real way, by local everyday lives and routines in households ... The processes involved are not one-way (as) consumption plays a key role in informing technology (re)design – through market research and consumer feedback. Consumers, rather than simply recipients of innovations, can thus be seen as playing a key role in the innovation process.[41]

Nokia has taken this a stage further than many of its competitors. Its website (www.nokia.com) invites visitors to suggest new uses and developments for its mobile communications products, exploiting their profile in the movie *Minority Report*. In the small print of Nokia's terms and conditions for e-mailing ideas, the company explains that once you click the send button, the intellectual property rights for the idea pass to them.

Many unofficial websites have been set up by enthusiasts of Nokia products. Subcultures of consumption are developing around many products, spurred on by the Internet as a means of creating global communities of users.

Consumption plays an essential role in the way that people creatively make their own lives – in their networks of friends and bonds of family, in their shared and individual leisure pursuits and ways of organising and conducting their work. For some people, particularly the young, consumption is highly expressive, individualistic and hedonistic – it marks out difference and provides pleasure. For others it provides a clearly identified set of codes to establish distinction and status. In a world in which most of us feel a lack of power and control – in both work and politics – consumption provides some source of choice and autonomy. As consumers we are neither passive victims nor liberated freewheelers. Our consumption has inherent constraints and no little degree of pressure, yet within these constraints we can construct our lives and equip them with meaning.

Consumer culture is a negotiated creative process. Designers are among those *cultural intermediaries* that provide goods and services with forms, packagings and presentations that imply *preferred readings*. However, as a negotiated process, those readings can be re-interpreted and retold. The essential task for designers is to understand how people make sense and meaning of the things they design, and how they create new experiences with them. It is a task that involves reconsidering the entire practice of design.

DESIGN AS THE MEANING OF LIFE?

Well, perhaps not quite. However, in this chapter we have explored the role of *consumption* in our culture and seen how it has become, not just a driving force for economic growth, but a key source of meaning and identity. The concept of *cultural economy* describes how the cultural and the economic have become more interwoven and interdependent. Consumption is now far more than a means of fulfilling functional needs. People today have a greater need for emotional, sensual and expressive experiences, in which the goods and services they consume play an essential part. We have seen how design, as a professional activity, *encodes* goods and services with symbolic meanings and interpretation, but this is by no means the end of the consumption story. In their *decoding*, consumers will identify new meanings, new uses and new experiential requirements. The task of design is therefore to place greater emphasis on understanding the processes of consumption – how people use the products of design and use them to design their own everyday lives and cultural meanings.

In our consumer culture we are all, to varying degrees, designers. We all make design decisions about the homes we live in, the clothes we wear, the entertainments we consume and the lifestyle we express. Such 'everyday consumption work', to quote David Chaney, 'exemplifies a notion of design as a way of using that is invested with significance'.[42] Consumer culture is a design experience that links production with consumption, professional designer with creative consumer. Designers, as *cultural intermediaries*, play a vital role in helping people find meaning, identity and sense in a highly confusing world.

NOTES

1. B. Eno (1996), *A Year with Swollen Appendices*, London: Faber and Faber, p. 317.
2. M. R. Solomon (1994), *Consumer Behaviour*, Needham Heights, MA: Allyn and Bacon, p. 536.
3. R. Williams (1961), *Culture and Society 1780–1950*, Harmondsworth: Penguin, p. 16.
4. T. O'Sullivan, J. Hartley, D. Saunders, M. Montgomery and J. Fiske (1994), *Key Concepts in Communication and Cultural Studies*, London: Routledge, p. 68.
5. J. Pilditch (1989), *Winning Ways*, London: Mercury Business Books.
6. D. Hebdige (1979), *Subculture: the meaning of style*, London: Methuen.
7. P. Dormer (1997), *The Culture of Craft*, Manchester: Manchester University Press.
8. F. Huygen (1989), *British Design: image and identity*, London: Thames and Hudson.
9. S. Lash and J. Urry (1994), *Economies of Signs and Space*, London: Sage, p. 57.
10. D. Chaney (1996), *Lifestyles*, London: Routledge, p. 157.
11. R. Bocock (1992), 'Consumption and lifestyles', in R. Bocock and K. Thompson (eds), *Social and Cultural Forms of Modernity*, Cambridge: Polity Press, p. 133.
12. M. Featherstone (1991), *Consumer Culture and Postmodernism*, London: Sage, ch. 2.
13. R. Cooper and M. Press (1995), *The Design Agenda: a guide to successful design management*, Chichester: John Wiley & Sons, p. 69.
14. Lash and Urry, *Economies of Signs and Space*.
15. Ibid., p. 15.
16. Ibid.
17. Ibid., p. 109.
18. P. du Gay, S. Hall, L. Janes, H. Mackay and K. Negus (1997), *Doing Cultural Studies: the story of the Sony Walkman*, London: Sage, p. 4.
19. T. Peters (1992), *Liberation Management*, London: Pan Books.
20. Ibid., ch. 46.
21. Ibid., p. 649.
22. J. Pine and J.H. Gilmore (1999), *The Experience Economy: work is theatre and every business a stage*, Boston: Harvard Business School Books.
23. http://www.amazon.co.uk
24. P. Townroe (1996), 'Sheffield: restructuring of a city economy over two decades', in N. Harris and I. Fabricius (1996), *Cities and Structural Adjustment*, London: UCL Press, ch.11.
25. C. Smith (1998), *Creative Britain*, London: Faber and Faber, p. 81.
26. http://www.sharinginnovation.org.uk – accessed 4 August 2000.
27. J. Baudrillard (1988), *Selected Writings*, Cambridge: Polity Press, p. 25.
28. For a fuller discussion see: A. McRobbie (1994), *Postmodernism and Popular Culture*, London: Routledge, ch. 10.
29. For interesting accounts see: J. Ash and E. Wilson (1992), *Chic Thrills: a fashion reader*, London: Pandora Press, part 2.

30. P. Bourdieu (1984), *Distinction*, London: Routledge.
31. A. Toffler (1970), *Future Shock*, London: Pan Books.
32. Ibid., p. 284.
33. Solomon, *Consumer Behaviour*, p. 448.
34. S. Nixon (1997), 'Circulating culture', in P. du Gay (ed.), *Production of Culture/ Cultures of production*, London: Sage.
35. Ibid., p. 207.
36. du Gay et al., (1997) *Doing Cultural Studies*, London: Sage, p. 69.
37. Baudrillard, *Selected Writings*, p. 50.
38. D. Hebdige (1988), *Hiding in the Light: on images and things*, London: Routledge.
39. McRobbie, *Postmodernism and Popular Culture*, p. 150.
40. S. Hall (1980), 'Encoding and decoding', in S. Hall, D. Hobson, A. Lowe and P. Willis (eds), *Culture, Media, Language*, London: Hutchinson.
41. H. Mackay (1997), *Consumption and Everyday Life*, London: Sage, p. 274.
42. D. Chaney (1996), *Lifestyles*, London: Routledge, p. 156.

2 Design in industry and commerce

I believe in Michaelangelo, Velasquez, and Rembrandt; in the might of design, the mystery of colour, the redemption of all things by beauty everlasting.
George Bernard Shaw, *Dramatic Opinions and Essays* (1907), vol. II, p. 52

Design has been a Cinderella subject in industry and commerce, particularly in the UK. Here designers, governments and design-led bodies have, since the formation of the Design and Industries Association[1] in 1915, and earlier, stressed the value of design; however, this commendation of design has often fallen on deaf ears. It seems that in other countries design has been more successful in proving its value. The Scandinavians, the Italians, the Germans, the French and the Japanese have used design to their competitive advantage. This has been reflected in buyer perceptions: studies[2] have indicated that each of these countries project excellence in some aspect of design, the Germans in engineering design, the French in fashion, the Italians and Scandinavians in furniture. These are, however, only perceptions; other studies over the last twenty years have looked increasingly at the contributors to success, and at new product development, particularly in manufacturing industry, where design is indeed one essential contributor.

DESIGN'S CONTRIBUTION TO SUCCESS

Before considering the wider notion of success and failure in industry and commerce and design's contribution to it, let us briefly consider how design is used by organisations. Quite simply, at least 50 per cent of what most organisations do, in various industries, is made possible through design. For example:

Manufacturing industry

Ford, for instance, design cars in designed plants through designed outlets, using designed brands and designed literature and advertising.

When consumers see a Jaguar on the road, we want the car itself to communicate what the marque represents — an elegant, sensuous original with refined power. When consumers see a Ford truck, we want the vehicle itself to communicate the tough, durable image it stands for.
Jay Mays, Vice President, Design[3]

Ford Motor Company has claimed to be heading in a new direction in design, but this has had nothing to do with the shape of its vehicles. Rather, the company has looked to use design as a communications tool that instantly and distinctly demonstrates each vehicle's personality, according to J. Mays, Ford's vice president of Design, speaking to the International Motoring Press Association. He said, 'The exterior design of a vehicle is the first visual signal that a customer experiences. In addition to being aesthetically pleasing, a vehicle's appearance should clearly communicate what the vehicle stands for – including a sense of quality, safety and reliability'. Under Mays's direction of seven design studios worldwide, Ford has aimed to create even more distinction between its various nameplates in the future.

The company also announced that the Ford Brand identification sign at Ford dealerships were to get a new look for the new millennium. Ford Division has been testing a new prototype blue Ford oval brand sign for durability and readability in Dearborn, Michigan. It is targeting the year 2003 for the signs to be installed at its 4,200 US Dealerships, timed to coincide with the celebration of the company's centennial anniversary. 'The blue Ford oval is the second most recognisable icon in the world', said Jim O'Connor, Ford Division president. 'The prototype Ford dealership sign was designed in partnership with our Ford dealers and with input from consumers. We believe it conveys the genuine, progressive and smart characteristics that define the Ford brand.'

Ford also has an environmental agenda. Through its environmental impact management efforts, existing plants are rebuilt to become more efficient – or transformed for entirely new uses. The Windsor Engine Plant has been rebuilt as one of the most environmentally responsible automotive manufacturing facilities in the world.[4]

Retail industry

Richards Stores, the womenswear retailer, sells designed apparel in designed outlets and using a designed brand image.

> Richards wanted a new approach to its store interiors that would allow repositioning as a more contemporary and feminine brand. Fitch succeeded in creating and implementing a new identity in selected stores in only four months. The new look completely reworked the image associated with Richards while avoiding alienating the existing customer base. With design as the only significant factor, the sales performance of the redesigned stores was significantly better than that of comparable old-style stores.[5]

Service industry

Osbourne Clarke, a firm of solicitors, uses design to develop a corporate identity and promote their services.

> Osbourne Clarke is a firm of solicitors based in Bristol and the city of London, serving clients throughout the UK and in six regional offices across Europe. Over the last ten years, regional firms

like Osbourne Clark have emerged as significant competition to the City of London firms. But in 1995, the partners decided that its existing identity did not convey the firm's size, expertise and growth aspirations, that it was too 'stuffy' and that it was too similar to other law firms' identities. The designers had to come up with a new identity which would position Osbourne Clarke as capable of competing with anyone in the UK or Europe, and that would increase awareness and understanding of the firm. The new identity was launched on July 1 1996 with mailings sent to thousands of clients, contacts and friends. A pack with full identity guidelines was distributed to all staff. Over the next few weeks, the change gained favourable comments from clients, colleagues and the press. Since launch day, turnover has increased by 30 percent, and the *Lawyer* magazine identified Osbourne Clark as the third fastest growing law firm in the country. Major new clients have been acquired, while the firm has had considerable success recruiting, with awards of the firm among prospective employees far higher than before the new identity.'[6]

Media

This large industry creates and delivers television, film and e-commerce, relying frequently on the skills of designers to visualise and communicate the product.

The website Ted Baker Online (Figure 2.1) had to give viewers quick access to the product ranges. 'It is designed around templates so it is easy to navigate', says Blueberry.Net e-commerce director Sam Stonier. 'Visitors can look at the clothes using a magnifying glass icon that zooms in on particular details of clothes. There is also a Flash animation box, containing information on promotions in the style of a shop window. ... There is also a two dimensional character christened Ted Bod, who is suitably enigmatic to show visitors around the site.' According to Blueberry.Net senior designer and art director of the website, Giles Routledge, 'the clothes come out from this two dimensional background. Blueberry.Net absorbs a percentage of the development costs in return for a percentage of the online profits, giving it a vested interest in making the site successful.'[7]

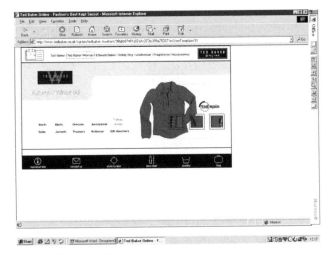

Figure 2.1   Ted Baker Online
Source: www.tedbaker.com

The public sector

The public sector uses design to address political and social agendas.

Great Notley Garden Village

'For several years Essex County Council has been pursuing a policy designed to integrate low energy and passive solar technology into educational and health authority buildings in the county'.[8] In 1997 it joined forces with the Design Council to run a design competition to design a sustainable low-energy, low-environmental-impact primary school. The competition attracted 91 entries and was won by an innovative young London partnership, Allford Hall Monaghan and Morris.

It is easy to cite examples of how the use of design has contributed to an organisation's commercial success in qualitative terms. There are, however, relatively few quantitative studies of the contribution of design to business and commercial success. There are several reasons for this. First there is the problem of defining success and failure.[9] Second, there are difficulties in measuring the 'qualitative' success factors and, third, in defining design and distinguishing the design contribution from the other potential contributors to success, such as those internal to the company, for example, contributions from marketing and sales effort, or external to the company, for example how the competitive environment affects its business.

The contribution of design to organisational success must be measured in more than monetary terms. Walsh, Roy, Bruce and Potter undertook one of the few studies of the contribution of design to business success in the early 1990s and in their book *Winning by Design* reported their results.[10] Table 2.1 illustrates the design factors measured as contributors to competitiveness.

The general results of the study indicated that design contributed to company success. Indeed, around 90 per cent of the implemented projects made a profit, a quarter opened up new home markets and 13 per cent resulted in new or increased exports. Other benefits included reduced manufacturing costs, stock saving, increased profit margins and improved company image.[11] Other studies have also found that design contributes to corporate success. Researchers at the University of Strathclyde, for instance, carried out a large survey of 369 companies, examining management attitudes to design and design management practices, making correlations with sales performance and major competitors. This study found that firms which linked technical and marketing skills, were committed to new product design and had design represented at board level while ensuring it was properly managed had greater market success.[12]

Although there is only a limited number of studies linking design's contribution to market and economic success, there are enough, particularly those undertaken in the late 1980s and early 1990s, to validate the proposition. Indeed, design has been

Table 2.1   Design factors as contributors to competitiveness

Factor in competitiveness	Influence of design	Reflected in:
Price	To reduce manufacturing costs	Sales price
	To determine cost of use and maintenance	Life-cycle costs
Non-price	Product performance, uniqueness, appearance, reliability, durability, safety, ease of use, etc,	Product specification and quality
	Product presentation, packaging, display, promotion, image	Company image
	To improve ease of development and to meet delivery schedules	Delivery to time
	To improve ease of service and repair	After-sales service

Source: Walsh et al. (1988), 'Competitive by design', *Journal of Marketing Management*, vol. 4, no. 2, pp. 201–17.[13]

given government backing both in Europe and the USA. In 1995 the UK government's Competitiveness White Paper stated:

> The effective use of design is fundamental to the creation of innovative products, processes and services. Good design can significantly add value to products, lead to growth in sales and enable both the exploitation of new markets and the consolidations of existing ones. ... The challenge is to integrate design into business processes.

In the USA President Clinton brought together 23 design professionals and industrialists to propose a national strategy for design that would contribute to the country's economy and cultural renewal.[14] In 1997 the UK's new prime minister Tony Blair, in launching the Millennium Products Initiative, stated

> I believe it is time to show a fresh face to the world and reshape Britain as one of the 21st century's most forward thinking and modern nations. I challenge companies to demonstrate that the UK can lead the world by creating products and services that exemplify our strengths in innovation, creativity and design.[15]

In Europe a number of initiatives have been funded to promote and encourage the use of design. For instance, through the European Commission's support of the

European Design Prize, the European Commissioner for Research, Education and Training states that the Commission is 'contributing to the increasing realisation that design has a decisive influence on the success of the innovations which come to the market.'[16]

There is, then, a convincing argument that design contributes to industrial success and improved economic performance, and to both price and non-price factors. Indeed, the design contribution can be defined in numerous ways, resulting in both lifestyle and economic impacts:

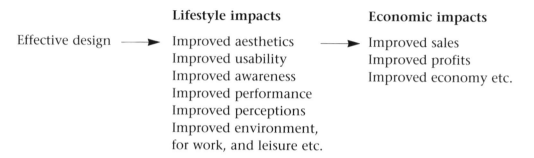

Design is now being recognised as a vital ingredient for two issues, which are foremost activities in most organisations and businesses: *innovation* and *identity*. Companies recognise that in both the national and global competitive environment they must innovate, develop new and better products and services and distinguish their business from that of their competitors by engaging and retaining their customers. It is recognised that designers and design bring creativity and innovation to the organisation.

DESIGN AND INNOVATION

Innovation is generally accepted as the major contributor to the ongoing success of any enterprise. To innovate is to change, to alter, to renew, to bring in something new,[17] and indeed most of the world is engaged in a constant process of change and renewal. Industries look to the process of innovation to enable them to develop and flourish. Frequently the terms design and innovation are used interdependently, possibly because they are both ambiguous terms that are used comprehensively and are both synonymous with creativity.[18] In fact the relationship between design and innovation is a complex one. In order to understand this relationship, it is important to clarify the meaning of each.

Because to innovate is to change, innovation can occur within any context. West and Farr,[19] writing on innovation at work, defined innovation as 'the intentional introduction and application within a role, group or organisation of ideas, processes, products or procedures, new to the relevant unit of adoption, designed to signifi-

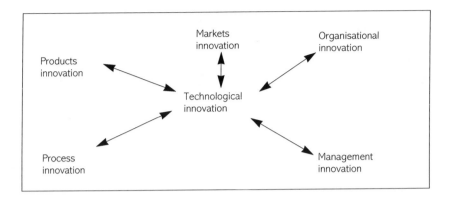

Figure 2.2   Innovation interrelationships

cantly benefit the individual, the group, organisation or wider society'.[19] In an industry context, therefore, one could have, for instance, management innovation, market innovation, process innovation and technological innovation and so on.

Earlier definitions of innovation subsumed all these innovations under 'industrial technological innovation'. Freeman described innovation as a process which includes: the technical, design, manufacturing, management and commercial activities involved in the marketing of a new (or improved) product or the first use of a new (or improved) manufacturing process or equipment (Figure 2.2).[20]

Many definitions of innovation ally it to product development process. Figure 2.3 illustrates how along the new product development process various types of innovation can occur. Jones describes two levels of innovation as breakthrough and incremental.[21] Incremental or low innovation involves the gradual improvement of a product through a series of steps or product variants. Breakthrough or radical innovation is associated with jumps or significant changes and will frequently require concomitant and significant organisational and procedural adaptations if it is to be successful.[22] Breakthrough or incremental innovation can therefore affect the design and development of products at any stage of the process.

The design process will often be central to product and technological innovation, and will also be a facilitator of process or market innovation. For instance, Cambridge Display Technology Company has developed light-emitting polymers, which means that TV screens could arch into incredible biomorphic shapes. Such polymers could replace traditional screens on electronic devices:

the revolutionary plastics allow for a myriad of original shapes and displays just one-millimetre thick, while being more light weight and durable than their glass predecessors. Applying a thin film of electrodes to plastic causes the screen to emit light. Such polymers are being applied to display screen in mobile phones and PDAs by Philips and Seiko Epson. However, CDT believe 'The Technology may ultimately replace paper. Thin and flexible, it's also easy to update with new information'.[23]

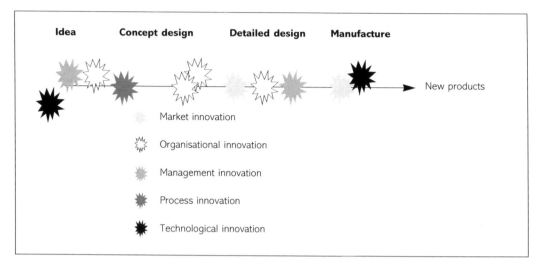

Figure 2.3   New product-oriented innovation process

This invention will only result in product innovation when the designers at Philips and elsewhere have used it in their product design and development process, indeed in developing further uses for the material, designers may enable market innovation or manufacturing process innovation in terms of new ways of producing existing products.

The concept of design as core to technological innovation is illustrated well by Roy and Bruce in their model showing the place of design and development activity (Figure 2.4). Design has a broader spectrum of operation in organisations and new product development; indeed, Walsh et al. contend that while invention and innovation involve a technical advance in the known state of the art of a particular field, designing normally involves making variations on that known state of the art. 'Designing sometimes involves no technical change at all, but may simply result in a product with a different form, style, pattern or decoration, for example a 'new design of chair or body styling for a car.'[24]

Piater described fashion design, for instance, as the creation of non-innovative novelties.[25] Such an example might be the Spring/Summer 98 collection of Issey Miyake the fashion designer, who,

> taking his cue from stocking manufacturers, designed a handful of basic styles spun out like paper dolls, each connected to the other. Individual pieces were separated but seams remained unfinished and could be cut following prescribed lines of indentation, allowing a variety of possibilities with the sleeve, neckline and length. Aptly named 'just before', the collection suggested a suspended state in the production of the garment. The wearer was very much part of the formative process. According to Nancy Knox, a spokesperson for Issey Miyake, 'The idea is to give a woman the choice to individualise her own clothing, so that an outfit takes on a bit of her personality'. Despite the fact that all pieces are cut from the same cloth, the effect is anything but cookie cutter.'[26]

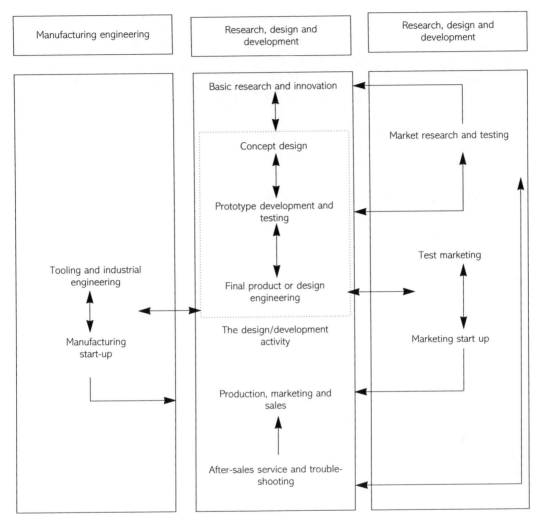

Figure 2.4   The process of technological or industrial innovation showing the place of the design and development activity
Source: R. Roy and M. Bruce (1984), 'Product design, innovation and competition in British manufacturing – background, aims and methods', Working Paper WP-02, Milton Keynes: Design Innovation Group, Open University.

Thus design and innovation are complementary, design being a core element of technical or product innovation yet also broader in its influence on product. Innovation is also broader than design in terms of the management areas in which it can occur alone. Together design and innovation are in effect the drivers of any successful business (Figure 2.5). We are all aware of examples of such synergy: Dyson cyclone vacuum cleaner (James Dyson, 1980s), the iMac (Jonathan Ives, 1998), first tubular chair (Mies van der Rohe, 1930) the London Underground Map (Henry Beck, 1933). They are in effect creating value through product generation.

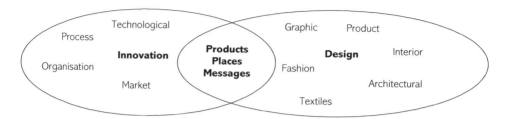

Figure 2.5   The innovation–design relationship

DESIGNING THE BRAND EXPERIENCE

As stated previously in this chapter design contributes to both price and non-price factors. Indeed, increasingly we are seeing trends that suggest that non-price factors are the basis on which most companies are competing; such 'non-price' factors include the *personality* of the company or product as represented through the brand.

The importance of *corporate image* and *identity* has been stressed for the last fifty years and indeed it is argued that Peter Behren's work at AEG (1907–14) created the first corporate identity (Figure 2.6).[27] More recently much of the work in developing the theory of corporate identity/image/personality has been undertaken by the designer Wally Olins, who over the last twenty years has written a succession of publications on this subject.

Figure 2.6   'AEG'
Source: *Design Week*, vol. 14,
no. 50, December 1999

The relationship between design and corporate identity lies in the role the designer takes in creating the symbols and images with which groups are represented: 'Groups always develop an identity, a personality and a behaviour pattern of their own, different from and greater than the sum of the personalities involved'.[28] Traditionally designers have been used to translate the values into the corporate identity. This is an activity that, over the years, has been ridiculed. In 1978 Wally Olins stated:

> After 25 years or so a cloud is beginning to grow over the corporate identity of Business. Businessmen are starting to ask themselves whether this is really another case where the Emperor has no clothes. Is all this fuss about corporate identity and image just a lot of nonsense about symbols, colours and a few bits of type? If these doubts grow the corporate design business will be in trouble and I and a lot of my colleagues will be out of work.[29]

Indeed, the designer decade of the 1980s did hype up design, and many companies saw a corporate identity change as the panacea for all their ills. This brought corporate design into disrepute during the late 1980s early 1990s recession. However, it also encouraged more reflection by organisations in terms of determining what they were aiming to do with their values as depicted by the brand or image. It is clearer today that it is an organisation's ability to communicate effectively that must be managed. This includes the development and monitoring of a corporate personality and an image that are perceived by that organisation's stakeholders. The designer is now one of a team, who must assess, develop and communicate the values and activities of the organisation. Thus we have now moved from purely corporate identity design (a logo, a typeface, colour and a corporate identity manual) to a managed corporate communication strategy.

ELEMENTS OF THE CORPORATE COMMUNICATION PORTFOLIO

The *corporate communication* theorists have developed from basically three fields: management/marketing/public relations; design; and organisational behaviour/ human relations, and each has its own angle on the subject. Marketing and public relations has looked at communications from an advertising and external communications perspective, design from a corporate identity, that is, tangible displays of communications, perspective, and organisational behaviourists have looked at communications from an internal corporate cultural perspective. Van Riel[30] sums this up by describing corporate communication as the integration of three forms of communication:

1. Management communication, that is, communication by (senior) managers with internal and external target groups in order to achieve one's goals, such as:
   – Developing a shared vision of the company within the organisation, establishing and maintaining trust in the organisational leadership

  – Initiating and managing the change process, empowering and motivating
    employees
  – Communicating the vision of the company in order to win support of external
    stakeholders
2. Marketing communication: advertising, direct mail, personal selling, sponsorship
   and so on.
3. Organisational communication – 'a general term used to cover public relations,
   public affairs, investor relations, labour market communication, corporate advertising, environmental communication and internal communication'.

From this perspective, then, corporate communications (like innovation previously)
encompasses everything the organisation is involved in. Van Riel goes on to suggest
that in order to orchestrate and manage corporate communications as a common
whole there should be a common starting-point (CSP) based around the strategy–
identity–image triangle. Van Riel translates the strategy into common starting-points
and further into what the organisation wishes to Promise to each target group, how
they wish to Prove this and the Tone of voice they wish to communicate (PPT). This
is subsequently translated into what they want the target group to know (knowledge),
to feel (attitude) and to do (behaviour) (Figure 2.7).

   This translation of strategy into the ways in which it will be delivered through a
process which includes both tangible and intangible goals is complex, and yet much
of the terminology used is familiar to the designer, whose skills lie in creating 'tones
of voice', of influencing and directing behaviour by manipulating the images and
objects of the world.

   Corporate communication in relation to the work of designers is no longer
purely about the consistent communication of a logo and the corporate colours
through products, environments and communication media. It is the complex
process of understanding the corporate strategy and managing all the manifestations
of that strategy in relation to the image perceived by the public or stakeholders of the
organisation (Box 1.1).

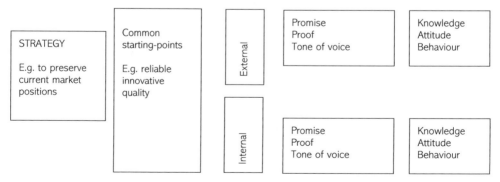

Figure 2.7   Translating strategy into corporate communication common starting-points
   Source: Van Riel (1995), *Principles of Corporate Communication*, Prentice Hall, London.
   Reprinted by permission of Pearson Education Limited.

Box 2.1   Corporate identity as corporate communication

Who you are, what you do, how you do it
Corporate identity manifests itself primarily in three major areas:

- Products or services – what you make or sell
- Environments – where you make or sell it
- Communications – how you explain what you do

Source: W. Olins (1984) *The Wolf Olins Guide to Corporate Identity*

Corporate image defined as the self portrayal of an organisation i.e. the cues or signals which it offers via its behaviour, communication and symbolism …
Source: Van Riel (1995) *Principles of Corporate Communication*

Corporate image
The set of meanings by which an object is known and through which people describe, remember and relate to it. That is, the net result of the interaction of a person's beliefs, ideas, feelings and impressions about an object
Source: G.R. Dowling (1986) 'Managing your corporate images', *Industrial Marketing Management*, **15**, 109–15.

The theory in relation to perceptions often refers to human information processing, by which we receive information via a stimulus; this enters our sensory memory via the senses, a sensory impression is formed by information about shape, colour, pitch, and so on.[31] At this stage, this is stored in the short-term memory and, if repeated, into the long-term memory. There are several views of the way in which images are stored in the memory network; in one such view 'objects can represent different values to people'; Reynolds and Gutman describe an image as hierarchically structured.[32] According to them, the image object has a number of meanings for the subject, which can be indicated by means of a hierarchical so-called means–end chain. Olsen and O'Neill have further elaborated this chain; see Figure 2.8.[33]

An image may also represent an attitude, based on experience or a general impression in the subject's memory. This approach to perceptions is often used as a basis for market research using Kelly's Repertory Grid or attitudinal surveys, semantic differential procedures or multidimensional scaling, comparing competing companies or products and so on. This type of deconstruction is also a demonstration of the important contribution of design to developing the bundle of attributes and attitudes held by an image object, whether a product, a space or a message. The designers again are the manipulators of our experiences and our senses. Taking the means–end chain further, design contributes at every level; it is therefore crucial that designers are aware of the power of their decision making in the commercial and social environment.

OBJECT FUNCTIONS	EXAMPLES	DESIGN
Terminal values		Whole Design Process
Instrumental values	Happiness, health Brazenness, integrity	User understanding/empathy
Psychosocial consequences	Status, attention	Social/cultural understanding awareness
Functional consequences	Leisure, save money	
Abstract attributes	Quality, style	Translated into tangible attributes – colour, materials, functions, shapes designed to be manufactured to a cost.
Concrete attributes	Price, colour	

Figure 2.8   Values of objects according to a means–end chain and design interpretation
    Source: Adapted from Olsen and O'Neill (1989), 'The image study: A worthwhile "Investment" for small retail securities firms', *Journal of Professional Services Marketing*, **4**(2) 159–71. Reprinted by permission of The Haworth Press.

DESIGNING THE BRAND

The key issues for designers are those of understanding the contribution they make and the ability to decode the attributes of an image. A great deal of attention to these issues has been paid in relation to *branding*. Branding is as important to a company as innovation. In the latter part of the twentieth century consumer choice in the developed world was a major factor in business and commercial success. In order to compete, companies must go beyond making and selling a commodity to *creating a brand*. This involves developing a brand image, encouraging brand loyalty, and developing a brand that has equity in the marketplace.

As Bruce states, the original thinking behind branding was to take a commodity and endow it with special characteristics through imaginative use of name, packaging and advertising.[34] Indeed, Aaker defined a brand as 'a distinguishing name and or symbol (such as a logo, trademark, or package design) intended to identify the goods or services of either a seller or a group of sellers and to differentiate those goods or services from those of its competitors'.[35] In both these situations it is easy to identify the role and contribution of design in terms of packaging, advertising and logo design. However, as with corporate identity the subject has become much more complex. As the development of Brands has become more competitive, so the art of branding has become more sophisticated.

In the mid-1980s Tom Peters is reported to have said, 'Perception is all there is'.[36] In 1999 Kotler suggested that marketing is largely the art of brand building and that having a brand name is not enough.[37] 'What does the brand name mean? What associations, performances, and expectations does it evoke? What degree of preference does it create?,' reiterating that perception is all there is. Image creation, like corporate image, is a major factor in building a brand, and thus the role of design and designers is central to its success. Walton suggests that 'a Brand might be defined as the blending of corporate reality – products, services, communications and the inter-actions among people inside and outside the organisation – with designs intended to convey and symbolise that reality'.[38]

Caterpillar, for instance, spent seven years training staff both internally and externally to understand the identity of the company and the values it projects, prin-cipally simplicity and strength. Bonnie Briggs, manager of corporate identity and communication for Caterpillar Inc., delivers and implements the corporate voice. She stated that 'giving people a working knowledge of our identity, defining Caterpillar's personality and developing a common approach to communicating that personality has helped us to reinforce the meaning of the brand ourselves and is helping us to know what makes the brand meaningful and powerful to others'.[39]

Branding is indeed the dominant issue, and often corporate identity is now just part of a branding exercise. Upshaw defined brands as Corporate DNA – the essential meaning of an organisation, service or product.[40] He defines brand identity as 'the meaning' of the brand (a sub-part of overall brand equity, which is the value of the brand). He goes further to suggest that brand identity is most often reflected in:

- brand positioning: here the customer is doing the positioning; the marketing team is simply selling cues into the marketplace. This is true for both the brand and the corporation,
- brand personality: this is often defined as the collection of human-like traits that a brand assumes. Upshaw cites IBM as having historically been masculine, well groomed, maybe a little on the dull side, while the Apple brand has a more femi-nine trait, with more artistic and friendly undertones.

> A key difference between personality and positioning is that the latter tends to be more rational in basis. Even the positioning of the most ephemeral brands – fragrances, for instance – is often based on a logical argument. But brand personalities are so important because no purchase is devoid of emotion. Oven cleaners, checking accounts, bottled water, rental cars, computer soft-ware all sound fairly mundane as products and services but purchasing them involves important emotions. A specific personality can give prospects an emotional 'handle' which consumers can better understand and relate to the brand.[41]

- identity distribution, 'the way in which the brand meaning is distributed in the market place', or how the identity is distributed, is important, as is the use of colour of symbols and images and the relationship between brands (brand networking).

Sue Whitehead, director of marketing at the Regal Hotel group, says 'it's [corpo-rate identity is] not just a new identity, but a rebrand and a rethink of how the company does business'.[42] Keiran Murphy, chief executive of animal pharmaceuti-cals group Vericore, described their new identity as a 'name change, business repo-sitioning and cultural change'. Therefore design groups such as Interbrand see themselves as branding specialists: 'We are no longer in the identity business but the brand business.'

Designers, however, should not forget their origin and their unique contribution – that of creativity and understanding the use of design tools and techniques to manipulate our senses and create perceptions. Understanding the business and understanding strategy are important, but the designer's unique contribution is translating and creating values. Take for example the traditional UK Pub: during the early 1990s the concept of the branded pub was launched. Chains such as the Pitcher and Piano and the Slug and Lettuce developed a brand and an excellent trade; however, as with most cycles the branding becomes formulaic and the chain begins to lose its value to the customer. The customer begins to see through the paint and rejects the pure marketing formula. There is a demand now, not just in pubs but in many areas of formulaic branding such as retailing, to provide individuality. The problems of Marks and Spencer in 1998/99 could be seen as a rejection by an increasingly sophisticated customer of the formulaic and bland use of branding and design. Steve Hall, designer associate at The Design Solution, suggests 'There is a need for more individuality while staying within the brand's family of design.'[43] This involves the use of subtle visual clues that are perceived subliminally by the customer, meaning that designers must be more completely in tune with design tools and customer pschology, for instance understanding the masculine and feminine needs in the interior design of a pub.

The Elbow Room, based in London's Westbourne Grove (Figure 2.9), is considered to be a good example of design that incorporates masculine and feminine elements in a balanced way: 'The Elbow Room takes a traditionally male venue and makes it attractive to women by including a sophisticated bar area, partially enclosing the pool area and providing a number of enclosed areas. Yet it retains an edge through masculine elements of design and materials, like iron from which the stools are made.'[44]

A further illustration of the development of brands as entities in their own right

Figure 2.9 'The Elbow Room'
Source: www.pauldaly.com

and a platform for the designer to create an image is seen through the use of personalities. The branding of Twiggy, the 1960s model, in the 1990s illustrates the way in which designing a brand relates directly to perceptions and translation by designers of a personality. The Twiggy brand, Twiggy & Co[45] set up by the model and actress, was to apply the Twiggy tag to a number of products, in association with existing manufacturers and retailers. The general brief in creating the identity centred around opportunities to market the brand in the fashion/health/cosmetics sector – all designs aimed to convey Twiggy's personality. 'Before we met Twiggy we had all sorts of preconceptions about what the Twiggy brand could involve. But the meeting focused our perception of her. What she does represent is health, vitality and beauty, plus a little bit of quirkiness.' This is the way a creative director of Springett Associates (the designers) saw his brief to create a brand (Figure 2.10). (Figure 2.11 shows ongoing development work, not the final design solution.)

This example illustrates just how much the brands rely on the designer to develop images that reflect and promote the value. However, one must not forget that the visual identity is just one aspect of the whole product. If the core product fails to deliver the values represented in every other aspect of the business, then the business will ultimately fail. For instance, the restaurant group Planet Hollywood used all the marketing hype and design power possible to develop a personality based on fame and the film industry. Yet once this standardisation became familiar to the sophisticated market, the customers reflected on the core product and many felt the food was purely expensive burgers.[46] Therefore, success always lies in designing the detail, developing individuality, and differentiation while maintaining the soul of the product or service, and keeping in touch with the increasing demands of the market place.

The increasing reliance on brand image demands more from designers. Designers

Figure 2.10 'Twiggy'
Source: design consultancy: Springetts; client: Twiggy & Co.

working in any arena must develop highly sensitive understanding of the design toolbox – colours, shapes, materials, movement, odours, space, texture and imagery. They must understand both tacitly and intuitively what is happening with the combinations of these tools in the environment of the contact – the consumer, the user, the stakeholder in that object, place or media. This means they must also understand the very nature of the human psyche, they are not only technicians, they are psychologists, sociologists and anthropologists.

THE DEVELOPMENT OF THE PRODUCT SERVICE PHENOMENON AND THE ROLE OF DESIGN

If we consider, then, that the nature of innovation and of branding owe much to the contribution of design as a function and an activity, we can consider the whole environment on which design has an effect. The *whole product model*[47] offers a comprehensive conception of a product, which incorporates elements beyond its technical capabilities. There are two reasons why this is useful:

- Product differentiation solely based on technical competence often deteriorates over time.
- Many customers, especially in industrial markets, rank intangibles such as service, worldwide presence, brand and quality as equally important as a product's technical capabilities. The whole product model (Figure 2.11) defines a product as the sum of core, expected, augmented and potential product phenomenon.

    As a market matures, expected and augmented elements become core elements. For example, intermittent windscreen wipers, originally developed for lorries, became an extra for the car market and are now seen as a core element. In parallel, the brand personality is wrapped up in this product model. As the elements are developed through design, so they represent the personality of the brand, illustrating the brand values developed through corporate and marketing strategy. Design strategy and the design brief of the product or service must represent the brand and the whole product model; the designer's role in innovation is to work with the 'DNA' so that the consumer/user stakeholder interprets and positions the whole product satisfactorily according to the organisation's strategy. In this way designers manipulate the corporate DNA which flows through every aspect of the organisation and its brands. The designer is thus the gatekeeper to the total experience.

    For any organisation, then, the designer is part of the team, determining and designing the experience. We are familiar with this in the most obvious way with theme parks and places such as the Millennium Dome, which has taken experience building to extremes. However in more subtle ways industry and organisations need designers to build the experience, through products, services, places and messages.

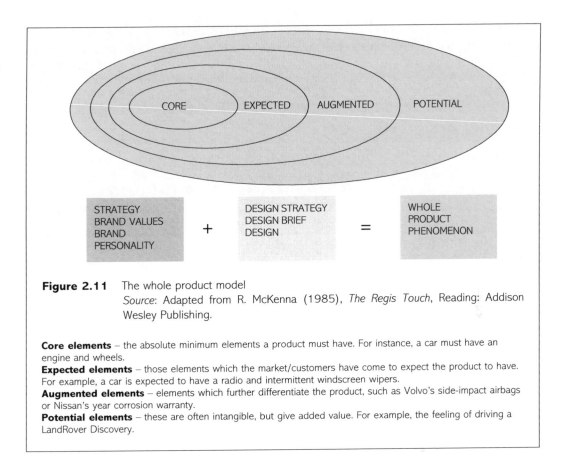

Figure 2.11   The whole product model
Source: Adapted from R. McKenna (1985), *The Regis Touch*, Reading: Addison Wesley Publishing.

Core elements – the absolute minimum elements a product must have. For instance, a car must have an engine and wheels.
Expected elements – those elements which the market/customers have come to expect the product to have. For example, a car is expected to have a radio and intermittent windscreen wipers.
Augmented elements – elements which further differentiate the product, such as Volvo's side-impact airbags or Nissan's year corrosion warranty.
Potential elements – these are often intangible, but give added value. For example, the feeling of driving a LandRover Discovery.

MANAGING DESIGN IN INDUSTRY

Design as a function or activity has been paid relatively little attention by management theorists. All other commercially critical business functions such as marketing, operations and finance have been studied, a body of theory developed and core curricula established in most business schools. Design has not had such treatment. It is only relatively recently that *design management* has appeared as a topic for research. In the UK, design management began with the Thatcher Government's Managing Design Initiative, which led to the development of a few courses in design and business schools which began to address the relationship between design and business. In the USA the predominant activity in this field has been led by the Design Management Institute, which was formed in the mid-1980s and has been producing case studies and a journal for over ten years. This is predominantly a practitioner-based group but has led the way in achieving prominence in, and discussion on, managing design.

There are now a number of core texts addressing the basic activities for managing design.[48,49] Generally managing design has been considered at two levels: managing design strategically and managing design at the operational level of the design process.

Managing design strategy

Managing design strategically is a complex issue, as this chapter has illustrated. Design's contribution to industry and commerce is extensive and it is a central feature in both innovation and image building. The subject therefore becomes elusive, ill defined if at all and perceived to be the domain of one or more of the dominant functions within an organisation. Marketing will define image creation or brand development as their domain; R&D will define innovation in products as theirs (Figure 2.12). Hence the development of the concept of 'Silent Design', that is, design by people who are not designers and are not aware that they are participating in design activity. Gorb and Dumas identified that this goes on in all organisations, even those that have formal design policies.[50]

Figure 2.12   Design straddles domains

In this age of 'experience', organisations must understand the experience they are providing and how design contributes to it. Therefore as a first step in design strategy development, the delivery of the experience through design must be deconstructed. Often this is referred to as a *design audit*, a systematic identification and analysis of design at all levels of the organisation, from the physical manifestations of design, to the external factors which might influence design decisions (Table 2.2).

It is now necessary to take this approach further, in order to deconstruct the total experience as perceived by stakeholders. It is important to analyse the elements which contribute to that experience, that is, to decode the attributes and the values they deliver. It may be useful to extend the whole product model to cover the entire experience (Figure 2.13).

Figure 2.13 illustrates the essential elements of the customer experience: the central core experience is of course the experience of the product, and this is augmented by the brand experience, the perceptions that the customer has of the brand before, during and after purchase. The touch experience may be a fleeting one – it may be an advertising hoarding, a brochure or the use of the product or service

Table 2.2   Areas for a design audit

Physical manifestations of design	Design management	Corporate culture	Environmental factors
Visual identity Corporate design standards Products Work environment	Design resources: human, physical, internal, external Design skills Design training Design management: process, procedures, guidelines Design funding: investment and return Design department: location, service, aim and objectives Project management	Corporate design strategies Design awareness/ understanding Design champions Integration of design and other functions Design activities undertaken	Market trends (which could affect design decisions) Design trends Legislation Standards Technology trends

at one remove, for example seeing a friend or colleague or receiving a recommendation. The potential experience is the experienced expected by the customer in the future, what are they looking for, what will delight them and maintain the overall values they have of the whole experience.

Techniques such as the use of object values to deconstruct each of the experiences may enable the company to understand the values, consequences and attributes necessary for the total experience. A design policy and strategy can then be developed from an understanding of this experience deconstruction. Table 2.3 illustrates how a matrix using values and experience can be explored.

The JBL case study illustrates the importance of understanding the customer and translating this into experiential-based design. 'Such experiential based design seeks to so thoroughly understand the customer's experience that it can identify the values he or she perceives as defining. It then fashions a product and marketing design strategy to mirror that experience in a brand culture underlying the product and inspiring passion.'[51]

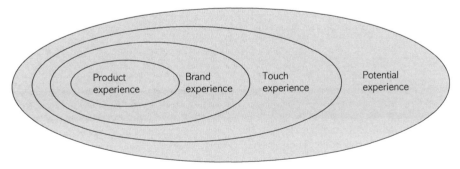

Figure 2.13   The whole product model as consumer experience

Table 2.3   Deconstructing the experience of BMW/car

		Product experience	Brand experience	Touch experience	Potential experience
Life values	Terminal values	Comfortable driving experience	Security	Excellence	Relationship
	Instrumental values				
	Psychosocial values	High status	Superior	Sophisticated	Solid
Consequences	Functional consequences	High-powered, fast, comfortable	Quality service	Quality	Advanced function
Attributes	Concrete attributes	Price, shape, engine power	Quality	Good customer service	Innovation
	Abstract attributes	Style, quality	Quality sophistication	Feeling valued, feeling important	?

Many international companies now build design centres or laboratories which seek to understand the users and their needs. For instance Texas Instruments has a User Understanding and Experimental Lab to identify user needs and to test the feasibility of concepts.[52] Design strategies and policies must evolve, from organisations' in-depth understanding of their markets, users, customers and other stakeholders, their need to define the experience that they want to give to these groups.

Organisations develop total product knowledge over time (see Figure 2.14). Beginning with products, they learn how to design and develop for the needs of their customers, building a sound understanding of user needs and desires. They build up the brand based on such knowledge, translating product ownership into brand values, and further into the manipulation of a sophisticated customer experience. The danger is that over time the focus is often lost, the company loses contact with the essence of the customer and is unable to use design to provide the product/brand/experience that satisfies the desires and expectations of the changing customer. This

Case Study: JBL Car Audio

In 1992 the consumer market for mobile audio electronics represented the fastest-growing and most profitable segment of the consumer electronics industry. JBL, one of the world's leading loudspeaker manufacturers, enjoyed wide consumer recognition for its home loudspeakers, but its car audio brand was relatively unknown among the Pioneers, Sonys, and Alpines. It controlled a significant share of the home loudspeaker market, but only a tiny percentage of the car audio market. Under the direction of Gina Harman, senior vice president of marketing and brand management, JBL retained Ashcraft Design to reinvent its car audio brand products and packaging.

The goals were threefold: to strengthen its brand image among car audio consumers, increase sales by 20 percent, and reduce manufacturing costs. To meet these goals, Ashcraft formed a multidisciplinary audit team to conduct an interactive customer audit that would define consumers' experience of car audio and how it contributed to the quality of their life.

JBL's existing brand market model rested on the assumption, formulated over years of selling audio components at retail costs of 15 percent to 20 percent higher than the competition, that consumers would pay a premium for quality materials and audio performance specifications. This strategy was directed toward the 'techno-spec' customer: male, 35 to 55 years old, economically better off, driving a mid to high end car. Industrywide, the war for market share was being fought through technical specifications. A competitive product audit revealed virtually no visual brand differentiation in competitors' product packaging. Packages were blue or grey, printed with photographs of the products and lists of engineering specifications. This tech-spec strategy left manufacturers struggling for brand recognition and market position in an ever-tightening spiral of increased engineering and power handling specifications. The customer found it difficult and confusing to discern the minute differences in the engineering specifications.

The interactive customer audit revealed an alternative market model. Sixty-five percent of the car audio market comprises young males between 18 and 24. Single or married, they work out, surf, snowboard, and 'cruise'. These are high-energy activities, and the customer's choice of music enhances and colours the quality of these pursuits. In many ways, music becomes the defining experience. These young men are value conscious but willing to spend disproportionately above their wages to purchase brands associated with their lifestyle. Most of all, they seek status, fun, and peer group acceptance.

They also associate the quality of their life experience with the quality of their car audio systems. The concussive bass-driven boomboxes on wheels currently jarring urban and suburban neighbourhoods are more than just popular among these young men: They represent a defining experience of young American manhood. Junie Vicente, a 25 year old resident of Oxnard, Calif., describes his Camaro's $11,000 stereo system this way: 'It's my wife, my baby, my Mona Lisa. It's me. It's who I am.'

For JBL, the battle for this consumer's mind would be fought through the high-energy experiences he associates with this music. To capture the market, JBL needed to strike at the core of these experiences. The challenge was to express the attributes of the culture driving this market throughout the market delivery system. Compared with the outmoded techno-spec customer model, the images with which these youthful customers associate their activities are more energy-driven, exciting and dynamic. Based on these images, Ashcraft formed a brand image design strategy identifying the quality of JBL's audio performance with the high-energy lifestyle of this core consumer group. Advertising, product, packaging, owner's manuals, point-of-purchase displays, trade shows, sales collateral materials, and employee training materials would all reflect and reaffirm the brand image design strategy.

This design strategy was woven through the product design, packaging design, advertising, point of purchase, brochures, and product labelling. Sales brochures and marketing communications developed the Loud and Clear concept to identify with the quality of the car audio experience. Package design and product graphics captured the energy of the customer's lifestyle, while advertising created TV spots that featured urban youths singing along with their favourite artists, associating the emotion of the concert experience with their life experience. The strategy was successful with both customers and retailers. In 1992 the coordinated experiential design program had reduced manufacturing costs and created defining objects that increased sales by over 30 percent the first year and maintained a consistent double-digit growth rate over the next three years.

Source: D. Ashcroft and L. Slattery, 'Experiential Design, Strategy and Market Share' *Design Management Journal* (Fall 1996), p. 42.

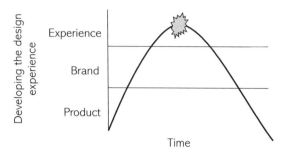

Figure 2.14   Developing the design experience

further emphasises the need for consistent and coordinated focus from multifunctional teams on the customer and possibly explains why management theory today emphasises that focus. This, however, is not the total solution: design skills and creativity are needed as core skills in developing the new world, the new experiences which the customer has never thought of but which are in tune with the values of the organisation. This balancing of customer needs, design visions and organisational values is crucial to the longevity of any business.

MANAGING OPERATIONAL DESIGN

When the experience required is understood, this needs to be translated into specific design briefs for all aspects of business, products, packaging, advertising, interiors and so on. Traditionally the design brief has been a stand-alone document developed usually by marketing and given to designers – either in-house designers or external designers.

Knowing that a business is based on the total experience means that the development of the brief requires enormous effort in capturing attributes and needs at the front end of the design process, the 'fuzzy front end', where no one really understands the concepts. This is the stage at which a rigorous *requirements capture process* should be undertaken.

Once the requirements capture process has been defined and is being managed properly, the product definition can then move into the product development process. This process, whether it is a service development, product, place or communication, has been subject to a great deal of debate: Cooper's model (Figure 2.15) is one of the most popular approaches and used by many practitioners.

Whatever the model used for new product development, it is important to understand how the design process within such a model is managed. Pugh developed a model in 1986, the total design activity model, in which he defined total design as systematic activity necessary from the identification of the market/user need – an activity that encompasses product process, people and organisation, that is, the integration of required coordinated inputs from different specialisms and something

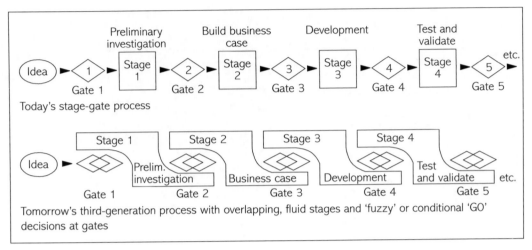

Figure 2.15   Third-generation model
Source: Robert G. Cooper (1994), 'Third Generation New Product Processes', *Journal of Product Innovation Management*, vol. 11, pp. 3–14.

from industry. This reinforces the need to bring the designer to the centre of a multi-functional team in order to understand and design the *total product experience*.

Figure 2.16 expands on the Pugh diagram by identifying all the stages of the design process and the activities involved. It also illustrates how it is a team-based activity. This model of the process was developed for SMEs who have little or no experience of sourcing, briefing, monitoring or evaluating designers.[53] It illustrates the degree to which design as an activity must be managed.

Sourcing design

Design as a function can operate both within an organisation (in-house design) or as a service provided by an independent consultancy (outsourced) or a combination of these two. The procurement of such services must be managed, as must any other organisational activity. Frequently this role has been undertaken by the marketing function; however, the specialist knowledge of both design and the design activity has led to a growth in the use of a design management function. (Chapter 6 illustrates by case study examples of such design managers.)

If organisations outsource design, there are principally two types of relationship: the *ad hoc* relationship by which a company contacts design consultancies as and when it needs to and chooses them using a bid process, based on skill and cost; and the partnering relationship whereby the designer is chosen as a preferred supplier or held on a roster of preferred suppliers, or, in the case of long-term partnering, the consultancy has an exclusive relationship with its clients. This relationship is often preferred by designers as it enables them to build a rapport with the company and its

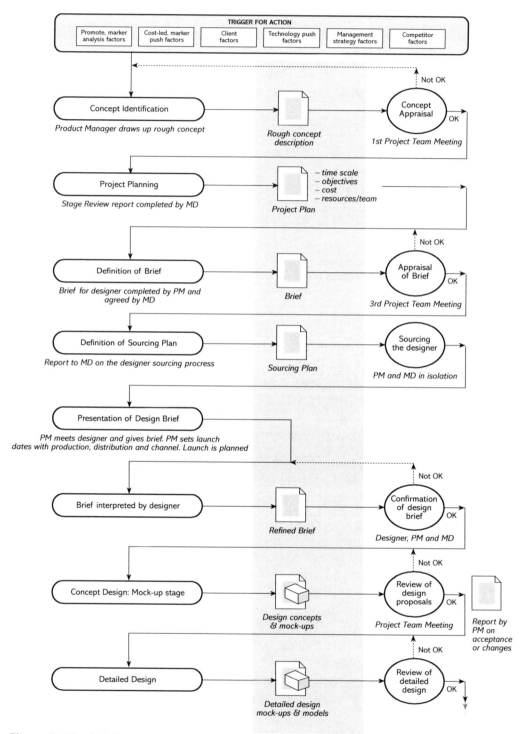

Figure 2.16   A design management process

Source: M. Bruce, R. Cooper and D. Vazquez (1999) 'Design – A Panacea for Enterprise Britain?', *The Design Journal*, vol. 2, Issue 3.

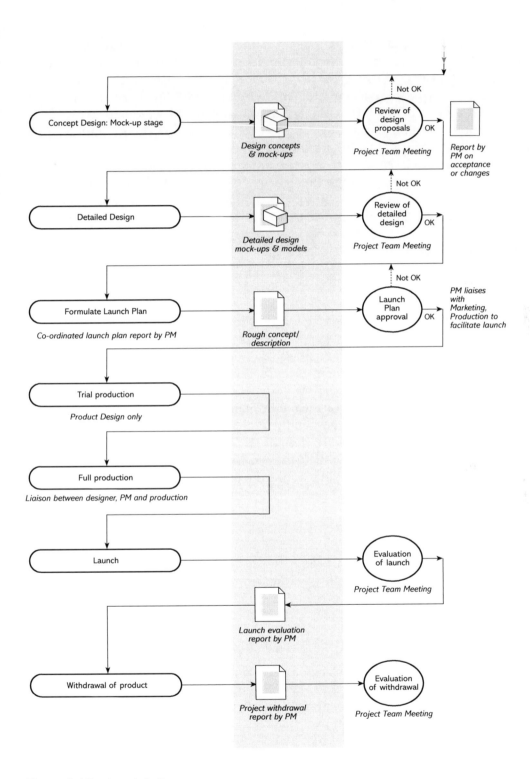

Figure 2.16   (concluded)

desired customer, and can thus engage with the product/service experience. Paul Smith, the fashion designer, is a good example of using a partnering arrangement. Ever since his days as a student at the Royal College of Art he has worked with Aboud Soudain, a design consultant, and student collegues, who design all retailing and promotional aspects of his international business. Again the product experience is built on a long relationship and a common product understanding and synergy between the customers and Smith and Aboud Soudain.

The sourcing of design expertise is a complex process. Many small companies have never used professional design expertise and may be wary of the potential costs of doing so. Other companies may not know the types of skills that designers have.

There are several different approaches to sourcing design.

• Personal recommendation
• Pitching
• Previous experience
• Yellow pages
• Qualified design broker (for example business links).

Some of the factors influencing the choice of designer are their reputation and the personal rapport that the client feels towards the designer. As design is a creative process involving both the client and the designer, the rapport or personal chemistry is a factor that should not be ignored. Commitment to the project may be an important aspect of sourcing, particularly when the project may last over a period of several months, which is typical for a product design. The comment by one marketing director of Ingersoll-Rand is apt here[54] 'the designer had to take some responsibility and put his own stake in as well. We didn't want someone to come and listen to our problems, go away and solve them and come back with a solution. We wanted someone who was part of the team.'

From the designer's perspective this may be more time-consuming than expected, and in this case the industrial designer said: 'You have to tell the client everything, otherwise at the end of the project, the product may not be acceptable. This takes a lot of time, and typically we have put in more than we wanted to.'

Preparing the brief

The nature of design is such that it requires an exchange of information between the functions of management and design, each having different perspectives and backgrounds, and effective communication between two different perspectives is not always simple.[55, 56] Studies have shown that the nature of the brief is of great importance to the success or otherwise of the final design work.[57] Studies have also shown that a designer needs a great deal of information/market intelligence, both overt and tacit, in order to produce an effective solution for the client.[58, 59] The designer needs to understand the market, the competition and the business environment of the client. In addition, the strategic direction of the company and of the product needs to be assimilated by the designer.[60] All this information should be communicated in the briefing process in order to enable the designer to understand the whole context in which he/she is creating. Chapter 5 discusses communication in greater detail.

A design brief should at the very minimum contain the following:

- Background to the company
- The design problem
- Design specifications, product attributes
- Consumer and market information
- Costs
- Timescales.

Briefing can also cover issues such as company structure, brand values, and explaining the business and the relationship with its suppliers.

Developing the brief is an interactive process and the designer can contribute to this by adding his/her perspective. In some cases, the designer may need to interview the senior managers to ascertain their views as to what is required and to obtain their input into the planning stages of the design. In corporate identity work, for example, the company name may be considered, the mission of the company and an assessment of the current logo may be undertaken in order to discover the best approach to take for the redesign. This process of fact finding and discussion may take considerable time and effort but is critical to the ultimate success of the project.

PROJECT MANAGEMENT

Project management means defining a project's goal, planning all the work to achieve the goal, leading the project teams, maintaining progress, and ensuring the project is completed successfully. Managing the design process effectively is extremely important to the outcome of the design and meeting project objectives. It is essential to establish resources early on in a project so as to determine the extent of the costs and to understand the tasks and assign roles and responsibilities of the project team members. A project team must be assembled consisting of the relevant people from the client firm. A representative from the design team should be present at all meetings.

Regular communication between the designer and client is vital to ensure that the designer's interpretation of the objectives is correct and that the project is running to schedule and budget. Companies need a *process with defined timescales* for meetings, contact reports, briefing, the first concept, detailed design and evaluation. Figure 2.16 provides such a project management tool for managing design.

DESIGN IS ABOUT VALUE CREATION

This chapter has discussed how design is central to industry and organisational activities, how it is related to both core products and the product environment – the product experience, thus revealing why it is important to manage design and understand its value. Design management now not only means managing the people and the process, but deconstructing and analysing the total product experience to enable the designer to work with the organisation team to understand and contribute to that experience. It is therefore important to understand designers and to manage the relationship between designers and organisations.

As our level of sophistication increases, so the demands increase on the designer to understand our relationship with the material world. However, the designer is not alone; organisations need to build the core skills around design thinking.

Edward De Bono suggests that the last millennium has not been a great success.[61]

> We have advanced in science and technology but not much in human behaviour. The thinking of the last millennium has been concerned with 'what is'. This is the thinking of analysis, criticism and argument. What we have not sufficiently developed is the thinking concerned with 'what can be' (creating value). This is thinking that is creative and constructive. This is thinking that seeks to solve conflicts and problems by designing a way forward. The emphasis is on design, not judgement and the only way we can move forward and make use of the opportunities offered by science and technology is by adopting this new thinking.

Design is a core skill, a central economic activity; it is intrinsic to industry/organisations not only as part of the innovation and image-building process, but also as a way of thinking about 'life experiences'. How we can create experiences, and how these affect human behaviour and the world, both material and immaterial, is the domain of design.

NOTES

1. The Design and Industries Association was formed in the UK in 1915 by Ambrose Heal and Harry Peach to promote design to industry. It was the forerunner to the Council of Industrial Design formed in 1944, and the Design Council formed in 1960.
2. M. Bannister and J. Saunder (1978), 'UK Consumer attitudes towards imports', *European Journal of Marketing*, **12**, (8), 562–70.
3. D. S. Halfhil (1980), *Multinational Marketing Strategy*, Management International.
4. *Ford Annual Report 1998*.
5. www. Ford.com 2000.
6. Design Business Association (1997), *Design Effectiveness Awards, Marketing Week* Supplement, p. 20. London: Centaur Communications Ltd.
7. Ibid., p. 9.

8. S. Bentley (2000), 'The Fabulous Baker Boy', *Design Week*, 14 January.
9. 'The Green Schoolbook' (1997/8), *Design*, Winter.
10. R. Cooper (1999), 'The Invisible Success Factors in Product Innovation', *Journal of Product Innovation Management*, **16**, 115–33.
11. V. Walsh, R. Roy and M. Bruce (1988), 'Competitive by Design', *Journal of Marketing Management*, 4 (2), 201–17.
12. S. Potter, R. Roy, H. Capon, M. Bruce, V. Walsh and J. Lewis (1991), *The Benefits and Costs of Investment in Design*, DIG Open University, July DIG–03.
13. V. Walsh, R. Roy, M. Bruce and S. Potter (1992), *Winning by Design*, Oxford: Blackwell Business.
14. L.M. Service, S.J. Hart and M.J. Baker (1989), *Profit by Design*, Scotland: The Design Council.
15. C. Pearlman, et al. (1993), Designing America, *Industrial Design*, March/April, 55.
16. Design Council (1997), *Millennium Products Brochure*, London: Design Council.
17. J. Thakara (1997), *Winners! How Today's Successful Companies Innovate by Design*, London: Gower.
18. *Oxford English Dictionary*.
19. R. Roy and D. Wield, (1989), *Product Design and Technological Innovation*, Milton Keynes: Open University Press.
20. M. West and J. Farr (1990), *Innovation and Creativity at Work*, Chichester, UK: John Wiley & Sons.
21. C. Freeman (1974), *The Economics of Industrial Innovation*, Penguin Modern Economic Texts, cited in Robin Roy (1996), *Innovation Design Environment and Strategy*, Readings Block 4, T302, Milton Keynes: Open University Press.
22. T. Jones (1997), *New Product Development, an Introduction to a Multifunctional Process*, Oxford: Butterworth Heinemann.
23. C. Freeman, *Economics of Industrial Innovation*.
24. A. Codrington (1998), 'Plastic Fantastic', *The International Design Magazine*, May, p. 28.
25. Walsh et al. (1992), *Winning by Design*, Oxford: Blackwell Business.
26. A. Piater (1984), *Barriers to Innovation*, London: Francis Pinter.
27. N. Herrman (1998), 'Bias Cut', the international design magazine, May, p. 26.
28. G. Julier (1993), *The Thames and Hudson Encyclopaedia of 20th Century Design and Designers*, London: Thames and Hudson.
29. W. Olins (1978), *The Corporate Personality*, London: Design Council.
30. Ibid.
31. Cees B.M., van Riel (1995), *Principles of Corporate Communication*, London: Prentice Hall.
32. J. F. Engel, R.D. Blackwell and P.W. Miniard (1990), *Consumer Behaviour*, Chicago: The Dryden Press.
32. T.J. Reynolds and J. Gutman (1984), Advertising in image management, *Journal of Advertising Research*, 24, 27–37.
33. R.A. Olsen and M.F. O'Neill (1989), 'The image study: A worthwhile "invest-

ment" for small retail securities firm', *Journal of Professional Services Marketing*, **4** (2), 159–71.

34. M. Bruce (1998), *The Concise Blackwell Encyclopaedia of Management*, edited by Cary L. Cooper and Chris Argyris, Oxford: Blackwell Business.

35. D.A. Aaker (1991), *Managing Brand Equity – Capitalising on the value of a brand name*, New York: The Free Press, ch. 1.

36. T. Walton (1997), 'Insights on the Theory and Practice of Branding', *Design Management Journal*, Winter, p. 5.

37. P. Kotler (1999), *Kotler on Marketing: How to create, win and dominate markets*, New York: The Free Press, p. 63.

38. T. Walton (1997), 'Insights', p. 5.

39. B. Briggs (1997), 'Building Brand Value', *Design Management Journal*, Winter, pp. 56–60.

40. Lynn B. Upshaw (1997), 'Transferable Truths of Brand Identity', *Design Management Journal*, Winter, p. 9.

41. Lynn B. Upshaw (1997), 'Transferable Truths'.

42. C. Thomas and C. Dowdy (1999), *Design Week*, 23 July pp. 17–21.

43. M. Barnard (1999), *Design Week*, 6 August.

44. Ibid.

45. Twiggy & Co (1999), 'Twiggy goes out on a limb', *Design Week*, 6 August, p. 9.

46. *BBC Breakfast News* item, Thursday 19 August 1999.

47. R. McKenna (1985), *The Regis Touch*, Reading, MA: Addison Wesley, T. Levit (1981), 'Marketing Intangible Products and Product Intangibles', *Harvard Business Review*, May–June, Reprint No. 81306.

48. R. Cooper and M. Press (1995), *The Design Agenda*, Chichester, UK: John Wiley & Sons.

49. M. Bruce and R. Cooper (1997), *Marketing and Design Management*, Oxford: Thompson Business Press.

50. P. Gorb and A. Dumas, (1987), *Silent Design*, Design Studies, (3), Oxford: Butterworth Heineman.

51. D. Ashcraft and L. Slattery (1996), 'Experiential Design, Strategy and Market Share', *Design Management Journal*, Fall.

52. C. Wood (1996), 'Vision Design: Building the User Understanding and Experimental Lab', *Design Management Journal*, Fall.

53. M. Bruce, R. Cooper and D. Vasquez (1999), 'Design – A panacea for enterprise Britain', *The Design Journal*, **2** (3).

54. M. Bruce and R. Cooper (1997), *Marketing and Design Management*.

55. W.E. Souder and M. Song (1997), 'Contingent Product Design and Marketing Strategies Influencing New Product Success and Failure in US and Japanese Electronics Firms', *The Journal of Product Innovation Management*, **14** (1).

56. Walker in Oakley (1990), *Design Management: A Handbook of Issues and Methods*, Oxford: Blackwell.

57. S. Potter, R. Roy, H. Cepon, M. Bruce, V. Walsh and J. Lewis (1991), *The Benefits of Costs of Investment in Design*, DIG Open University, July DIG–03.
58. Cooper Press, *Design Agenda*.
59. Oakley, *Design Management*.
60. Bernsen in Oakley, *Design Management*.
61. E. De Bono (1999), *New Thinking for the New Millennium*, London: Viking.

3   Designing the experience

Joseph Campbell wrote, 'What people seek is not the meaning of life but the experience of being alive.' This provocative view challenges us to look inside ourselves and at the work that we do. What does it take to provide enlivening experiences for others? I find that professional training and years of experience are not enough. By themselves, they seem somehow inadequate in our evolving world, in which design and technology come together. What is vital is our humanness: who we are and the ways in which we express our fundamental human qualities in our work. When these qualities are included as an integral and natural part of the design process, everyone benefits: those for whom we are designing, as well as ourselves.

Lauralee Alben, interactive designer[1]

PUT IT ALL DOWN TO EXPERIENCE

Are you a product designer, or a designer of textiles? Do you design ceramics or interactive media? Perhaps graphics, packaging or craft objects are your thing? The design professions are traditionally defined by the physical objects that they each produce. This stems, in part at least, from many designers being 'thing' people rather than 'people' people – it is the using, conceiving, designing, making and fitting together of things that inspires, motivates and drives designers. This apparent obsession with things – with material objects – provides the spur to developing the skills and knowledge that are essential to good design practice. It has also led to some truly dreadful, irrelevant and self-indulgent design in which objects fulfil no apparent need, are difficult to use and have little appeal to anyone other than the designer. We are not stating a matter of taste here, but a matter of fact. As we will explain later in this book, most design ideas are commercial failures, and the chief reason for failure is that these ideas fail to connect meaningfully or effectively with people's lives.

A theme we keep returning to is that the designer is not just a creator of objects, but is an enabler of experiences – and it is this idea of experience that should be the starting point and focus of design. But don't just take our word for it. For a designer brimming over with creative vision, it is perhaps strange that Eric Chan talks so much about invisibility. This New York based industrial designer has designed telephones, banks' cash machines, lighting and a range of other products that have picked up sixteen major international design awards. According to him:

it's essential to soften the technology, to make it transparent. As designers we have to think about how users enjoy the experience of whatever it is that they're doing, not the object. The object should become transparent – it's the action that people want the object to do, and the experience of doing it that is important'.[2]

It is an obsession with *material culture* – not just material objects – that would appear to mark out the successful, or at least relevant, designer. Material culture is, if you like, the frame that surrounds the object – its social context, ways of using it, its commercial value, the meanings it provides to users and the overall experience that its use or ownership enables. As such, products are 'an expression of who and what we are that shapes how society can proceed'.[3]

So how can designers understand experience? What experiences are most meaningful to people? How is experience shaped by the design process? In what ways can designers 'design experiences'? How important is the idea of experience to the future of material culture? How should designed experiences help to shape society in the twenty-first century?

This chapter considers these and other key questions. It bridges the cultural context of design presented in Chapter 1 with the business context of design practice raised in Chapter 2. These two perspectives are not mutually exclusive – indeed they are mutually dependent, as we aim to demonstrate. The concept of *experience* is essential as a unifying issue between the culture and economy of design, as a means of understanding the context of design today, and as a window through which to view the possibilities and challenges facing design in the future. We begin by presenting models of design experience that enable us to understand the nature of our interaction with products and services. Then we focus on experience issues that designers are likely to be increasingly concerned with in the years ahead, such as those required of an ageing population and sustainability. Finally we consider how this affects the very process of design itself.

A focus on experience – the sensations, feelings, desires, aspirations and social relations that arise through our interactions with the designed world – inevitably strengthens the 'humanness' within design, as Lauralee Alben suggests in the quote at the start of this chapter. The history of design in the twentieth century could be characterised as pursuing the art of the possible. It is our hope that design in the new century pursues the art of the relevant and meaningful – in other words, that it more fully meets the needs of the people it purports to serve.

MODELS OF DESIGN EXPERIENCE

Viewed in its commercial context, design is a business activity that begins with a corporate objective and applies design thinking and processes to turn that objective into a physical solution that can be delivered to the market cost-effectively. Corporate identity design, for example, translates an organisation's mission and values into a visual language that symbolises those values – through a logo, packaging, environmental design, and so on. Industrial design can communicate corporate identity, together with providing a product that meets the need of the target market, thereby strengthening market share. Even a contemporary craftmaker is driven by business objectives – to design and make objects that earn the maker at least a reasonable living.

All design users – from craft businesses to transnational corporations – use some sort of market research to inform the design process more specifically about the requirements the design must fulfil. What do consumers prefer? What are competitors supplying? How is the company perceived? What unmet market niches exist? How much are people willing to pay? But as Chicago based design research consultant John Cain points out; 'missing quite often from the repertoire of information that shapes product and service strategy is an understanding of what happens to those products and services once they are handed over to real people'.[4]

Cain advocates an approach to new product development that he terms *experience-based* design (EBD). He argues that designed artefacts occupy a place between two arenas – the first is business, while the second is everyday experience. EBD aims to bring these two arenas together by reframing the design problem in terms of the conditions of use and experience that give rise to a business problem, rather than the other way around. This involves using detailed *ethnographic research* to understand user experience. Cain illustrates this with the example of mobile (cellular) phones. Rather than define the problem in terms of increasing a company's market share of mobile phones for the business market, the manufacturer would first explore the attitudes and perceptions of phones and communication in the workplace, the patterns of behaviour surrounding communication, and examine specific instances of use. We examine ethnographic research in more detail in the next chapter. At this stage it is sufficient to think of it in terms of ways of understanding people's behaviour and social use contexts from which business and design opportunities can be identified.

As a first step in understanding the human experiences that design makes possible, let us consider the properties that objects have and the experiences that each property can provide us with. We will make use of a typology provided by sociologist Tim Dant[5] and apply it to a product we first met in Chapter 1 – the Apple iMac computer (Figure 3.1). We use this example simply because it displays all properties identified by Dant, as we would expect from most consumer electronics.

Our experience of a product's *function* is that it extends or enhances at least one of our physical actions. A computer can make the task of writing more efficient, especially when we have to edit and rework our text. Writing this book using a computer, for example, was faster than using a pen. Our very experience of writing changes – we can play around with text more easily, cut and paste from previous drafts and try different page designs as we go along. The computer, of course, has transformed the experience of designing. The concept of on-screen hypertext has also changed how we read and explore information, breaking down the linear paths of narrative that the written word provides and creating new forms of interactive engagement with information.

Through its *signification* a product signifies membership of a social group – as we

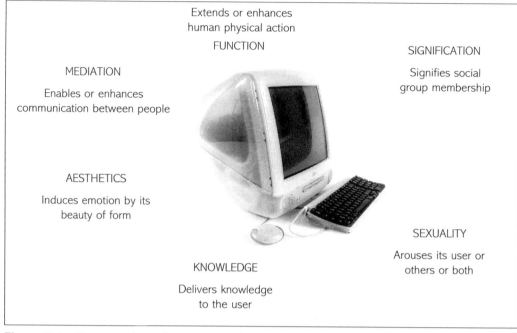

Figure 3.1   The properties and experiences of designed objects
Source: Adapted from T. Dant (1999), *Material Culture in the Social World*, Open University Press, Buckingham, p. 12.

saw earlier, it marks our difference. The Apple iMac user may wish to identify with the creative, think-different ethos that is used to market the product, to mark it and its users out from the beige corporate image of the Windows PC market. Part of the experience of using an Apple computer is often having to justify your purchase to PC owners. There is also a significant subcult of iMac users with their own websites, magazines and social activities. So on one level the iMac is a high-tech equivalent of a Manchester United scarf.

By *sexuality*, we mean that a product is sexually arousing in some way or signifies sexual identity or activity. Perfume, jewellery and clothing are among products that can exhibit this property, but so too with cars and consumer electronics. For some iMac owners the product's distinctive 'sexy' styling may act as a fashion accessory to enhance their own self-image.

The property of *knowledge* exists in a product when it imparts knowledge or information to the user. Designed to provide Internet access as easily as possible, the iMac demonstrates this property particularly effectively. Of course knowledge products – whether maps, train timetables, books or computers – facilitate all kinds of rich human experiences. A map shows us where we are, and makes journeys possible, a timetable helps us to plan our journey, a book provides distraction as we travel, and a laptop means that we can work on the move, so our experience of working changes.

Aesthetics provides an emotional experience based on the form, style or sculptural content of a product. The iMac stands out in the computer market in that it possesses strong aesthetic properties. These may or may not appeal to particular individuals, but it is unusual to find a person who does not have an emotional response one way or the other to this product. We are moved by a work of art, a craft object, but also increasingly by the products of industrially based design. It is all part of the *aestheti-cisation* of our *material culture*.

And finally to *mediation* – the ability of a product to enable or enhance communication between people. The iMac allows the user to write, to e-mail, to engage in online chats and discussion forums. As we have seen, possession of an iMac can lead to spirited discussions defending your purchase decision to PC owners or to membership of one of the many iMac clubs in existence. Few of the products we purchase or use do not involve any form of mediation, if only a brief exchange with the salesperson. All designed objects to a greater or lesser extent are part of social life. Of course, while the computer does enable new forms of mediation, it can also reduce those opportunities, as some concerned with the insularity of game-oriented 'mouse potatoes' argue.

So we can see that the Apple iMac provides a range of different experiences, from changing the way in which we read and write, through providing forms of social identity and difference, aesthetic responses to the product, and enabling new forms of social relationships. We cannot of course disengage the design of any product or service from the way it is advertised and packaged, the context in which it is sold, the different phases of use and experience it provides and the manner by which we complete our use or ownership of it. The example we used above helps us to understand the relationship between an object's properties and the experiences that they provide, but we now need to explore the dynamic nature of those user experiences – how they change over time, interact with each other, and in themselves create demand for new and different experiences. Recognising this holistic cycle of experience is critical in appreciating the rich and diverse challenges and opportunities for design.

THE DESIGN EXPERIENCE MODEL

According to marketing specialist Darrel Rhea, 'the real challenges come when we step back and reassess all the ways a design might influence and benefit customers – physically, emotionally, intellectually, and culturally. It is, in fact, customers' every experience with a product that reveals opportunities to use design in innovative ways'.[6] Rhea developed *the design experience model* as a conceptual tool to understand the entire cycle of experience, from when customers are first aware of a product, through purchase and use, to disengagement and the integration of the entire experience into their lives. This is shown in Figure 3.2.

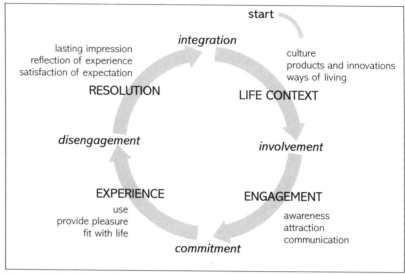

Figure 3.2   The design experience model
Source: Adapted from D. Rhea (1992), 'A new perspective on design: focusing on customer experience', *Design Management Journal*, vol. 9, no. 4, pp. 10–16, p. 12.

Life context

The cycle of experience starts at *life context* – the cultural and social background to any new design. This equates to Cain's conditions of use and experience – the world in which a new product or service will seek to find a place. This includes people's behaviour, patterns of living and working, shared cultures, concerns and beliefs, together with all the other products and innovations that help to shape that context. This determines our responses to any design, and the different ways in which we may use or experience it. It is itself a world of experience that in turn shapes other experiences and can help us understand the changing expectations people have of the experiences provided by goods and services (see Box 3.1). The central importance of life context explains why companies such as Pepsico and Nike commission extensive cultural lifestyle studies of young people – to ensure that their brand adapts to changing values and their products meet the needs of emergent patterns of behaviour.

Engagement

According to Rhea, the next stage in the cycle of design experience is *engagement*. This begins in a transitional phase he terms involvement, during which consumers first become aware of the design. During engagement, design must undertake three tasks – it must make people aware of its distinctive presence, it must attract and hold interest, and it must communicate the product's key attributes. As Rhea explains, this

Box 3.1   Dining and designing

Our changing eating habits vividly reflect social and cultural shifts and provide new rituals for new ways of living. When in 1999 the OXO family met for the last supper of its thirty-year run of TV commercials, it was a sign that the dinner table no longer provides the focus for family cohesion. Families are less likely to eat together than they once did, and if they do, then TV dinners on trays take the place of the table. Convenience and informality now typify our eating habits, and the food that we eat. From the 1980s food became fashion thanks to TV chefs, restaurant culture and the marketing strategies of leading food retailers. And with the fashionability of food came the fashionability of tableware, with many people now expecting their tabletop to change with the times.

At the same time multiculturalism has exposed us to a range of different *cuisines* and eating rituals that have been absorbed into hybridised Western culture, which appears capable of enjoying dim-sum, Yorkshire pudding and an espresso – all in the same meal. Home entertaining has placed new demands on the tableware and cookware that we use. They must be versatile enough to prepare and serve a range of different foods in different settings – at the table, in front of the TV, in the garden, or in bed. They must also signify the values of a culture that is less status-oriented and less formal in its rituals.

This changing life context, and its impact on eating habits, has led tableware manufacturers to design products that are more appropriate to the experiences demanded of consumers. Wedgwood's Weekday Weekend range has provided a design styling that took some of the classical forms and pattern elements consistent with Wedgwood's brand image, but reconfigured them for contemporary taste. The range has encouraged a mix-and-match approach consistent with the needs of creative home living, and has been marketed to engage with changing lifestyles. Described by some as casual dining, this development in tableware design illustrates how designers are responding to a new life context.

Life context research drove the Weekday Weekend range. Simon Stevens, Wedgwood's senior designer 'approached food advisors and looked at marketing reports on modern-day eating habits. He walked the aisles of supermarkets to see what sorts of food people are actually eating. And he looked at his own lifestyle'.[7] The range has been designed and marketed to enable new eating experiences to be enjoyed.

stage may only last a matter of seconds, but whatever its duration, design must fulfil its three key tasks.

The task for design in this stage of the cycle could be summarised as communicating values that are relevant and engaging to the consumer. Los Angeles-based designers Daniel Ashcraft and Lorraine Slattery have provided a succinct definition of the task that integrates product design, marketing strategy and branding:

Experiential-based design seeks to so thoroughly understand the consumer's experience that it can identify the values that he or she perceives as defining. It then fashions a product and marketing design strategy to mirror that experience in a brand culture underlying the product and inspiring passion. A successful brand culture cannot be contrived or dishonest. It must be authentic and consistent with corporate values to connect on an intuitive level with the consumer's experience of the defining object.[8]

Let us consider an example of such experiential design which picks up on a case raised earlier in this chapter. The mobile phone market is a competitive and complex one, so service providers must be distinctive enough to engage consumers in appropriate ways and communicate positive values and experiences. Hutchison Microtel a UK service provider that by the early 1990s had invested £1.5 billion in the infrastructure for its digital network, commissioned Wolff Olins to design a corporate identity and overall consumer experience that would create brand awareness, customer attraction and communication of core values. Hutchison Microtel turned Orange.

The market for mobile communications up to 1993 was generally perceived as business-oriented, exclusive and male. The opportunity was therefore to propose a consumer experience that was personal, providing clear value for individuals. As two members of the design team explain, they were seeking the identity to emulate the success and appeal of a previous high-tech product: 'If it was to deliver "mobile for the rest of us" in the way that Apple had (with personal computers) then it needed to have broad appeal, to be for everyone. The service should talk to them in a language they could understand'.[9]

Wolff Olins came up with a position called 'It's My Phone'. At the core of this concept were two central propositions – outstanding value and future-proof, supported by five values: refreshing, honest, straightforward, friendly and dynamic. This was translated into the brand name – Orange – and corporate identity guidelines that ensured that the brand's values, or personality, were communicated comprehensively to the consumer. 'We made sure the five values were present not just in Orange's advertising media but also in the way customer service handles calls and, later, how point of sale was handled in the stores'.[10] The brand image design is reinforced in all contact between consumer and service – through packaging, retail design, advertising, billing and tariff structures and the website.

Within three months of the brand's launch, Orange was polling 45 per cent consumer awareness and within one year beat all UK mobile and fixed-line telecom providers in terms of TV awareness. As a brand which attracts consumers and communicates appropriate values, Orange succeeded in becoming a leading service provider and was described as 'brand of the decade' when Wolff Olins won the UK's Design Effectiveness Award in 1996.

Engagement, as a part of the design experience cycle, can be gained through effective branding, packaging, advertising and product design, all working together harmoniously to mark out a distinctive consumer experience that communicates values that gain awareness and attraction.

Experience

Successful engagement, in Rhea's cycle, leads to commitment, whereby the consumer buys the product. This leads on to the next stage in the cycle – *experience* – in which the product or service is used and becomes part of life experience. The challenge here is not only to satisfy consumer expectation, but to go beyond this and provide extra, unexpected benefits. As Stefano Marzano, head of the Philips Design Group, explains, 'What really delights people is when you give them something nice they hadn't expected. And this may be something that they didn't expect simply because they had never even thought of it; or if they had thought of it, they never believed it would be possible'.[11]

Up until this point in the design experience, the consumer has experienced primarily the symbolic design elements – the brand position, distinctive styling, packaging and other communicative components all driven by an understanding of life context. Now the product or service itself will actually be used – be experienced – and in this phase must prove usable, provide pleasure and generally fit in with how consumers live their lives. It is at this stage that functional aspects of design become critical to the experience of the product or service. This is often informed by research into *usability* – how people use products, what they want to do with them, how they perceive a product's functionality, and how the product performs over time.

There is a danger in assuming that the *fashioning* of all areas of consumption puts style above substance, form above function. But this process of stylised consumption places even greater demands on the effective use of functional design and its integration with a holistic stylistic approach to product design and development – the user experience demands it.

Take shoes, for example. The sports footwear market is perceived as a high-fashion industry, with the emphasis on branding, high-cost advertising and continual stylistic change. It has connected with a youth culture that has woven sport and fashion into its lifestyle. Fashion sportswear's dominant position in popular consumerism has enabled it to attract some of the leading designers, film makers and cultural stylists to create and sell its product. Journalist Dylan Jones has claimed, with little exaggeration, that 'if Botticelli were alive today he'd be working for Nike'.[12]

Alongside McDonalds' golden arches, and Coca Cola's dynamic ribbon motif, the Adidas three stripes have almost universal brand recognition, with footballer David Beckham ensuring that the brand lives on the eyes and desires of a new generation. So, we have a brand that connects with life context, styled to engage with its target consumers and their need for fashionable feet. However, the company's multi-billion-dollar business rests ultimately upon its ability to design and engineer a sports shoe.

Adidas needs its materials engineers as much as it needs icons like Becks. Its 'Feet you Wear' brand position was based on minimising materials to increase the efficiency of the foot. This demands a research and development programme into materials that absorb shock, provide protection and ensure the full movement of the foot, together with testing equipment in use. Tom Peters's idea of *embedded smarts*, introduced in Chapter 1, is much in evidence in an Adidas trainer. 'The shoe bristles with extra smarts: conforming prosthetics that form to the underside of the foot, breathable materials which track away the whiff, not to mention a nickelodeon of flash styling materials on the outside intended to attract the attention of the passing Olympian'.[13]

The design experience finds its focus in the actual use of a product or service. A teacup, mobile phone or sports shoe may look desirable, it may express our life values and communicate who we are – but if the cup's handle falls off, the phone only works in built-up areas, or the trainers give us blisters, then we feel short-changed. It must work. But more than this, it must exceed our expectations of how it works. The critical objective is to create a product that provides rich sensory pleasure.

The cup must feel balanced in the hand, easy to hold and drink from, and it may provide tactile stimulation through the use of texture. It may provide an opportunity to mix and match from its range, enabling users to create their own table settings and to complement their colour schemes. It may attract the compliments of guests and thereby act as a *mediating* object. If we break one, we are reassured if the company has a policy to continue the range for some time to come. In these and other ways the cup is usable, provides pleasure and fits in with our life – in other words, it fulfils the needs of a positive design experience.

Leading designer Bill Moggridge argues that designing experience is the essential focus for design. He takes the example of a champagne glass to illustrate the different sensory design experience challenges: 'Does the stem give the tips of your fingers a little tingle of pleasure? Does the aroma of the wine float towards you as you lift the glass? Does the rim feel just right against your lips? Does the sound of the material ring true and clear as you touch your glass against another?'[14]

Moggridge goes on to compare the champagne glass with the mobile phone. Both are hand-held, intimate objects designed to provide a range of different sensory experiences. The difference between them derives from the latter's technological complexity and the need for multidisciplinary teams to consider all aspects of the user experience – from the tactile qualities of the phone, to the design of the software, the clarity of the sound, and the ease of maintenance. But the central point is that from the simplest to the most complex of products, the experience of use is vital.

Resolution

At a certain point in our experience we *disengage* from the product and enter the phase of *resolution* (see Box 3.2). It's time to upgrade to an Internet mobile phone, the trainers have worn out, the tableware's looking dated – or we've simply just finished our can of Coke. We resolve our experiences in different ways, depending on the specific nature of the product or service. In the case of a consumable – such as a can of Coke – we literally expect it to leave a pleasant taste in the mouth. Increasingly we feel reassured about our experience if the can displays a recyclable logo, as we could then take it to the recycling centre and resolve our experience with the can, safe in the knowledge that we have done one small thing to save the planet.

In all cases we reflect on the *experience* phase of consumption, use or ownership. Did it satisfy? Did it exceed our expectations in some way? Did it fit in with our life context? How did it enrich our experience of being alive? The design objective is to move users through this phase positively so that they integrate their experience into

---

Box 3.2   Nike – from running track to MP3 track

Successful **resolution** can be exploited by applying a brand to a wider range of products or services, thereby enhancing the brand experience. Virgin exemplifies this approach, applying the brand to an airline, railway, financial services and a range of consumer products. Nike's leading position in the footwear trainer market is now being used as a bridgehead into the fast-growing wearable digital technology business with its new nike[techlab division. 'Essentially, Nike has stuck a wire in sports,' said Clare Hamill, Vice President of Nike Equipment. 'Keeping the athlete in mind, [techlab will pioneer products that fuse sports and technology for the benefit of today's digital athlete'.[15]

Among the first products launched during summer 2000 were an MP3 player, a heart monitor and a personal communication device. Nike's challenge is to keep ahead of the changing life context of its customers, provide products that are consistent with the company's core values, and build further on the idea of wearable technology that is applied to trainers. When Nike's profits halved in 1997, it was a sign that new products were needed to shift the company away from reliance on traditional sportswear. Collaboration with digital product specialist S3 and Diamond Multimedia provides access to technology to which can be applied the Nike brand experience. Taking this concept further, www.nike.com will provide appropriate content for the MP3 player. Nike is demonstrating the features of design in the age of consumer culture described in Chapter 1, such as design coordination, complexity and customisation.

---

their life context, and begin the cycle again. If successful, then drinking Coke, wearing Adidas trainers and using the Orange phone system become a part of life context, so we stay with the brand, repurchase the product or pay again for the service.

By considering the properties and experiences of designed objects, and the cycle of experience that all products and services go through, we have underlined the critical challenge facing design today. Designers do not just design products; they are not just aesthetic stylists; they are not just problem solvers – they are all these things and more. Above all, they are creators of experiences that enrich the fundamental human experience of being alive. Therefore their greatest concern is – or should be – with the humanity of our material culture.

Our concern in this chapter so far has been with the micro-level relationship between design and human experience – our day-to-day interaction with products, services and brands, and the integration of that interaction within our life context. However, these processes must also be seen in terms of macro-level changes that will radically change our material culture. Demographic change and sustainable development are two major forces which are destined to transform the nature and experience of design in the twenty-first century. After considering each of these in turn, we will draw together some conclusions on trends and issues that will shape the nature of design experiences.

EXPERIENCING DEMOGRAPHIC CHANGE

During the first two decades of the twenty-first century those aged over 50 in the UK will increase in number by 20 per cent, and by 2020 half the population will be 50 or over.[16] This trend, common throughout all advanced industrial economies, is even more acute in Germany and Japan. This dramatic demographic shift is accounted for by longer life expectancies, decreasing birth rates and the 'baby boomer' bulge. In 1901 life expectancy for men was 45 years; because of improvements in health, lifestyle and working conditions, it is now 75, and is likely to be around 90 in 2101. Since the 1960s, when contraception and abortion became more freely available, the birth rate has gone down. Europe needs every woman to produce 2.1 children to replace the population, but the women of Europe with their new-found right to choose have chosen only 1.59 offspring. The old live longer, fewer babies are born, and the baby boomers are entering retirement – together these developments are creating a huge social and design challenge.

The fundamental challenge concerns constructing new models of ageing appropriate to the twenty-first century. While ageing is indeed a biological process, our experience of it is conditioned more by the socially constructed process of ageing – how our society views the various stages of our life course. Figure 3.3 summarises the social construction of ageing over time.

Childhood, as a distinct phase of our lives, is a relatively recent social invention, as in the Middle Ages children were more in charge of their own lives, being independent of rather than dependent on adults. Adults themselves had little civilising influence to mature their personalities, therefore the behaviour of adults and children was very similar. Childhood became defined as a period of dependence – as a distinct phase of life – during the nineteenth century. One factor that differentiated adulthood from childhood was the so-called 'civilising process' – the increasing role of etiquette in the regulation of social behaviour. This process also associated ageing with 'offensive' characteristics, such as incontinence or dementia. This negative view of ageing was reinforced by the twentieth century's cult of youth.

The growth of psychology and the work of psychiatrists such as Freud identified a distinct phase of our lives known as adolescence, and from the 1950s the adolescent gave rise to the cultural construct of the teenager, typified by James Dean and Elvis Presley. The teenager was created when the adolescent was given serious money to spend, and from this period we have the blossoming of youth culture which elevated youth to the ideal – expressed through music, advertising, fashion and our bodies. To look young is the ideal, even if you are old. The effect of this obsession with youth is to distance us even more from ageing – especially from very old age.

The social construction of ageing not only changes over time, but according to social class. The middle classes view their 20s as a period of extended adolescence, of self-discovery and perhaps of world discovery. By contrast, the working class regard their 20s as a time for acquiring responsibility – getting married, having children and making a home. The period from 40 to 60 differs greatly according to class – for the

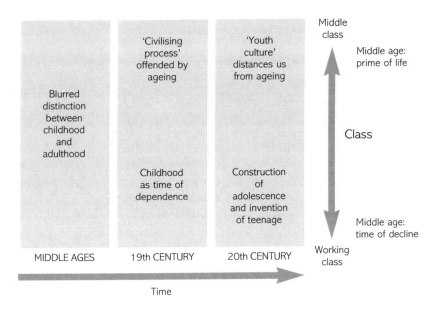

Figure 3.3   The social construction of ageing

middle class it is the prime of life and career fulfilment, but for the working class it is more a time to look back on lost opportunities, maybe of enforced redundancy, a time to look forward only to a state pension.

We can only speculate on how this will change in the years ahead, but change it will given the demographic shifts taking place, fast-changing social attitudes and one fairly crucial economic imperative – the old have money, while the young have relatively less – giving rise to the grey pound and the silver dollar.

Data for weekly disposable income per head for UK adults according to age is displayed in Figure 3.4. This shows the highest levels of disposable income for the 50 – 75 age groups, with those aged 50 – 65 having over one quarter as much more to spend than the under 30s. Given the population distribution by age group, it is now clear that the over 50s already account for at least half of all spending power, and one recent estimate suggested that they control over 80 per cent of all wealth in the UK.[17] It is worth noting that the general trend of increased disposable income for older people as a consequence of pension schemes and greater inherited wealth disguises an enhanced polarisation of income among those of pensionable age. Too many older people in industrialised countries continue to live below the poverty line.

The co-existence of a cash- and time-rich older population, enjoying a good income and a lifestyle that will enable a long life expectancy, together with an impoverished older population, having low income and shorter life expectancy, highlights a critical feature of ageing – older people are not all the same. In his study of design for an ageing population, American industrial designer James Pirkl makes the following point:

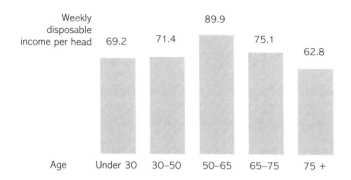

Figure 3.4   UK weekly disposable income by age group
Source: Family Expenditure Survey

Many people – old as well as young – harbour a false notion; the idea that, as a group, older people become more alike. This simply is not the case. With increasing age, the elderly grow more dissimilar. In fact, diversity among the elderly is greater than between the young and the old. In most aspects, other than advanced chronological age, they are a diverse, heterogeneous group of older adults who defy characterisation.[18]

The experience of ageing has changed radically in the latter half of the twentieth century. For many more people, retirement is no longer a brief respite from a work-dominated life, characterised by declining health and low income. It is fast becoming a new stage in our life course enabling new lifestyle choices and leisure activities that are as diverse in their nature as those of the youth. Peter Laslett uses the term 'Third Age' to describe this extending period of personal fulfilment between work and responsibility and death.

The 'Third Age' fits into a broader picture of our life course, from the First Age of youthful dependence, through a Second Age of work and responsibility, leading to a lengthening Third Age and a shortening, less common Fourth Age of final dependence, decrepitude and death. These ages provide a far more useful and positive way of considering the life course, and the experiences that they give rise to. But as this century continues, it is likely that the Four Ages model may be replaced by more diverse life course patterns providing even more challenge for designers and industry. Our current linear life plan is already shifting towards a more cyclical life plan, as shown in Figure 3.5. Life-long learning will provide education opportunities throughout life, and flexible employment patterns are likely to punctuate periods of work with periods of leisure, at times enforced. Already there are indications that employers are valuing the unique skills and knowledge that older employees possess, providing opportunities for work after formal retirement age.

Designing the products and services that enable the new ways of living and experiences required by 'Third Agers' requires us to develop a more balanced and less prejudicial view of the physical consequences of ageing. We tend to associate old age with

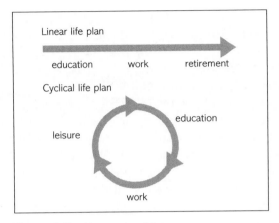

Figure 3.5   New ways of living

advancing disability, vulnerability to disease, dementia and general physical weakness. While 10 per cent of those over 65 have some form of dementia and 12 per cent are effectively house-bound, we must recognise one crucial fact: growing old is not the same thing as getting sick or becoming disabled. Current levels of sickness or disability for older people are consequences of lifestyle and vulnerability to risk factors which have accumulated over lifetimes in which exercise, healthy eating and non-smoking have only been relatively recently acknowledged as contributors to good health. Those currently entering their Third Age are doing so with far healthier lifestyles. However, it is a normal consequence of ageing that all senses – including vision, touch and hearing – decline in sensitivity. We also experience some limitations in bodily movement, some of which can be caused by arthritis. While arthritis can affect young and old, those who are older tend to be affected to a greater degree (Pirkl provides a comprehensive overview of the physical effects of ageing).

The demographic shifts taking place have highlighted the profound shortcomings of the designed world to provide for needs of those other than the able-bodied. Jars that are difficult to open, type sizes that are difficult to read, colour-coded information that takes no account of reduced colour perception, environments that are difficult to negotiate with impaired movement – all these and more make the experience of living less enjoyable and harder work – for all of us.

While the burgeoning Third Age market suggests that there is money to be made from text in big type and easy-to-grip jam jars, these opportunities also remind us that physical limitations affect all people of all ages. Anyone who has worn spectacles since childhood, was born colour-blind, has suffered a sports injury, broken or lost a limb, experienced temporary hearing loss (for example, following a loud rock concert), been pregnant or is registered 'disabled' will have experienced problems created by a world geared in the main for the able-bodied. Since this includes over 80 per cent of all people, then there is clearly a compelling case for claiming that design, as it is currently practised, could do far more to improve the experience of being alive – for all people.

Universal design has arisen as a design methodology aimed to maximise usability and to enhance inclusiveness and adaptability in the design and use of products, services and environments. The Centre for Universal Design in the USA has detailed seven principles upon which this methodology is based, and the guidelines that follow from them. These are shown in Box 3.3.

Universal design is being applied in the UK by the supermarket chain Tesco, whose low store shelves, shallow trolleys and home shopping systems have been introduced with the needs of older consumers in mind. It is behind recent investment and developments on the London Underground given London Transport's stated wish that 'we don't want to ghettoise the underground as somewhere only for the young, fit and healthy'.[19] Universal design is also linked to a gradual move towards presenting positive images of ageing. The tired and offensive stereotypes of age are simply untenable in a society in which most of its members will soon be aged over 50.

Box 3.3   Universal design

The design of products and environments to be usable by all people, to the greatest extent possible, without the need for adaptation or specialized design.

Principles

1   Equitable use

The design is useful and marketable to people with diverse abilities.

- Provide the same means of use for all users: identical whenever possible; equivalent when not.
- Avoid segregating or stigmatizing any users.
- Provisions for privacy, security, and safety should be equally available to all users.
- Make the design appealing to all users.

2   Flexibility in use

The design accommodates a wide range of individual preferences and abilities.

- Provide choice in methods of use.
- Accommodate right- or left-handed access and use.
- Facilitate the user's accuracy and precision.
- Provide adaptability to the user's pace.

3   Simple and intuitive

Use of the design is easy to understand, regardless of the user's experience, knowledge, language skills, or current concentration level.

- Eliminate unnecessary complexity.
- Be consistent with user expectations and intuition.
- Accommodate a wide range of literacy and language skills.
- Arrange information consistent with its importance.
- Provide effective prompting and feedback during and after task completion.

Box 3.3 (concluded)

4   Perceptible information

The design communicates necessary information effectively to the user, regardless of ambient conditions or the user's sensory abilities.

- Use different modes (pictorial, verbal, tactile) for redundant presentation of essential information.
- Provide adequate contrast between essential information and its surroundings.
- Maximize 'legibility' of essential information.
- Differentiate elements in ways that can be described (i.e., make it easy to give instructions or directions).
- Provide compatibility with a variety of techniques or devices used by people with sensory limitations.

5   Tolerance for error

The design minimizes hazards and the adverse consequences of accidental or unintended actions.

- Arrange elements to minimize hazards and errors: most used elements, most accessible; hazardous elements eliminated, isolated, or shielded.
- Provide warnings of hazards and errors.
- Provide fail safe features.
- Discourage unconscious action in tasks that require vigilance.

6   Low physical effort

The design can be used efficiently and comfortably and with a minimum of fatigue.

- Allow user to maintain a neutral body position.
- Use reasonable operating forces.
- Minimize repetitive actions.
- Minimize sustained physical effort.

7   Size and space for approach and use

Appropriate size and space is provided for approach, reach, manipulation, and use regardless of user's body size, posture, or mobility.

- Provide a clear line of sight to important elements for any seated or standing user.
- Make reach to all components comfortable for any seated or standing user.
- Accommodate variations in hand and grip size.
- Provide adequate space for the use of assistive devices or personal assistance.

Source: NC State University, The Center for Universal Design
http://www.design.ncsu.edu:8120/cud/univ_design/princ_overview.htm

Compiled by: Betty Rose Connell, Mike Jones, Ron Mace, Jim Mueller, Abir Mullick, Elaine Ostroff, Jon Sanford, Ed Steinfeld, Molly Story, Gregg Vanderheiden.

As a methodology to enhance general usability, it is misleading to pigeonhole universal design as 'design for the old and infirm'. As one recent commentary suggested: 'Perhaps a better question than 'how to design products for old people' would be: should we be designing products for a society where age becomes irrelevant?'[20] Or to put it another way, we are moving away from an age in which design's principal concern is for the young and able-bodied. As Oscar Wilde said, 'the old fashioned respect for the young is fast dying out'.

EXPERIENCING MORE FOR LESS

The design of garbage should become the great public design of our age.
Mierle Ukeles, Artist in Residence, New York City Department of Sanitation, 1995

No longer is the environment simply a resource to be squandered or a sink for waste. Companies are now seeing it as an opportunity and as a valuable asset. In short, the view of the environment as a business constraint has undergone a paradigm shift and it can be now demonstrated to provide opportunities for innovation and competitive advantage. This shift is one of the most significant changes in business philosophy of the last 50 years.

Design Council

The quality of life experienced by most people in the industrialised world can only be sustained if significant improvements are made in the efficient use of resources. One commentary suggests that we need to be four times more efficient, although Enzio Manzini – one of Europe's leading design researchers – argues that a ten-fold increase in efficiency is required.[22] A study by the US National Academy of Engineers in 1993 revealed that of all materials used, 93 per cent is discarded before final production, and 80 per cent of that passed on to consumers becomes garbage within six weeks.[23] In other words, in the USA at least, 98 per cent of all materials used is thrown away within six weeks. This is unsustainable.

The concept of *sustainability* is central to environmental responsibility and is being seen increasingly as a key objective for governments, corporations and the design community. Sustainable development was defined by the 1987 World Commission on Environment and Development as development that 'meets the needs of the present without compromising the ability of future generations to meet their own needs'.[24] It is in pursuit of this objective that the European Union has over 200 items of environmental legislation under way. The history of the twenty-first century will certainly be marked by increasingly radical steps taken to move the planet towards a sustainable future.

Climate change, increasing problems of waste disposal and pollution, tropical deforestation, and the consumption of finite energy resources are among the well-documented environmental problems that are creating the compelling case for sustainable development.[25] However, sustainability does not necessarily require any reductions in the quality of life. One commentator has suggested that 'it is possible for seven billion people in the world to reach a consumption level and a standard of living compatible with corresponding current European levels just by using very efficient technologies'.[26] It is sustainability that provides the key for all the people of the world to enjoy an experience of living marked far less by want and despair.

The ecological limits imposed on our use of resources, together with the issues raised by sustainability, have led to new definitions for terms such as 'standard of living' and overall are characterised by a shift from quantitative to qualitative measures. Measuring standard of living crudely by the level of economic activity – through Gross Domestic Product (GDP) – is giving way to assessments of life quality, such as the United Nations Human Development Index, which includes health, education and environment measures. Perhaps, then, life experience is finally counting for more than economic growth.

The regrettable but inevitable answer is no – in a system driven by the pursuit of profit, the economic bottom line determines priorities and values. However, part of the 'paradigm shift' suggested above is the competitive advantages that arise from environmental sustainability. In a discussion paper by the Design Council, seven such advantages were identified:[27]

- **Cost savings** – through improvements in industrial design and process engineering, considerable savings can be made in manufacturing costs, by reducing energy and materials input.
- **New environmental market**s – environmental technologies themselves represent a considerable and growing market, forecast to reach £325 billion worldwide by 2010.
- **Marketing benefits** – some companies have used their environmental credentials as core marketing strategies – such as the Body Shop. The evidence suggests that many customers will pay more for an eco-friendly product.
- **Supplier requirements** – suppliers of products and services to retail traders are increasingly under pressure to ensure that they address issues of sustainability in their supply. The recent example of GM crops in the UK demonstrated how supermarket chains were quick to drop suppliers who used GM technologies.
- **Satisfying legislation** – legal 'green tape' in Europe, the United States and elsewhere is providing a regulatory framework to which companies must adhere if they are to avoid fines and adverse publicity.
- **Satisfying stakeholders** – while shareholders remain the paramount interest group for any business (according to UK law at least), others who are affected by its operations – employees, consumers, local communities, etc. – increasingly have their views considered.
- **Consumer demand** – the evidence is now suggesting that consumer demand for ecologically responsible product is real, and growing. What was an added value niche in the early 1990s has now become a mainstream issue – again, the widespread unease over GM crops demonstrates this.
- **Achieving product differentiation** – as the Design Council argues: 'In today's

increasing competitive global marketplace, any form of product differentiation is welcome. There are a number of examples of businesses that have used environmental sustainability to achieve differentiation'.[28]

These advantages have led some companies and design teams to adopt product development strategies that take into account the environmental implications of all aspects of the product life cycle – the *cradle-to-grave approach*. Techniques such as *life-cycle analysis* (LCA) equip designers with environmental data on all aspects of materials, manufacture, use and disposal. Figure 3.6 identifies some of the design issues that need to be addressed at different stages of the product life cycle.

The term *ecodesign* is commonly used to describe 'design which addresses all environmental impacts of a product throughout the complete life cycle of the product, whilst aiming to enhance other criteria like function, quality and appearance'.[29] There are many well documented cases of ecodesign, ranging from product case studies such as kettles[30] and washing machines[31] to community transport systems.[32] Less detailed cases can be found in the winners of the UK's Millennium Products[33] and the European Design Prize.[34] Analyses of the strategic development of ecodesign by industry and in design teams have also been undertaken.[35]

In the case of some companies, ecodesign forms an essential element of clearly defined, distinctive design philosophies that focus and guide product development at both strategic and practical levels. South Korea's Samsung Electronics has developed 'Balance of Reason and Feeling' as a concept to describe their design culture. Innovative, lifestyle-driven and aesthetically coherent, the philosophy claims to

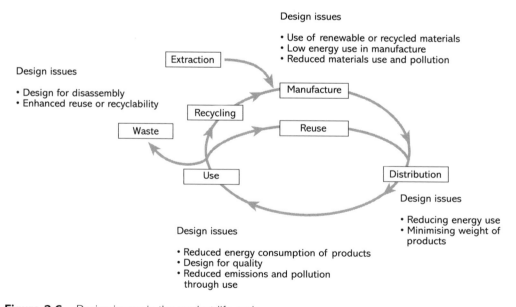

Figure 3.6   Design issues in the product life cycle

'harmonize with environment ... [and] contribute to the development of a better world for all people'.[36] Half a world away at Philips, the term 'High Design' is used to describe a design philosophy that aims 'to create a harmonious relationship among products, people and their environments, both natural and man made'.[37]

Samsung and Philips would appear to be acting on the apparent logic described by design expert John Thackara: 'The beauty of sustainable design is that it can be a 'win-win' strategy. When limits set by regulators, or by consumer pressure, are embraced, the quality and profitability of products is often found to improve ... Inefficient production is poor-quality production – and quality is what consumers want'.[38] On its website, the domestic appliance manufacturer Electrolux echoes Thackara's sentiment: 'It's a win-win situation for the household economy and the global ecology, in other words real EcoEco savings!'[39]

Like universal design, ecodesign promises to enhance our experience of products and services through increasing quality, and literally to sustain that experience into the future. However, the key problem is that the current state of ecodesign is a confusing mix of isolated good practice by generally smaller companies, individual entrepreneurs and university-based designers, overblown marketing hype by some of the larger corporations, and corporate structures that conspire to restrict ecodesign aspirations to the head office. Reporting on a UK national survey of nineteen manufacturers that examined ecodesign in the electrical and electronics industry, Matthew Simon acknowledges the positive position adopted by Electrolux and the championing of ecodesign from the board downwards. However, he also notes: 'a thick ecodesign manual developed by Electrolux in Sweden made little impact at a small refrigerator plant in the UK (now closed) even though the manual was specifically for the refrigerator division'.[40] His study suggests that the role of committed individuals within companies is more crucial than corporate policy.

A separate study of UK manufacturers based on interviews with design managers concluded thus: 'Our research findings, so far, suggest that design measures in the UK to improve environmental performance – in the guise of 'green' or 'ecodesign' – has the following characteristics: predominantly short term; generally requires low financial investment; reactive in its stance towards legislation and customer needs'.[41] Despite these problems, the study acknowledges that ecodesign is beginning to make a positive impact. First, as companies realise that they have to respond to environmental pressures, design's contribution is taken far more seriously than before. Second, product-based and single-issue opportunities are being taken up, often by smaller companies or individual ecodesign/entrepreneurs. It is notable that of the 81 'environment-driven' Millennium Products selected by the Design Council, 35 of these came from firms employing 20 or fewer people.[42]

Small and medium-sized companies (SMEs) are already playing a critical role in applying the principles of ecodesign, and in some cases base their business start-up on an 'eco-product'.[43] There are also increasing numbers of craft-based designers in jewellery, furniture, fashion accessories and other areas who have been working with recycled or waste materials, and in so doing 'exploring the aesthetic of sustainability'.[44] Eco-activists are also translating their commitment into business plans and developing a currently embryonic eco-economy providing a range of new goods and services. The Green Map System, which we met in the Introduction, is a powerful example of a wholly new enterprise model – a virtual transnational, linking committed activists throughout the world to develop a set of related projects, all aimed at changing perspectives, attitudes and behaviour. This is fundamental. A sustainable future will inevitably bring radically different forms of consumer experience, far beyond that of enjoying a slightly lower energy bill. The eco-entrepreneurs are perhaps going further than the large corporations in proposing such experiences.

Craft recyclers can change aesthetic attitudes to 'throwaway' material, while those who develop wholly new materials from waste, though the ecological attributes may be largely invisible to the consumer, introduce new design possibilities and could promote forms of eco-DIY. Craft, fashion-based or industrial products with recycled material have included drawers made from sardine cans and designs incorporating a range of found, post-consumer materials. Figure 3.7 details three other broad approaches to ecodesign enterprise and the impact on consumer experience. The many eco-product innovations from the SME sector include the first low-cadmium rechargeable battery, water-efficient toilet flushing systems and the popular Freeplay wind-up radio. The latter has already proved its worth in developing economies, bringing the experience of radio to rural communities, while in the West it has developed a strong niche as a fashion product – and in so doing has perhaps reminded consumers of the value and convenience of clockwork mechanisms. The Green Map System is just one example of many new information services, in this case combining paper-based and on-line access. Such new information products are already leading directly to new activities and opportunities for consumers and businesses.

Most commentators agree that the drivers for change – including legislation, consumer attitudes and the innovations of the eco-entrepreneurs – will shift us further along the road of ecodesign towards more radical design objectives. Hans Brezet suggests four phases in the development of ecodesign:[45]

1. Single issue attempts to reduce environmental impacts such as design for recyclability or design for disassembly and incremental design improvements that have been the main focus to date.
2. The more radical redesign of products and application of life cycle methods to product development.
3. 'Function innovation' including strategies such as dematerialisation, through the conversion of products to services.
4. 'System innovation' that involves the wholescale redesign of systems to move us closer to true sustainability.

These ecodesign phases can be plotted against the four design experience stages presented earlier to suggest how they form part of a progressive shift in consumer values and experience, as shown in Figure 3.8. In the eco-cosmetic phase, consumers

Entrepreneurial ecodesign focus	Example		Description	Consumer experience
Materials innovation using waste material	Ttura glass-resin composite developed by Sheffield Hallam University		A new structural material developed using 80% waste glass involving very low energy input, with applications in furniture and flooring.	• More diversity available for domestic interiors. • Could promote eco-DIY. • Largely 'invisible'
Product innovation	Freeplay wind up radio – invented by Trevor Baylis		Clockwork mechanism and solar panel integrated with radio	• In developing countries, can bring the radio to rural areas. • In the West, can re-value labour-intensive technologies
Information systems	Green Map System		A worldwide network of projects that produce city maps detailing eco-businesses, environmental projects, natural and cultural assets, etc.	• Provides new insights into urban environments • Promotes ecological lifestyles. • Encourages links between eco-businesses

Figure 3.7   The focus for ecodesign enterprise
Source: Wendy Brawer, *Modern World Design* (Green Map System); authors (Ttura and Freeplay)

primarily see cost advantages in the 'eco-lifestyle', while manufacturers are driven by the market and legislative context. As consumers begin to engage with the issues, increasing opportunities are provided for more radical design approaches and there is a greater expectation on companies to be genuinely committed to ecological values. This currently represents a significant market niche. The eco-active phase is so far very marginal in the market, but is likely to grow significantly. In this stage ecological responsibility is more firmly embedded in everyday life and requires wholly new, often dematerialised products to enrich and give pleasure to the experience of this new lifestyle. The sustainable phase involves a root-and-branch overhaul of the systems, products and services that sustain human life for the full resolution of the issues and problems we currently face. Models of this phase are thin on the ground, but The Eden Project in Cornwall and The Earth Centre in South Yorkshire are initiative which aim to explore and demonstrate different elements of such systems. In terms of a truly sustainable future, we remain in the realm of vision and imagination.

Research suggests the critical role played by individual designers in moving us further down the road of ecodesign either as entrepreneurs or as in-house 'ecodesign champions'. In her detailed study of ecodesign in the textile industry, Jo Heeley argues this:

Designers in the future could take a leading role in integrating environmental criteria into a product's overall marketing and communication strategy. The designer is the central connection to

Eco-lifestyle stage	Key design experience phase	Design priorities	Eco-design strategy	Example	
Eco-cosmetic Producers driven by market and legislative context Consumers driven by cost advantages and eco-guilt	Life context	• Become consistent with user context • Gain design improvements that offer economies to producers and consumers • Emphasis on marketing	Incremental design changes based on market research	"Eco-friendly" washing machines	
Eco-concerned Consumer values 'engage' more fully with ecological issues	Engagement	• Provide real advantages to user • Stronger commitment to ecodesign • Distinctive marketing focus	Radical redesign of existing concepts	Freeplay radio	
Eco-active Ecological responsibility more embedded within everyday life, beyond consumption	Experience	• Significant functional advantages • Provides new pleasurable experiences • Promotes ecological lifestyle beyond the design itself	Alternative product and service concepts	Green Map System	
Sustainable Balance achieved between social, economic and ecological systems	Resolution	• Fundamental changes for life context • Pleasurable eco-lifestyle enabled • Satisfactory resolution of most product lifecycle design issues	Redesign of whole systems providing full sustainability	Eden Project	

Figure 3.8 Eco-lifestyles and design strategies
Source: Wendy Brawer, *Modern World Design* (Green Map); authors (others)

the marketplace, acting as the bridge between the manufacturer who produces the goods and the consumer who desires them.[46]

The challenge for the designer is to gain the specialised knowledge necessary to design the sustainable experiences of the future.

IT'S DESIGN, JIM ...

By thinking about the kinds of situations or experiences that products will participate in and create, we can ensure that technology makes meaningful contributions to people's lives ... Once we have the option of designing situations, of designing the activities of people and groups of people, we also have the option of changing what individuals and groups of people do. In a sense, products and services have the potential to be seen as abstractions of better ways for people to work and play – and to maximise their own potential.

John Rheinfrank, Executive Vice President, Fitch RichardsonSmith[47]

This chapter has considered design's contribution to experience. We began by considering the experiential qualities of the objects around us, and how our experience of them changes as they move in and out of our lives. Then we turned to our experience of living and of growing older to see how this places new demands on the objects we use, the places we inhabit and the information we require. Finally, we considered how the need for a more balanced relationship with our environment would involve changes in consumption, in design, indeed in our overall experience of the world. We also saw how the goal of sustainability is linked to another goal – to enrich the 'experience of being alive' for the majority of those living on this planet, not just a materially affluent minority.

The key point we are making is that the focus of design is moving inexorably beyond the product or service towards the experience – the culture of use in which people negotiate, gain and express meaning from the designed world around them. This necessarily means that the practice of design must change – indeed it is already changing. It is design, but perhaps not quite as we know it.

In John Rheinfrank's view, designers should be in the business of making 'meaningful contributions to people's lives'. He has presented a useful framework for understanding what designers do in terms of transforming technologies into useful tools and cultural artefacts. Figure 3.9 sets out his three kinds of design transformation, to which we have added the design priorities that are implicit in each, together with a relevant example.

Most commonly, design is about *developing* products. This involves understanding product technology and user needs to produce a distinctive, easy-to-use product. He suggests a 'dumbing down' of products to achieve this universal usability, an example of which is the point-and-click camera.

Designers are *optimising* products when they iteratively refine technologies and consider more critically their 'fit' to the context of use. User participation in product

Design transformation	Process	Objective	Design priorities	Example
Developing	Designers gain understanding of technology and people and create products	The development of a 'fool proof' product for 'everyday' use	• Usability • Stylistic differentiation • Product first	Single-use camera
Optimising	Designers refine technologies or existing products to make them functionally and aesthetically appropriate to their context of use	Continuous improvements in design that increase the relevance of products	• Usability • Functional and aesthetic differentiation • Customisation • Technological innovation • User involvement • Consumer first	Bulthaup kitchens
Metamising	Designing beyond (or through) products to consider the experiences that surround or could surround the product	Design experiences in which a product is situated in its context	• Designing experience • Rethinking function • Customisation • Individuality • Context first	Tac-tile sounds system

Figure 3.9   Design transformations
Source: Adapted from J. Rheinfrank (1993), 'The technological juggernaut: objects and their transcendence', in S. Yelavich (ed.) *The Edge of the Millennium*, New York: Whitney Library of Design

development is common, and this form of transformation aims to maximise the potential for customisation. European Design Prize winner Bulthaup produces kitchens, the designs of which are continually informed by new technologies and lifestyle trends. Their top-end ranges use a modular design with high-quality materials to ensure that they can be tailored to individual needs. While fabrication is standard, the assembly of modular units allows for tailor-made installation.

Rheinfrank's final transformation is described as *metamising*, by which we 'design beyond (or through) products'. Designers begin by considering the experience that they wish a product or service to create, then focus the design thinking on the hardware and cognitive support for such activities. As a consequence the final design is highly relevant and meaningful to the user, and may enable customisation to be taken to its individualised conclusion. Rheinfrank claims that such an approach ensures 'that technology makes meaningful contributions to people's lives'.

The Green Map System encountered earlier is an example of metamised design. The original Green Apple Map of New York City was not conceived as a design exercise in cartography (although it clearly developed new cartographic methods), but rather as a tool to change people's views and experience of the city. A further example is that of the Tac-tile sounds system – a therapeutic sensory device for people with

Macro change	Experience driver	Effects
Social change Fundamental changes in social structures that will effect changes in everyday life	**Demographic change**	A highly significant force behind new attitudes and lifestyle change. Will lead to development of new services and products meeting lifestyle and functional requirements of older people. Changes the experience of ageing.
	Family structures	The continued erosion of traditional family structures will be accompanied by changing gender roles, greater active involvement of children in family decision making (changing the experience of childhood) and new flexible models of parenting.
	New consumer values	Older consumers may be more cynical about 'branded' experiences. Quality and durability may become more highly valued, and environmental values will become far more critical. Consumers unwilling to pay for on-line digital goods and services.
	Patterns of work	Flexible employment, portfolio working lives, home-based working and cyclical life plans are all part of the future of work. This will be linked to new patterns of learning with a blurred distinction between education, work and leisure.
Political issues Issues that are likely to be pursued by governments	**Environment**	Greater legislation on all aspects of the environment – energy, use of resources, recycling, product specifications – can be expected. Along with greater penalties will be incentives for companies and consumers to shift towards more sustainable activities.
	Creative economy	The 'creative knowledge economy' will be furthered by government policies covering education and support for business. This is likely to further support 'creative industries', including design.
	Democratic systems	Governments will use new interactive communications media to increase participative and consultative democracy. This also provides opportunities to further regional and local government.
	Crime and copyright	The fight against crime will increasingly employ new technologies and design, and could lead to fundamental changes in product and retail design. The issue of copyright raised by technologies such as MP3 could lead to radical changes in the law.

Figure 3.10   Experience drivers

profound sensory disability. As a modular system of 'vibrating stools' which allows for individual configuration, one of its uses is to convey the emotions of music and meaningful sounds to deaf children. This Millennium Product was developed by Paul Chamberlain at Sheffield Hallam University's Design Innovation Research Unit, and has become a market leader in its field. The project began through Paul's chance encounter with a clinical specialist in vibro sound therapy working with deaf–blind children, who explained that the lack of effective or appropriate therapeutic equipment had restricted the application of this form of therapy. Paul's starting-point in the design process was to work with clinicians on developing a therapeutic experi-

Macro change	Experience driver	Effects
Market forces Pressures driven by consumer demand and producers	**Product differentiation and innovation**	Consumers demand difference and consuming pleasure. This – more than price competitiveness – will drive new product development strategies at least in the immediate future. New technologies and diversifying markets provide the source of difference.
	Usability	Ageing populations greatly increase the demands on usability – mainly because they are experienced consumers who expect things to work. Success of Internet technologies, interactive TV, 3G phones, will rest ultimately on their usability.
	Customisation	In the age of post-mass consumption, consumers expect far more individuality from products and services. Customisation is already a driving force for change in many companies and will continue to be so.
	Eco-lifestyles	Consumers simply will no longer tolerate excessive packaging, high-energy-use products, and companies which pollute or use hazardous technologies. The move towards sustainable lifestyles is now irreversible.
Technology Technological developments and trends	**Body-based technology**	There will be a confluence between bio-engineering, consumer electronics, fashion and jewellery. Technology in and on the body is likely to be a key area of interest for manufacturers and consumers alike.
	Communications systems	The Internet, digital TV, digital radio, WAP, Bluetooth, etc. The proliferation and refinement of communications systems will continue to create new working, leisure, education and community-based activities.
	Smart systems and materials	Smart materials, products and systems. Innovations in materials science, manufacturing systems and digital technologies are among those embedding intelligence in products and services.
	Smart organisations	Virtual corporations and communities, learning organisations and creative teamwork all demonstrate how technology and new ways of working can develop organisational structures with collective vision, imagination and intelligence to make change happen.

Figure 3.10 (concluded)

ence that would have a positive impact on the children's behavioural and communication problems. This process was interwoven with refining a design brief for a product that could deliver the clinical experience and developed through a programme of field trials. For Paul Chamberlain, whose award-winning furniture is in London's V&A Museum, the challenge and excitement of the project was 'the prospect of designing products where the focus was shifted away from the visual and more towards issues related to the senses of touch, taste, smell and sound, in which one sense is enhanced by the absence of another'.[48] In other words – to design through the product to the wider realm of sensory and cognitive experience.

Designing the experience is indeed a challenge. To design through the product, we must first be able to see the world beyond the product – the social, technological, political and market forces that shape our world, and determine the hopes and fears, joys and pains that form the diverse experiences of being alive. In Figure 3.10 we have summarised the key experience drivers that are reshaping the design agenda and creating new challenges for today's and tomorrow's designers.

We cannot predict how these drivers will interact to form new experiences, or how designers and others will develop creative responses to them. For example, we know that new communications systems, on-line communities and digital technologies are beginning to create new ways of consuming and enjoying music. Napster and similar systems allowed the something-for-nothing consumer values encouraged by the Internet to result in a free global exchange of MP3 music ripped from CDs, at a daily rate of 15 million downloads at the time of writing. The music industry regards this as piracy, while the MP3 community sees it as the death knell of the music industry, neither of which appears a tenable position. The industry is responding by seeking legal and technical fixes, which appears to avoid addressing the question of what they can do to enhance the consuming experience that surrounds the music. Systems like gnutella attract music consumers precisely because they provide an engaging and interactive experience around the music, and enable consumers to customise their music collections track by track. They also provide a cultural space for consumption more similar to intimate collectors' record shops rather than impersonal megastores. There was a time when the music industry itself provided an engaging experience around the music – gatefold sleeves, lyric sheets and posters often came folded around the vinyl disc providing engagement and experience beyond the listening experience. The CD and Mini Disc with its 4 point type and cheap plastic simply does not provide such tactile and visual enjoyment. Perhaps it is time for the music industry to get physical again – think engaging real product, think consumer pleasure. Of course, it may just keep its head down and think lawyers.

The issue of music illustrates the unpredictable nature of change, and the shifting sands upon which designers have to think and work. If designing the experience is the new challenge, then it places new demands on the working methods of designers, and in particular the research that underpins their practice. It is to this issue that we turn in the next chapter.

NOTES

1. L. Alben (1997), 'At the heart of interaction design', *Design Management Journal*, **8** (3), p. 9.
2. Cited in M. Press (1995), 'Buddy, can you spare a paradigm?', *co-design journal*, **1** (3).
3. T. Dant (1999), *Material Culture in the Social World*, Buckingham: Open University Press, p. 12.

4. J. Cain (1998), 'Experience-based design: towards a science of artful business innovation', *Design Management Journal*, **9** (4), 10–16, p. 12.

5. T. Dant, *Material Culture*, pp. 55–6.

6. D. Rhea (1992), 'A new perspective on design: focusing on customer experience', *Design Management Journal*, Fall, 40–8, p. 41.

7. T. Blanchard (1999), 'Bowled over', *The Observer Magazine*, 6 June, pp. 66–7.

8. D. Ashcraft and L. Slattery (1996), 'Experiential design: strategy and market share', *Design Management Journal*, **7** (4), pp. 40–5, page 41.

9. D. Hamilton and K. Kirby (1999), 'A new brand for a new category: paint it Orange', *Design Management Journal*, **10** (1), 41–5, p. 43.

10. Ibid., p. 44.

11. S. Marzano (1998), *Creating Value by Design: Thoughts*, London: Lund Humphries, p. 23.

12. D. Jones (1999), 'The golden fleece', in S. Andrew, (ed.) (1999), *The Design of Sports*, London: Lawrence King, p. 85.

13. R. Seymour (1999), 'The song of Pebax on Kevlar', in S. Andrew, (ed.), *The Design of Sports*, p.44.

14. B. Moggridge (1999), 'Expressing experiences in design', *Interactions Journal*, July/August, pp. 17–25, p. 18.

15. http://www.nikebiz.com/media/n_techlab.shtml, accessed August 2000.

16. R. Coleman (ed.) (1993), *Designing for our Future Selves*, London: Royal College of Art.

17. Design Council (2000), 'Growing your market through inclusive design', paper on Design Horizons website, http://www.designhorizons.org.uk/trend.htm, accessed 1 May 2000.

18. J. Pirkl (1994), *Transgenerational Design: products for an aging population*, New York: Van Nostrand Reinhold, p. 37.

19. Design Council (1999), 'Exploring the opportunities of inclusive design', paper of Design Horizons website, http://www.designhorizons.org.uk/bookpdfs/explorin.pdf, accessed 1 May 2000.

20. Ibid.

21. Design Council (1998), 'More for less', discussion document, http://www.design-horizons.org.uk/bookshelf.htm, accessed 4 August 2000.

22. S. Manzini (1998), 'Products in a period of transition: products, services and interactions for a sustainable society', in T. Balcioglu (ed.), (1998), *The Role of Product Design in Post-industrial Society*, METU Faculty of Architecture Press.

23. P. Hawken (1993), *The Ecology of Commerce: how business can save the planet*, London: Weidenfeld and Nicolson.

24. World Commission on Environment and Development (1987), Our Common Future, Oxford University Press, p. 43.

25. D. Mackenzie (1991), *Green Design: design for the environment*, London: Laurence King. Ch 2 contains a discussion on these as related to design.

26. P. Burrall (1996), *Product Development and the Environment*, Aldershot, UK: Gower, p. 10.
27. Design Council (1998), 'More for less', discussion document, http://www.design-horizons.org.uk/bookshelf.htm, accessed: 4 August 2000.
28. Ibid., p. 5.
29. P. Goggin (1996), 'Glossary: key concepts and definitions', *co-design journal*, nos. 5–6, pp. 5–7, p. 6.
30. A. Sweatman and J. Gerkakis (1996), 'Eco-kettle: keep the kettle boiling', *co-design journal*, no. 5–6, pp 97–9.
31. R. Roy (1996), 'Designing a greener product: the Hoover "New wave" washing machine range', *co-design journal*, no. 5–6, pp. 34–9.
32. S. Potter (1999), Managing the design of an innovative green transport project, *Design Journal*, 2 (3), pp. 51–61.
33. www.sharinginnovation.org.uk
34. J. Thackara (1997), *Winners! How today's successful companies innovate by design*, Aldershot, UK: Gower.
35. J. Heeley (1996), 'Designing for cleaner textiles', *co-design journal*, no. 5–6, pp. 23–7; M. Simon (1999), *Ecodesign cultures in industry*, Proceedings of the third European Academy of Design Conference, Sheffield Hallam University, 30 March–1 April 1999.
36. T. Hardy, K.H. Chung and S.T. So (2000), 'Strategic realisation: building fundamental design values', *Design Management Journal*, 11 (1), pp. 65–9, p. 67.
37. S. Marzano (2000), 'Suffusing the organisation with design consciousness', *Design Management Journal*, 11 (1), pp. 22–7, p. 23.
38. J. Thackara (1997), *Winners!*, p. 343.
39. Electrolux (2000), 'Electrolux ecosavings, http://www.electrolux.com/node1001.asp, accessed 8 August 2000.
40. M. Simon (1999), *Ecodesign Cultures in Industry*, p. 275.
41. E. Dewberry and P. Goggin (1996), 'Spaceship ecodesign', *co-design journal*, no. 5–6, pp. 12–17, p. 16.
42. www.sharinginnovation.org.uk
43. A. Van Hemel (1998), *Ecodesign Empirically Explored: design for environment in Dutch small and medium-sized enterprises*, Delft: Delft University of Technology.
44. M. Press (1996), 'All that is solid melts into craft: crafting a sustainable future from today's waste', essay in Craftspace Touring (1996), *Recycling: forms for the next century – austerity for posterity*, exhibition catalogue.
45. H. Brezet (1997), 'Dynamics in ecodesign practice', *UNEP Industry and Environment Journal*, Jan–June, pp. 21–4.
46. J. Heeley (1996), 'Designing for cleaner textiles', p. 25.
47. J. Rheinfrank (1993), 'The technological juggernaut: objects and their transcendence', in S. Yelavich (ed.) (1993), *The Edge of the Millennium*, New York: Whitney Library of Design.

48. P. Chamberlain, J. Roddis and M. Press (1999), *Good Vibrations: a case study of design-led collaborative new product development in the field of vibro sound therapy*, Poceedings of the third European Academy of Design Conference, Sheffield Hallam University, 30 March – 1 Apřil, vol. 3, pp. 18–39.

4 Research for design

A STAB IN THE DARK

The myth of the designer as a lone visionary does not quite match up to that of the film director. As the cinema lights go down, we sit in expectation waiting to enter the film-maker's own imagination. Many cinema-goers entered the nail-biting world created by Adrian Lyne when *Fatal Attraction* became a box office hit in 1987. In Lyne's climactic scene, a knife-wielding Glenn Close came to a prolonged gory end at the hands of Michael Douglas. Adrian Lyne clearly has a vivid and vengeful imagination, or perhaps not.

In this case it was suburban American movie-watchers who provided 'the cinematic vision'. At a test screening of the film in which the original cut ended with Ms Close taking her own life, the outraged audience was baying for more blood than her own suicide provided. Their reaction persuaded Paramount to sink over $1 million into filming a new more violent ending.

Coming up with a box office hit is no longer the stab in the dark that it once was, and neither is developing a successful product or designing software. Through *focus groups*, *hall tests*, and a range of other methods, consumers inform the design process through their reactions to new concepts and prototype products. At Sweden's Orrefors Glass factory an annual conference of buyers and distributors is held to review new ranges and suggest design adaptations for different national markets, while at Hilti Powertools users work with designers in assessing new product ideas. Microsoft's designers subscribe to e-mail discussion lists of the products they design to ensure that the next version of their software addresses the problems faced by users.

Whether we create a film, glassware, a powertool or a word processor, we need appropriate methods of ensuring that it satisfies people's needs and expectations. Especially in the design of products we must also ensure that an advantage over competing designs is offered, and that our work reflects changing trends and developments in design, technology and culture.

This chapter examines why research is necessary, how it can be used to underpin an approach to design in which experience is central, and examines some of the main methods used. In particular we focus on methods that have been refined in recent years to meet the challenges of new consumer cultures and technological possibilities.

RESEARCH AND THE DESIGN PROCESS

Most designers would not like to consider themselves as researchers; however, very often that is just what they are. Nijhuis and Boersema[1] (Figure 4.1) provide us with two models, one of the design process and one of applied research.

The commonalties are obvious in that both go through a process of identifying a problem, undertaking a series of steps to investigate that problem and provide a useful solution. Each step involves research or a process of searching for knowledge, which will inform all those stages of the creation process. Indeed for designers engaged in practice, design research is primarily about the process of searching in the three following areas.

Searching for understanding

Designers, in order to design effectively, need thoroughly to understand the context in which they are designing. This does not mean that they are always researching consciously; many designers have the innate skill to be in tune with the environment, with people and their needs, with colours, shapes, and materials; indeed a type of delving into the material world. This enables them, in turn, to use that knowledge during the act of designing. However, there is often a need to collect information about markets and product stakeholders (including customers, users, manufacturers), and there are tools and techniques and other disciplines that contribute to this activity.

Searching for ideas

During the process of designing, the designer is looking for ideas to shape products – their functions, materials and aesthetics – and here again the designer's intuitive knowledge is brought to bear, yet frequently this must be enhanced by research activities. This depends on the designer's creativity and ablility to use knowledge to trigger it. Having understood the context for the design problem/activity the designer then searches for ideas. A number of creative idea generation techniques, are available to stimulate this creative process (see Box 4.1). These have been referred to as design methods.[2]

Searching for solutions

Finally, in developing design concepts and solutions, designers are undertaking research, they are testing ideas, both formally and informally. This involves all the creativity techniques but also methodical searches for processes, materials, technologies and ideas. Frequently designers maintain their own repository of information. Design consultants PSD, for instance, have a trend and technology room where materials and trends are stored for designers to use on an *ad hoc* basis.

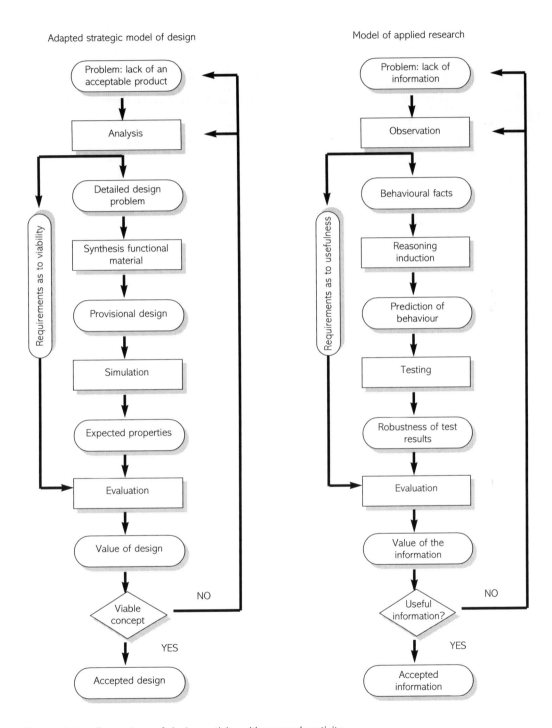

Figure 4.1   Comparison of design activity with research activity
Source: W. Nijhuis and T. Boersema (1999), 'Cooperation between graphic designers and applied behavioural researchers', in H. Zwaga et al. (eds), *Visual Information for Everyday Use*, Taylor & Francis, London.

Box 4.1　Creativity idea generation techniques

Brainstorming

A group participation technique for generating ideas for tackling a stated problem

Objectives tree

A method of listing the design objectives and sub-objectives in a project and construction of a diagram of hierarchical relationships between them

Counterplanning

This requires examining the assumptions and underpinning the problem, decision, plan or design and, through a process of proposing and considering conflicting assumptions, coming to a revised decision, plan or perception

Interaction matrix

A method of exploring and setting out a chart based on the interaction between a number of elements within a problem

Interaction net

The development of an interaction matrix into representation of spatial or other patterns of relationship between elements of a problem

Forced connections

A way of generating innovations by searching for possible connections that do not presently exist between components of a product or system

New combinations

A method of devising new combinations of alternative components that may not previously have been combined.

Source: Adapted from OU Design Methods Module

These searching activities are of course interdependent: each informs the others. There is an overlap between understanding the context, searching for ideas, and testing the concepts (Figure 4.2).

THE DESIGN PROCESS

These searching activities are not undertaken sequentially. There is an ebb and flow throughout the design process. This can be illustrated by considering the four basic categories of the design process: formulation; evolution; transfer and reaction.[3]

Formulation is concerned with identifying the need and planning the problem definition. This front end of any new product design and development process is often referred to as the fuzzy front end. It is where both the designer and other partic-

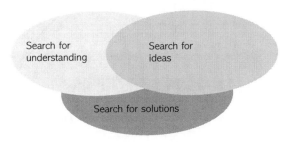

Figure 4.2   The designing environment

ipants in the product development process seek to understand the needs, requirements and desires of the stakeholders in the product. This is the stage which results in idea generation – idea triggers.

There are perhaps two parts of the process (Figure 4.3). One is the general environmental scanning, where the designer and other functions such as sales and marketing personnel in companies watch trends, collect general market data, observe users and customers, and monitor product use and feedback. Frequently the designer only takes responsibility for watching trends and observing users. This process may be conducted formally but quite frequently it is undertaken informally. The designer may go to exhibitions, roam a retail outlet, watch TV and collect market and user knowledge in an *ad hoc* manner. Market research and sales personnel often collect such data in a more formal way. The aim for the designer is to understand intuitively the world for which he/she is designing, to enable the generation of ideas, and to trigger the creative process – searching therefore for understanding and for ideas.

Once a problem or a concept is defined, the searching becomes more methodical. Research techniques can be introduced; this is often referred to as the *requirements capture process* (Figure 4.4). This procedure of gathering and transforming information to generate requirements uses formalised techniques often originating in market

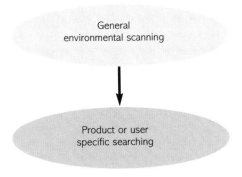

Figure 4.3   Research at formulation stage
of the design process

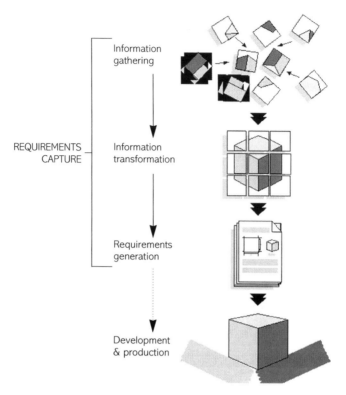

Information
gathering

REQUIREMENTS
CAPTURE

Information
transformation

Requirements
generation

Development
& production

Figure 4.4   Requirements capture process
Source: Wootton et al. (1998), *A Generic Guide to
Requirements Caputre*, University of Salford, Salford.

research; however, as the more ethnographical techniques are introduced, the most
important aspect of this process is that of recording the research results and monitoring their use and value throughout the product development process – a process
of requirements management.

Evolution deals with the idea, concept and detailed design generation. It is during
this stage of the process that the designer is searching for ideas, using knowledge and
information and creativity techniques to develop concepts, searching technologies,
materials and processes to stimulate ideas and develop solutions, and, finally, testing
design concepts and revising the designs based on an understanding of contextual
and user responses to that design.

Transfer covers implementation of the design in production and launching or
delivering the product to the user or consumer. Here the research is concerned with
ensuring a smooth transfer of the design into production, most of which will have
been undertaken in the earlier planning stages. But knowledge and experience will be
gained at this stage in terms of an understanding of the production and implementation process. This will be valuable for the future design problems.

Reaction addresses the outcome of the design, evaluation of the outcome in terms of user and stakeholder response – evaluation also of the whole process and the knowledge gained. This is part of the personal and often the organisational learning process. All such knowledge contributes to the search for understanding of the design experience.

Research, the designer's activity of searching and the design process are therefore interrelated and iterative, a constant process of learning and knowledge management. Linking the research activities described in more detail later in this chapter with the concept of searching and the design process, Figure 4.5 illustrates clearly that

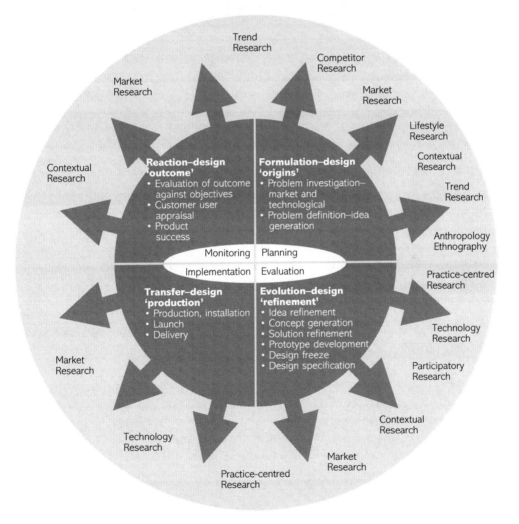

Figure 4.5   The design research cycle
Source: Adapted from D. Bennett et al. (1988), 'The design of products and services', in M. Bruce and R. Cooper

much research activity is the domain of the designer, particularly at the front end of the design process. The next issue is why do it and what research is best.

RESEARCH TO MINIMISE RISK

All design is a risk. We can never be certain whether an idea will work or not, but the evidence suggests that effective research helps to minimise the risk. According to Gillian and Bill Hollins, of all those design ideas generated in industry, less than 5 per cent result in a commercially successful product.[4] Around 80 per cent get weeded out before a design is specified, many of them nevertheless a necessary part of the idea generation process. But the further a design travels through the new product development process, the more expensive it becomes. Given that only one in three products launched on the market is a commercial success, there is a need to identify the factors that lead to successful products. This will reduce the risk and the cost of failure.

Cooper and Kleinschmidt analysed 203 new products – winners and losers – that were launched into the market.[5] Their research identified nine factors that had a significant relationship to new product success, three of which had the strongest impact:

- Product advantage: the product offered unique features for the customer; it was of a higher quality, innovative, offering better value for money and solved a problem faced by the consumer.
- Proficiency of predevelopment activities: successful products had made use of a range of up-front activities, such as initial screening, preliminary market assessment, detailed market research and financial analysis.
- Clear product definition: there was a clear definition prior to the product development stage of the target market, customer needs, wants and preferences, the product concept and product specifications.

In other words, successful products were rooted in a thorough understanding of the customer, the overall market and the new product concept's advantages over competing designs. Gaining this intelligence is often a specialised business. In-house marketing departments, market research consultancies and other specialists help to steer the design process towards success. However, designers need to understand the nature of the research tools available, and know how to adapt them to their own use during the process on smaller-scale projects.

COMPETITOR RESEARCH

If successful design involves offering an advantage over competing products, it is essential to analyse and assess the competition with care. This can help to identify gaps in the market that can be designed for in terms of price, functionality, style, or any other design criteria. Conversely, close scrutiny of the competition may suggest that we should not compete at all.

A number of companies strip down competitors' products to discover how they are designed and manufactured. Ford Motors undertook such reverse engineering in 1960 on the BMC Mini. Studying the car down to the last spot weld and carefully costing its assembly led the Ford engineers to the conclusion that it was being produced at a loss. Competing on price with the Mini was therefore not an option. Designer James Pilditch discovered on a study visit to Japan that all the electronics companies he visited undertook such reverse engineering on competitors' products.[6]

Market research reports are a useful initial source of information on leading competitors in a product market, but rarely do they provide detailed or visual information. Many designers will embark on some form of critical design analysis, pulling information from a range of diverse sources. Trade fairs and exhibitions, industry journals, *Which?* reports, *Kompass* (a 'who makes or sells what' directory found in most libraries), and observant window-shopping are all sources of competitive research. Once the designer is equipped with sales brochures, price lists, reviews and other data, they can begin to make sense of it.

MARKET RESEARCH

Buyers of ceramic tableware in Wales are 5% more likely to use colour as a purchase criterion than buyers in Yorkshire. Durability of plates is less important to those over 65 than those under 25. Mancunians are more price conscious than other buyers of china. 56% of men bought a t-shirt last year. When shown it, 96.5% of consumers positively disliked a particular prominent 'designer' kettle …

Such observations of consumer preferences and behaviour are to be found in market research (MR) reports. The MR industry collates information from manufacturers, retailers and consumers, usually through the use of large-scale surveys. In some cases companies will commission a survey for its exclusive use in comparing its products with those of competitors.

Such 'formal' market research is clearly an important source of consumer intelligence, although not all companies make use of it. Research carried out by the Design Innovation Group in the UK discovered that nearly 90 per cent of successful non-UK companies made use of formal MR in product planning, compared with less than half of the UK firms surveyed.[7] Their findings suggested that successful companies used a wide range of information sources in the design and product planning process,

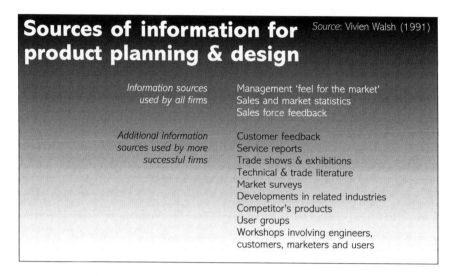

Figure 4.6   Sources of information for product planning and design
Source: based on Walsh, V. et al (1992), *Winning by Design*, Oxford: Basil Blackwell, p. 185.

complementing formal MR with other methods. Figure 4.6, drawn from the research, lists information sources used by successful firms. Less successful companies tended only to use the first three sources listed.

As we will see later, formal MR is often too general, too imprecise and too reactive to help designers adapt products or come up with new concepts that predict future needs. The term 'creative marketing' has been used to describe MR techniques, which are more qualitative in nature, providing richer information on consumers' views of products and alternative concepts. It involves teams of researchers, designers and consumers discussing product ideas before the brief is specified, and again when prototypes have been manufactured.

One method employed to elicit the views of consumers is the *focus group*. A group of typical users, usually around six to eight people, is brought together to assess an existing product or a new concept. Chaired by a facilitator, the group is encouraged to express and discuss their views and suggestions in an informal, open manner. A well-used method in new product development, focus group research was used by Tony Blair as a means of developing the principles and policies of 'New' Labour. Leaving aside the ethical question of whether political choices should be determined by market research, there are also questions concerning the efficiency of the focus group method and its inherent limitations.

Recent research conducted at Loughborough University has examined the involvement of designers in focus groups as a means of evaluating existing products.[8] This concluded that there were clear benefits for designers in that their involvement increased their empathy with and understanding of end-users, and lifted their confidence in designing for diverse consumer groups. Useful design-related data was gained, although the process was time-consuming. However, one of the world's leading specialists in usability research is more critical. According to Donald Norman, focus groups 'reveal what is relevant at the moment, not about what might happen in the future. Users have great trouble imagining how they might use new products, and when it comes to entirely new product categories – forget it'.[9] Norman makes a further point, that focus groups tap into the rational part of human behaviour, which is not necessarily consistent with actual human behaviour. In short, what people say they do and what they actually do are often very different.

This is especially true with children – they lie. This is not through any inherent dishonesty but, as any parent will tell you, children are notorious for providing adults with answers that they think the adults want to hear, rather than their real reaction. Giving them a prototype toy and asking their views on it is therefore an undependable method of research. Fisher Price in the USA has developed a system of research known as Playlab. The company takes a group of carefully selected children, places them in a room packed with new toys, and watches them play from behind two-way mirrors. The researchers soon discover which toys sustain interest and activity.

So, is this the secret to effective design? Just wheel in a few consumers, design to their needs and wait for the orders to flood in? As in any method of research, we must be cautious. We have to be sure how representative they are of consumers as a whole, and indeed the process seems to benefit if we have more forward-looking consumers than people who are less open to innovation.

Tom Peters, in his book *Liberation Management* shows how one firm overcame this problem.[10] Hilti, the manufacturer of professional powertools, used a method pioneered by Professor Eric von Hippel of the Massachusetts Institute of Technology. The Lead User Market Research Method involves identifying those users most open to new ideas and innovation. They are then involved in product development workshops where they help to develop and assess design ideas alongside marketers and designers. Used as part of the new product development process, lead user research succeeded in slashing Hilti's development costs in half.

LIFESTYLE RESEARCH

Sony's design boss Yasuo Kuroki has been reported as saying: 'I don't believe in market research – it doesn't help us develop new products'. As Christopher Lorenz has explained, at first sight Sony would appear to have a point.[11]

In 1960 the American electronics giant General Electric shelved its plans for producing portable TVs after market research concluded that consumers saw no need for the concept. That same year Sony launched an 8-inch set retailing at nearly twice the price of 21-inch sets. The product was a runaway success, providing a springboard from which Japanese companies would eventually dominate the US television market.

However, Sony's success was not due to ignoring market research, but rather in using new and more appropriate methods. Instead of being influenced by the views of consumers, who are often sceptical or uncertain about change, Sony focused instead on analysing behaviour patterns and cultural change. Virtually all American homes had a TV set, were being offered a growing number of channels, and were experiencing a cultural fragmentation as youth culture created divergent forms of entertainment. Put all of these facts together and there had to be a need for an additional set for the kids to watch Elvis on, or for the housewife to be entertained by Lucille Ball while she cooked.

Lifestyle research is now a key activity in many leading Japanese companies. Some in-house design departments have established units known as Trends Research Centres or Lifestyle Centres where sociologists, psychologists and anthropologists work alongside industrial designers. At Mazda design research is not just reading technical reports on carbon fibres. Required reading for the teams include *Vogue* and *The Face*, and designers are sent on people-watching trips where they sit around in European bars and restaurants.[12] This has evolved into a richer form of ethnographic research, which we will consider later in this chapter.

TRENDS RESEARCH

Increasingly design is about meeting 'soft' needs: lifestyle, fashion, changing tastes, cultural relevance. Woven in with design trends are rapidly evolving technological developments, which create new design fields and needs. How is the designer to make sense of these processes of change and predict their future evolution?

The forms, shapes, colours and materials that are popular at any given moment affect the nature of designed artefacts. A range of factors determines communications and environments. The possibilities of technology are obviously critical. Plastic moulding, for example, is a key factor in the dominant aesthetic of the 1950s and 1960s. Computer image manipulation led trends in graphic design in the 1990s, and new manufacturing technology and materials are enabling a greater diversity of design.

The state of the political economy clearly has an impact on design trends. The fashion historian James Laver has gone so far as to argue that the length of hemlines in women's clothing has a direct relationship with the state of the economy. Economic growth and hemlines, he argued, rise and fall in apparent harmony.[13]

Then, of course, there are social and cultural attitudes. Our attitude to the environment has transformed over the last 30 years. In place of the 1960s disposable furniture, we now have an emphasis on the use of recycled material. The slippery fishes of taste and fashion also drive product styles. What we need to be particularly aware of today is that fashion is far more diverse than in the past. Indeed, design trends are themselves more diverse.

Rather than be overwhelmed by the diversity and increasing pace of change in design trends and fashion, we need to find ways of disentangling some of these threads and understanding the factors that determine change. In this way we may be able to predict future change.

Technological change – microelectronics, information technology, new materials, advanced manufacturing and biotechnology – will continue to transform all areas of design (Box 4.2). It is clearly essential to keep up with new developments and plot their future course. In textiles, for example, metallic fibres and holographic printing offer new opportunities for designers. New textile innovations developed for industrial application are being adapted by fashion designers, such as Helen Storey's work for ICI in developing fashion concepts using a material designed to insulate greenhouses. In the years ahead, technological confluence is likely to drive design innovation. This will result in new product hybrids that combine functions and technology.

As any historian will explain, seeing into the future is easier if you have a clear view of the past. One method which can be used to make us more conscious of the nature and pace of change is change charting. Putting together a change chart involves looking back at the evolution of design in a general product field, or in the products of a particular company. Such charts help to show the speed of change, and can be used to prompt ideas for further development and refinement. They can be made particularly detailed by using photographs, detail on performance and functions, prices, sales figures and so forth. Change charts can help the designer to see the pace and nature of stylistic and technological change. They may suggest whether or not the time is right for design changes and can indicate gaps in the market.

Predicting future change in fashion, in terms of colours, styles and forms, is the concern of the more than 50 trend forecasting agencies which have been established in the UK since the 1960s. Once used exclusively by the clothing industry, these

---

Box 4.2 When clothing meets electronics

Philips Design launched its Wearable Electronics in 2000, representing a combination of electronic and textile technology. Design specialists in electronics, consumer products and fashion worked together on developing the clothing with its integrated electronics. According to Peter Saranga, head of Philips Research Laboratories in the UK that developed the concept clothing, 'People are already carrying around more and more electronic products – mobile phones, palm-top computers, personal hi-fis – and more are on the way. It makes perfect sense to actually start integrating the products INTO our clothes'.

Advanced textiles that integrate cabling provide a wearable 'network' into which various components can be attached according to need. For children, mobile phones and tracking systems allow parents to keep in touch, while play-based systems can provide a fun element. For clubbers, interactive fabrics could be used to change a club's music or lighting, while Philips also proposes 'pageable knickers' which light up if someone with shared interests is close by.

Source: Philips press releases – http://www.research.philips.com/pressmedia/releases/990802.html, accessed 16 August 2000.

agencies now count retailers and manufacturers such as Ford among their clients. Forecasters make their money by doing, what they claim designers should be doing, but simply don't have the time. They examine cultural and social trends, market research, developments in fashion, media and music, and distil all these data into elaborate 'mood boards'.

A QUESTION OF TASTE

A few years ago one of us was engaged in a live radio debate with the managing director of a ceramic tableware producer, which centred on the apparent unwillingness of his industry seriously to embrace diverse contemporary design.[14] Defending his company's reliance on century-old designs, the MD finally said, 'At the end of the day, design is a matter of personal taste'. The company in question recently went into receivership.

To a degree, the MD did have a point. Design policy in the UK was founded historically on a mission to 'raise' the taste of the mass market, with the Design Council's key task being to define standards of 'good design'. And this evangelical pursuit of the 'cultured middle classes' did not accord with industrialists and their allies. In 1951, an internal Treasury report recommended abolishing the Council, as it saw no future in 'good taste'. According to the report: 'It appears that the worse an object is designed the better it sells in the export market. China dogs apparently are really popular abroad'.[15]

If modernism's mission was to smash the china dog and all that it stood for, post-modernism's concern is to have more and varied dogs, preferably plastic and manufactured in China. Globalism, diversity and consumer choice have replaced the questionable tenets of 'good taste', with the Design Council long since abandoning its role as the arbiter of taste. As we saw in Chapter 1, taste is a system of distinction and differentiation that literally marks out who we are, giving form to our identities. Design is no longer an attempt to impose modernist tastes on the mass market, but rather a matter of understanding the tastes of specific consumer groups, and giving products forms and feelings that express the underlying meaning of those tastes. Form no longer follows function – form follows meaning.

Mirja Kälviäinen, of Finland's Kuopio Academy of Design, considers that an understanding of consumer taste must be embedded in the design process: 'The element of taste in designed objects should not be based on designers' own beliefs. Reflexivity, the opening to question of the designer's own concepts of taste is fundamental in design processes where customer taste is taken into account'.[16] Kälviäinen proposes three practical areas of research to guide the designer in understanding the tastes of users:

1. **The objective framework**. This concerns the demographic characteristics of the user group, the context of use and the history of the product within this context.

2. **The making of meanings.** Here the interest is in symbolic meaning in which the life histories of users and the ways in which they make meanings from consumption are examined.
3. **The network of influences.** The social world of the user, comprising the social codes and rituals, rules of interaction and key influences, is explored by the designer.

In summary, Kälviäinen argues that empirical research into the world of the consumer, viewed through theoretical perspectives from the social sciences that seek to explain the creation of meaning in consumption, and underpinned by a reflexive self-questioning on the part of the designer, can provide an essential understanding of consumer taste. A number of consultancy firms are already specialising in such areas of research. In the USA, Image Engineering has developed a qualitative research method that claims to elicit consumers' emotional responses to the visual symbols of brand and product design, thereby mapping out their 'making of meaning'.[17] Research into consumer tastes is essential for design that aims to connect with the emotional world of the user. Taste is part of the 'soft' function of any product or service and, as McDonagh-Philp and Lebbon have argued 'soft functionality cannot simply be applied like a gloss. It has to be inherent within the design concept. It will only add value if it is culturally and emotionally significant to the target audience'.[18] Understanding taste and emotional engagement with the material world is a job for the anthropologist.

ANTHROPOLOGY – ACTIVE ENGAGEMENT WITH CONTEXT

In California's high-tech hub of Palo Alto, the job vacancies for anthropologists almost outstrip those for software engineers. A leading article in the finance section of *USA Today* in February 1999 entitled 'Hot asset in corporate: anthropology degrees' explained how 'no survey can tell engineers what women really want in a razor, so marketing consultant Hauser Design sends anthropologists into bathrooms to watch women shave their legs'. Anthropology is very cool.

Indiana Jones was perhaps the first anthropologist to demonstrate just how cool it could be. Harrison Ford's character was an archaeologist who used the study of artefacts to understand human beings and their cultural systems. Archaeology is one field within anthropology and is concerned with the study of historical cultures. Another field – applied anthropology – uses the study of cultural systems and human behaviour applied to real-world problems, although arguably Indiana Jones was doing just this in his efforts to outwit the Nazis.

Ethnography draws upon the methods, practices and theories of anthropology together with those of other social sciences such as psychology, sociology and communications and has been defined as 'a methodology used to represent the perspective of everyday life'. Judy Tso is an anthropologist whose consultancy Aha

Solutions Unlimited (www.ahasolutions.org) applies ethnographic methods to product development needs. As she explains,

> Ethnography was once the province of those intrepid anthropologists who spent years doing field-work in faraway places. Doing fieldwork required the anthropologist to spend long periods of time living with and observing the people under study. It is an approach to qualitative investigation that is also a narrative or literary form. The anthropologist would observe and participate in a locale and then, after one or more years of study, summarise his or her observations, stories, and narrative into a document called an 'ethnography'.[21]

If you want to know about water, don't ask a fish. One of the problems of conventional market research methods that rely on structured survey methods is that fundamental needs, goals, habits and values are so deeply embedded in the culture of a group of consumers that they cannot be expressed or rationalised. If we seek to understand life context, then it is the observation and analysis of the behaviour and interaction between people that is likely to provide a richer understanding. By studying the activities and movement of fish we can actually learn a great deal about water. Or photocopiers.

Anthropologist Lucy Suchman, working for the Xerox Palo Alto Research Centre (PARC), carried out one of the first ethnographic studies in the high-tech sector in 1979. Her film of office workers making heavy weather of photocopying tasks on a Xerox machine led the design team to see ease of use as more important than the range of features. The design outcome was a large green button that provides a single straightforward copy, still seen on even the most feature-heavy Xerox machine. Suchman's work was groundbreaking for product development, and paved the way for anthropologists to find a place in virtually every high-tech company.

More recently, Kodak made use of ethnographic studies as part of its Global User Experience (GLUE) programme. This research aimed to develop product and user interface designs for Kodak in the markets of Japan, China and India, and combined ethnography, product and user interface prototype development and validation focus groups in all three countries. Detailed documentation of this research in *Design Management Journal* provides strong evidence of how ethnography can contribute directly to the design process.

While Kodak is very obviously in the business of developing consumer products that need to be informed by contexts of use, Intel would at first sight appear to be just a high-tech component supplier. However, Intel employs a team of anthropologists to research a diverse range of use contexts that may find a place for a device with an Intel Inside. Genevieve Bell is a team member who has worked for the company since 1998. According to her, ethnography 'is based on the idea that you can best absorb a culture by being there and doing it. An old professor of mine called it "deep hanging out". You've got to actually be there, hang out with people, and participate in their daily activities'.[23] 'Deep hanging out' is used by Intel to identify new uses and users of computer power, thereby increasing the market for their microprocessors, as Box 4.3 explains.

Box 4.3   Intel outside

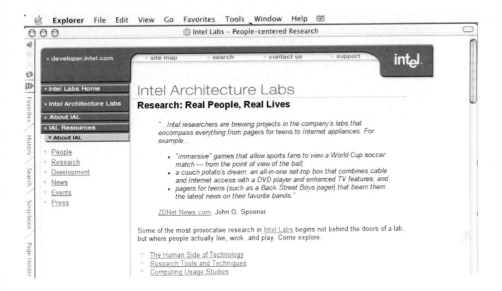

To get its microprocessors inside more digital products, Intel goes outside. On one recent investigation the company sent its anthropologists out shopping. The aim was to set design briefs for e-commerce web designers and to advise Intel on technologies for future development. The methods used by Genevieve Bell and her team included interviewing shoppers, e-commerce enthusiasts, e-retailers and traditional retailers. Historical research also revealed the openness of the American market to new shopping experiences.

They also joined a group of women from Seattle and filmed them on a day's shopping trip. Their film revealed the tactile, social and play-acting elements of shopping, which provided insights to the needs of e-commerce: 'None of that happens on the Web – you can only view a photo of the item and the price. We need to think about the expectations that people already have about shopping as we design e-commerce and m-commerce sites [m-commerce is mobile commerce which is popular in Japan]'.[24]

The research proposed a model of shopping ecologies, shown below. Maintenance shopping includes buying petrol or renewing insurance, while Consumption shopping is about self-indulgence. The Provisional model centres around home-making and family care, while Pilgrimage is social, event-centred shopping. Each model poses different design constraints and opportunities. The researchers also note national differences with, for example, household food acquisition being 'Provisional' in the USA, while possibly more of a 'Pilgrimage' in Italy. Defining and understanding these ecologies has helped to develop appropriate e-commerce models.[25]

Box 4.3 (concluded)

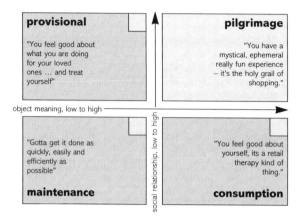

Some of Intel's outside research has a far more focused outcome. One ethnographer visiting an Alaskan salmon fishery discovered that the tender who collected the day's catch from the fishermen had a notebook computer taped to the outside wall of his cabin. It was simply the most convenient spot for the data to be entered. The resulting study, titled 'Fish and Chips', led to Intel designing microprocessors capable of operating in sub-zero temperatures.[26]

Ethnography has been described as a mapping of the mundane. Alongside quantitative methods, researchers make use of participative observation, interviews, oral histories and, of course, deep hanging out. Stream-of-behaviour chronicles involve observing or videotaping people's behaviour, which is particularly appropriate for research in workplaces. The tape can be studied by researchers to develop questions or hypotheses about the activity, and stimulated recall can be used during which a subject provides a running commentary on the tape. Finally, researchers can categorise and index activities on the tape.[27] Ethnographic interviews include a range of approaches and techniques, which can include grand tour questioning, which asks a subject to 'show the researcher around' the space of their living or working domain, and 'personal experience' questioning which seeks to explore examples of experiences.[28] The process is an iterative cycle of observing, recording and analysing, resulting in a considerable quantity of written notes, video and audiotapes and collections of artefacts. It is open-ended and discovery-oriented, aiming to see the inside and the outside perspectives. Fundamentally, 'ethnography holds the philosophical position that people themselves have the answers and understand the most about their lives, problems and circumstances'.[29]

Ethnographic research for new product and brand development is big business. Cheskin (www.cheskin.com) is one California-based consumer research consultancy that has developed ethnographic techniques to meet the needs of its clients. 'Applied

Figure 4.7   Cheskin Digital Ethno
Source: Cheskin

exploration' investigates consumer behaviour to arrive at actionable outcomes with an emphasis on studying life contexts to gain 'consumer insight'. Examples of this approach include designing a new dealership experience for Mitsubishi, based on ethnographic research of car buyers, and analysing teenage lifestyles for Pepsi.[30] With Digital Ethno™, Cheskin is connecting ethnography to the Internet (Figure 4.7):

> While traditional ethnographers physically immerse themselves in distinct places and cultural formations, digital ethnographers capitalize on wired and wireless technologies to extend classic ethnographic methods beyond geographic and temporal boundaries ... Consumers can be given powerful tools and technology to observe and record their own worlds. They then communicate these worlds via the Internet and other digital technologies.[31]

Meanwhile, over at the Brand New Corporation, Getting Closer™ uses what the company describes as 'photographic ethnography' to 'enable participants to investigate their own lives and behaviour by using a camera. It captures participants' motives, attitudes and intentions in very deep ways. This method is like qualitative research in that it uses small numbers of participants, and it looks and feels like a focus group. But that's where the similarity ends'.[32]

From specialist consultancies and in-house teams is coming increasing evidence of the value of ethnographic research:

- Canon's first colour printers targeted at the home market had unimpressive sales figures when they were launched in 1995. The company commissioned GVO, a Palo Alto consulting firm, to research what kinds of printed material families create and exchange. Their study of refrigerator doors and bedroom walls led to Canon Creative, software that now comes bundled with printers for producing posters, t-shirts and greetings cards.[33]

- Kimberly-Clark's ethnographic research into potty-training revealed issues, concerns and fears that traditional methods, such as focus groups, would not have discovered. This led the company to develop Huggies Pull-Ups, post-nappy (diaper) training pants that went on to secure a $400 million market.[34]
- A study undertaken in China by Motorola discovered that business people who were based in rural areas without telephone services had themselves developed an elaborate system of sending coded messages using their pagers. Following this, Motorola developed a two-way pager for the Chinese market.[35]

Ethnography – it's deep, it's cool and it's a very lucrative design consultancy service. There have yet to be any objective assessments of the efficacy of ethnographic methods in new product development. Most of the current literature, limited as it is, concentrates on individual case studies, journalistic accounts and accounts written by ethnographic consultants themselves, although Morrow's survey of literature covering the use of anthropology in product development is a useful source.[36] However, from the documented cases that do exist, some benefits for design teams are suggested, which can be summarised as follows:

- **Design serves the needs of users, not designers**. As Marietta Baba, chair of the Anthropology Department at Wayne State University explains: 'In the old days, you had a bunch of white middle-aged guys sitting around saying, "this is what I like and this is what my wife likes, so let's make that"'.[37] An ethnographic foundation ensures that design is rooted in the life context, needs and preferences of users.
- **Research can reveal unforeseen users or use situations**. Technologies have diverse applications and use contexts, which may be revealed by ethnographic methods, such as the case of two-way pagers in China cited above. Markets and product variations can thus be broadened.
- **A focus on meaning and identity**. Ethnography is concerned with the cultural meaning of objects, rituals and other activities, together with the social identities bound up with them. In an age of consumer culture, in which products represent expressions of meaning and identity, this perspective ensures that cultural experience informs the design process.

It is this final advantage that is crucial. As cultural historian W. Bernard Carlson argues, 'Successful products are more than just a bunch of technical solutions. They are also bundles of cultural solutions. Successful products, unlike inventions, succeed because they understand the values, institutional arrangements, and economic notions of that culture'.[38]

TOWARDS DESIGN EXPERIENCE RESEARCH

Our experience shows that consumers can tell you that they want bigger buttons, fewer features, or a better price. But these are relatively superficial needs. As we probe deeper, we find that consumers have a hard time articulating, or even envisioning, the kinds of products they won't be able to do without over the next few years.[39]

Robert Logan is head of user interface design at Thomson Consumer Electronics. Becoming more consumer-oriented to develop new desirable products that enhance user experience has been a critical goal for the company. To this end Thomson has developed a new method and organisational focus for the company called 'the New R&D', or research and design.

Thomson has built on the experience of companies such as Apple Computer and Xerox that have adopted similar approaches in experience-driven design. The New R&D brings together three groups of specialists to work on product development, as shown in Figure 4.8. The artist group includes industrial and graphic designers, fine artists, photographers and new media designers, while the humanists include ergonomists, marketers, psychologists and anthropologists. The technologists include mechanical engineers, CAD engineers and computer scientists.

While each group has defined responsibilities for research and design, all members actively participate in all types of research, enabling different insights to be

Specialists	artists	humanists	technologists
research responsibilites	• track aesthetic evolution • identify emerging trends • research tools and techniques	• task analysis • ethnographic observation • usability testing • focus groups • participatory design	• track technological evolution • identify emerging technologies • identify synergies
design responsibilites	• voice and personality • branding • aesthetic • bitmaps	• overall usability and ergonomics • mental models • research	• engineering to design translator • prototyping • specifications

Figure 4.8   Research and design responsibilities at Thomson
Source: Adapted from R. J. Logan (1997), 'Research, design and business strategy', *Design Management Journal*, vol. 8, no. 2, pp. 34–9, p. 35.

drawn upon in all parts of the process. According to Logan, 'research tasks are intended to define today's consumer space, track trends, and facilitate insights into future opportunities'.[40] Combining subjective, impressionistic research with highly objective measured techniques, Thomson's approach to research is a mix of the raw and the cooked.

If the realm of experience does indeed exist at the confluence of art, technology and humanity, then Thomson's approach would appear to be an appropriate one. In the previous chapter we considered the idea of designers *metamising* technology – designing beyond (or through) products to address the meaningful user experience, a variation on Pine and Gilmour's idea of inging the thing that we encountered in Chapter 1.[41] The case of Thomson is one example of how research and design can be organised to achieve this. It reflects a general trend in design management through-out the 1990s and into the twenty-first century, to develop far richer research methods aimed not just at product differentiation and competitive advantage, but at the enhancement of user experience.

As we have seen from the examples elsewhere in this chapter, the consumer elec-tronics and software sectors have driven much of this change. They have had to adapt from a reliance on 'early adaptor' consumers – for whom technology and innovation are all-important – to a far more mature phase reliant on a more diverse market in which technology counts for very little, and convenience, reliability and a positive experience are critical. This shift is reflected in the writings of psychologist-turned-design specialist Donald Norman. Published in 1988, '*The design of everyday things*' is his definitive text on usability – a powerful argument and set of practical methods for designers and manufacturers to create products that are intuitively easy to use.[42] Using examples such as doors, cookers and telephones, Norman makes a case for 'user-centred design' 'with an emphasis on making products usable and understandable'.[43]

A decade later, in *The invisible computer*, Norman has moved beyond usability and design to a broader idea: human-centred product development.[44] This he defines as a multidisciplinary process in which 'the goal is a technology that serves the user, where the technology fits the task and the complexity is that of the task, not of the tool'.[45] For Norman, user experience is a critical element in products meeting the needs of today's markets: 'When the technology matures, customers seek conve-nience, high quality experience, low cost, and reliable technology. A successful product sits on the foundation of a solid business case with three supporting legs: technology, marketing and user experience'.[46]

Donald Norman regards user experience (UE) as a multidisciplinary activity within product development requiring six sets of disciplines:

1. Field studies specialists, based on skills in anthropology and sociology.
2. Behavioural designers, with backgrounds in cognitive science and experimental psychology.
3. Model builders and rapid prototypes, rooted in computer programming, engineer-ing and industrial design.

4. User testers, who are skilled in rapid user-testing studies and may have a grounding in experimental psychology.
5. Graphical and industrial designers, 'who possess the design skills that combine science and a rich body of experience with art and intuition'.
6. Technical writers, 'whose goal should be to show the technologists how to build things that do not require manuals'.[47]

Norman's UE is not dissimilar to Thomson's New R&D. Both place design within a multidisciplinary context that embraces relevant humanities and technological disciplines, and both see the appropriate enrichment of the user's experience as the primary objective. This demands that we see design's organisational, disciplinary and research interfaces in a broader way than we have in the past. Research and practice within design management have until now emphasised the relationship between design and marketing, with some studies explaining how marketing can act as a 'trigger' for design, and detailing design's contribution to each element within the marketing mix: product, price, place and promotion.[48] What has been given far less attention in the literature is the design–experience interface, and the research issues that arise from it. To complement the 'four Ps' of the marketing mix, we propose the 'fours Cs' of the experience mix – context, connection, consumption and closure (Table 4.1). These follow broadly the phases of Rhea's design experience model described in the previous chapter.[49]

Each of the four experience phases – its context, initial emotive connection with the consumer, sustained consumption, and closure or disengagement – can be explored by a range of different research methods in order to understand the experiential requirements and to ensure that these are enabled by the various design elements. Brand, packaging, product, environmental and information design need to work in harmony to provide a holistic experience of use.

Market research and forecasting methods can contribute to a definition of context. Taste research and other visual research techniques can provide useful insights to connect a product with its intended consumer. For example, Ashcraft Design has developed a method entitled Interactive Customer Audit in which a multidisciplinary team (marketing, engineering, sales, design) examines the entire product experience to discover the values within it that can be developed for a brand image strategy.[50] In terms of everyday consumption, focus groups, conventional usability testing and other methods can be useful. TSDesign has developed a method for online designers called the User Experience Audit that provides a design analysis of a website from the users' perspectives. This method involves a team of designers, information architects and business strategists auditing a website in terms of the stated business objectives for the site.[51]

Two methods in Table 4.1 require particular attention as they offer great benefits to designers. While both are rooted in the design of work-based computer systems, their application is broadening and they are being used increasingly for the design of interactive media and, to a lesser extent, industrial design.

Table 4.1   Research for the four Cs of user experience

Experience elements	Key question	Design and research issues	Appropriate methods
Context	What is the cultural, functional, market and technological context?	Life context Consumer space Ways of living Aesthetic trends Technologies Market trends	• Ethnographic research • Contextual inquiry • Competitor analysis • Trend research • Market research
Connection	How should the design engage emotionally with the consumer?	Communication Engagement Promotion Desire Brand values	• Taste research • Customer audit • Concept testing • Market research
Consumption	What are the functional and emotional requirements of everyday use?	Use Fit with life Usability Pleasure of use Usefulness	• Usability testing • Focus groups • Experience audit • Contextual design • Participatory design
Closure	How can the user's disengagement become a positive experience?	Lasting impression Overall satisfaction Integration with life Resolution	• Ethnographic research • Lifecycle analysis • Focus groups

CONTEXTUAL INQUIRY

The Microsoft Usability Group uses *contextual inquiry* (CI) to define the needs of new software packages,[52] while Hewlett Packard has made use of it to define new needs for the computer printer market.[53] Again, CI has its roots in the high-tech industries, but, as a research methodology, is certainly not restricted to it.

CI is an applied anthropology research method that has been most widely used to understand processes, activities and needs of people at work. The originators of the method, Hugh Beyer and Karen Holtzblatt, describe CI as:

> An explicit step for understanding who the customers really are and how they work day to day. The design team conducts one-on-one field interviews with customers in their workplace to discover what matters in the work. A contextual interviewer observes users as they work and asks about the users' actions step by step to understand their motivations and strategy. Through discussion, the interviewer and user develop a shared interpretation of the work'.[54]

CI has two critical characteristics that mark it out from many conventional methods of understanding user needs. First, researchers, using a model of craft apprenticeship to guide them, conduct the fieldwork, and second, the research is conducted by designers rather than anthropologists or other specialists in user research. Both of these characteristics add significant benefits to CI as a research tool.

CI developed from a growing realisation that traditional methods from market research were inadequate in meeting the needs of design in fast-moving technological fields. In particular they reinforced a distancing between users and designers – quantitative surveying does little to foster any real understanding of or empathy with consumers' real needs. In seeking a more appropriate research model that overcame this shortcoming, Beyer and Holtzblatt identified the relationship between master craftsmaker and apprentice – in the same way that an apprentice learns skills from a master, so designers want to learn about customer needs from the customer. Just as a master craftsmaker teaches by doing and talking about it while doing it – not by formal teaching – so too a customer can impart knowledge about their work in the same way. Seeing a person work reveals what matters, the detail of their craft and the structure of their work. Technique and strategy can thus be imparted without direct explicit articulation. Using this model to guide the research means that the researcher does not take a list of prepared questions, but follows the process as it evolves.

The use of designers, rather than other specialists, is important to the effectiveness of CI 'because it is the designers who have to understand the customer in order to design ... We find that the data gets in the designer's head better if designers and specialists conduct interviews and interpret them together, rather than if specialists conduct all the interviews'.[55]

Providing methodological details is beyond the scope of this chapter, although there are several good sources available.[56] CI has evolved into a more holistic approach to software design called Contextual Design, which is described in fuller detail by its originators at their website (www.incontextenterprises.com).

PARTICIPATORY DESIGN

Participatory design (PD) has its origins in the Scandinavian social democratic model expressed in its commitment to industrial democracy – involving workers and their trade union representatives in the management of industry. The issue of new technology in the workplace from the late 1970s initiated a number of projects that aimed to give working people a say in the technologies and systems that were to shape their jobs. One such project that pioneered the principles of participatory design was UTOPIA. A researcher worked with the Nordic Graphic Workers' Union with the overall objective of 'developing powerful skill enhancing tools for graphic workers',[57] so some progress was made in developing computerised newspaper layout systems that built upon and enhanced the skills of the print and graphics workers.

In the UK there were similar initiatives on the fringes of the trade union movement, most notably the Lucas Aerospace Joint Shop Stewards' Committee attempts to design and develop a whole range of 'socially useful' products that their ailing defence sector factories could manufacture.[58] However, the Scandinavian culture of codetermination that led to UTOPIA, was in marked contrast to the UK politics of the

1980s that aimed to weaken trade union influence in the workplace. From the perspective of Thatcherism, new technology's main asset was in smashing the power of the trade unions.

Imposing technology on people did perhaps have some short-term political benefits for the Right. However, two decades on from the pitched battles of Wapping through which Murdoch finally put an end to the power of the print unions, we can perhaps view it as part of a wider, more problematic attitude. With some exceptions, UK industry has tended to devalue both working people's own knowledge and experience of the jobs that they do, and consumers' own needs and ways of living. The fate of the UK motor industry best expresses the consequences of failing to value the quality of working life and the quality of the consumer experience. Bad jobs and bad products have no future.

So yet again we look to the American computer and multimedia industries as the engines of change, which have seen in participatory design ways of getting closer to the consumer. Tec-Ed Inc. is a consultancy that has implemented participatory design projects for Sun Microsystems, Logitech, Cisco Systems and other companies. According to their account of participatory design,

> a team of people who represent the major stakeholders in a product design effort work together to create product designs that reflect the way customers will actually use the product in their own work. Users play a central role in the participatory design sessions, telling us about their work environments and the tasks they're trying to accomplish, including what works for them and what doesn't when they use their current tools. This proactive user input can both result in better designs and help shorten product development and testing cycles.[59]

At the Digital Equipment Corporation, designers worked with a group of chemists on the development of a portable torque-feedback device in a participatory design process that comprised five phases:[60]

1. **Building relationships**. Identifying a group of users to work with was done initially through electronic bulletin boards, which was followed by meetings to familiarise the users with the issues and technologies.
2. **Contextual inquiry**. The principles and methods of CI were applied in order to understand the users' work context.
3. **Brainstorming sessions**. These were developed with the users to identify possible design approaches.
4. **Storyboarding**. Users and computer designers developed the more fruitful brainstorming ideas into illustrated scripts of a 'day in the life' of a user.
5. **Iterative design**. Storyboards became design specifications for engineers, who built prototypes that were tested by the user–participants and the design continued in an iterative process.

In this example, 'Participatory design has steered computer engineers and chemists in some new design directions. This experience indicates that participatory design can be used to develop new computer technology as well as new computer-based application systems'.[61]

Participatory design offers a number of advantages to a design team. First it can draw upon the 'tacit knowledge' of users to identify design issues and solutions that may otherwise elude a non-user team. Through this, the design can enable a 'better fit' with real-world needs and use context, enhancing the experience of use. In designing for a specific group of users or use environment, PD can make users feel more valued and empowered and give them a sense of 'ownership' in the new design.

PRACTICE-CENTRED RESEARCH

The final 'method' we will consider is less an actual method than a set of approaches that better integrate the tacit knowledge and creative practices of design within a clearly articulated set of research priorities. *Practice-centred research* has arisen over the last decade as a means for design practice to be regarded as a component within a research degree submission.[62] While the methodological debates that continue to surround practice-centred research are beyond the scope of our discussions, there are some issues that have arisen from this debate, and from the few documented exemplars of such research that exist, that we should consider.

Theory and practice have had at best an uneasy relationship within design. The design methods movement of the 1960s and 1970s was seen as an attempt to graft a rationalist cricket bat of method on to the delicate intuitive tomato plant of practice. While the movement raised relevant questions, its distancing from the everyday practice of design (and the real world of designers) consigned it to a marginalised academic role. As a consequence the theoretical base of design has remained to a large extent impoverished, vulnerable to anti-intellectualism and, perhaps justifiably, 'few practising designers now see the relevance of what they know of design theory to what they practice'.[63]

At the time of writing, practice-centred research can be viewed as a diverse range of approaches that in differing ways aim to bridge practice and theory. One approach regards practice as research, claiming that a designed artefact embodies knowledge and thus can stand virtually alone as a research outcome, with only a minimal requirement to elaborate its theoretical implications. This model is perhaps more rooted in some research derived from fine-art practice. Elsewhere other models are emerging that seek to gain communicable design knowledge and theory through design practice that is informed by theory. This latter model reflects a new confidence within design to assert its own creative and tacit methodologies within academic inquiry, while acknowledging the need to connect with other disciplines and methodologies. Some of its advocates have referred to the historical contribution of craft and design practice to the growth of knowledge, and indeed to the theory that draws upon that knowledge.[64] Kevin McCullough makes the case that a fusion of theory and practice – design praxis – should be the goal of design: 'practice informed by theory, and theory informed by practice'.[65]

This is a far more viable prospect today than it was in the days of the Design Methods movement for two key reasons, first, because design is a far more complex, research- and theory-dependent activity than it was in the 1970s. What was then a cottage industry is today an international hotel industry – global in scale, technologically more complex and connected to more diverse organisational functions than before. The methods we have described in this chapter are not theoretical constructs that we have dreamt up, but are based on the practices of design teams that we have witnessed in London, Seoul, Palo Alto and elsewhere. Second, design departments in today's universities and colleges of art and design have strong financial incentives to fuse theory and practice in new relevant ways.

Some within the design research community are making the case for design to become a more 'science-based' profession, stressing that this is not at odds with the art and craft that lies within design practice (Box 4.4). Ken Friedman and Antti Ainamo are two of the strongest advocates of this view:

> Science and the scientific method does not necessarily mean positivism. Modern science and scientific method can involve diverse kinds of relationships between theory and practice, and not only a positivistic one. What matters is that we strive to make conscious design knowledge, to understanding how things are and how they work based on fundamental principles. The central difference between design as science and design as art is that with design as science one does not start with the look and feel, but rather with the parameters of the problem. Look and feel and tone and feeling and flavour emerge in the solution phase once the parameters of the problem establish the basic requirements of a solution. Thus, the scientific approach to design does not contradict the artistic aspect of design.[66]

The issue of practice-centred design has triggered a healthy and welcome re-evaluation of design's relationship with theory, science and methodology in an academic context. The diverse nature of design disciplines means that in some cases artistic practice will legitimately drive research, as is the case with the applied arts, but for industrially oriented design a key priority has to be to ensure that design practice is rooted in the social sciences of culture. This will ensure that real needs and meaningful experience drive design.

THE RESEARCH EXPERIENCE

Design in the twenty-first century is a research-driven activity, informed by an understanding of culture and technology, bridging art, science and humanity. This places new responsibilities and demands on designers. Perhaps one of the key demands is on reconciling the apparent need for rigorous research with the pressures of time imposed by the competitive product development process. With this in mind we conclude this chapter with our 'top five tips' for the time-challenged (Table 4.2).

Box 4.4   Hand-made research

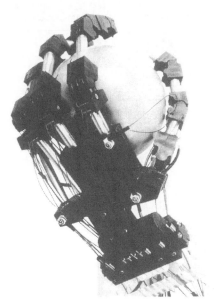

Photograph reproduced with permission of Sheffield
Hallam University

A PhD project at Sheffield Hallam University provides one example of practice-centred research that addresses user experience. Industrial designer Graham Whiteley's investigation of the design of upper-arm prostheses uses creative design practice and craft techniques to address problems normally considered to be the province of the scientist or engineer.

The project has resulted in physical models of a naturally articulated skeletal hand and arm which follow, dimensionally and functionally, the bones and joints of the anatomy of the arm. The models also provide attachments for analogous 'tendons' which could allow muscle-like actuators to provide motive power to the 'arm'. The research provides a useful and accessible demonstration of practice-based design research in a multidisciplinary context. A significant aspect of this is the way in which the knowledge developed and embodied in the models produced can be fully and quickly recognised by the various specialists and user groups who have reviewed the work without the need for supporting text. Whiteley and his supervisor, Chris Rust, have published reflections on developing design research based on creative practice[67] and, significantly, have engaged in academic discourse both within design[68] and Clinical Engineering.[69, 70] The project has demonstrated the value of design practice as a means of testing usability, and as a focus for the integration of theory from a range of different disciplines.

Table 4.2   Quick and dirty research – the top five tips

E-mail	There are e-mail discussion lists for most communities and user groups, ranging from users of specific products, such as Nokia mobile phones, to people dealing with specific life problems, such as parents of babies with sleeping problems. These can often give great insights into user groups.
User trip	This exposes the designer to the complexity of a design situation by becoming a user – a critically observant user. A user trip involves undertaking a task in the guise of a user, noting down actions, ideas and impressions. It aims to get the designer thinking more deeply about the situation users find themselves in.
Rapid ethnography	This is ethnographic research for the time-challenged, providing data that are just 'good enough' to support design development, rather than data gained through full scientific rigour. Condensed interview methods and passive video observation are among methods used by the Human Interface Design Centre at Apple Computer, and have been documented in a case study.[71]
Hang out	It doesn't need to be deep. Hanging out in a 'consumer community' by shopping, going to social events, 'people watching' and generally being immersed in the target group can provide essential insight and understanding.
Dog fooding	This derives from the old marketing adage that dog food manufacturers should 'eat their own dog food'. This is established practice at Microsoft, where product teams install and use the new software they are working on. According to David Cortright, program manager for Microsoft Office Macintosh Edition 'everyone on the team gets to feel the pain of the user and most of the usability issues can be found and addressed before the product ships'.

From the experiences of designers themselves we have drawn up our 'top five quick and dirty' research tips. Design may well need to become more science-based and certainly must be informed by scientific knowledge and methods. However, as Donald Norman argues, 'Applied science does not need the precision of the traditional scientific method. In industry, it is good enough to be approximately right. Speed comes before accuracy'.[73]

Good design is an expression of knowledge and understanding; poor design is an admission of ignorance. This chapter has made the case for research to underpin and inform the design process, to ensure that user experience is enhanced by our designed world. In particular we have shown how techniques from market research, ethnography and other fields make the crucial difference between success and failure. We have seen how users are not only a source of market information, but can become vital partners in the processes of design. We have also seen how design practice can act as a central plank in clearly articulated research programmes that extend our knowledge and better integrate the theory and practice of design.

NOTES

1. W. Nijhuis and T. Boersema (1999), 'Cooperation between graphic designers and applied behavioural researchers', in H. Zwaga, T. Boersema and H. Hoonhout (eds), *Visual Information for Everyday Use*, London: Taylor & Francis.

2. J. Christopher Jones (1980), *Design Methods*, Chichester, UK: John Wiley & Sons.
3. D. Bennett, C. Lewis and M. Oakley (1988), 'The Design of Products and Services', in M. Bruce and R. Cooper (eds) (1997), *Marketing and Design Management*, London: Thompson Business Press, pp. 46–69.
4. B. and G. Hollins (1991), *Total Design: managing the design process in the service sector*, London: Pitman Publishing, p. 22.
5. R. G. Cooper and E. J. Kleinschmidt (1987), 'New products: what separates winners from losers?' *Journal of Product Innovation Management*, **4** (3), 169–84.
6. J. Pilditch (1989), *Winning Ways*, London: Mercury Books, pp. 89–90.
7. V. Walsh, R. Roy, M. Bruce and S. Potter (1992), *Winning by Design: technology, product design and international competitiveness*, Oxford: Basil Blackwell, ch. 6.
8. D. McDonagh-Philp and H. Denton (1999), 'Using focus groups to support the designer in the evaluation of existing products: a case study', *The Design Journal*, **2** (2), 20–31.
9. D. Norman (1999), *The Invisible Computer*, Cambridge, MA: The MIT Press, p. 192.
10. T. Peters (1993), *Liberation Management*, London: Pan Books, pp. 83–5.
11. C. Lorenz (1986), *The Design Dimension: the new competitive weapon for business*, Oxford: Blackwell, pp. 32–5.
12. We have provided a fuller account of this in our previous book: R. Cooper and M. Press (1995), *The Design Agenda*, Chichester, UK: John Wiley & Sons, pp. 124–9.
13. J. Laver (1983), *Costume and Fashion: a concise history*, London: Thames and Hudson.
14. For further elaboration of this argument see: M. Press (1995), *From Mean Design to Lean Design and a Smarter Future*, Proceedings of the 7th international forum on design management research and education, Design Management Institute, 9–12 July, Stanford University.
15. P. Maguire (1991), 'Designs on reconstruction: British business, market structures and the role of design in post-war recovery', *Journal of Design History*, **4** (1) 15–29.
16. M. Kälviänen (1999), *Customer Taste as a Challenge in the Design Process*, Proceedings of the third international conference, European Academy of Design, Sheffield, 30 March – 1 April, vol. 2, pp. 78–102.
17. M. Sack (1998), 'Using research to create visual and verbal agreement', *Design Management Journal*, **9** (4).
18. D. McDonagh-Philp and C. Lebbon (2000), 'The emotional domain in product design', *The Design Journal*, **3** (1), 31–43, p. 37.
19. Cited in J. Tso (1999), 'Do you dig up dinosaur bones? Anthropology, business and design', *Design Management Journal*, **10** (4), 69–74.
20. T. Salvador, G. Bell and K. Anderson (1999), 'Design ethnography', *Design Management Journal*, **10** (4), 35–41, p. 36.
21. J. Tso, 'Dinosaur bones', p. 72.
22. D. Harel and G. Prabhu (1999), 'Designing for other cultures: a strategic approach', *Design Management Journal*, **10** (4).

23. Intel Architecture Labs (2000), Genevieve Bell, Ph.D., Anthropology, http://www.intel.com/ial/about/people/bell.htm, accessed 16 August 2000.

24. Intel Architecture Labs (2000), Ethnography projects, http://www.intel.com/ial/about/people/projects.htm, accessed 16 August 2000.

25. Salvador et al. 'Design ethnography'.

26. P. Kupfer (2000), 'Designing products based on real life: high-tech firms seek clues in anthropology', *San Francisco Chronicle*, 31 January, http://www.sfgate.com/cgi-bin/article.cgi?file=/chronicle/archive/2000/01/31/BU74422.DTL, accessed 16 August 2000.

27. For a documented case study of this method see J. Ramey, A.H. Rowberg and C. Robinson (1996), 'Adaptation of an ethnographic method for the investigation of the task domain in diagnostic radiology', in D. Wixon and J. Ramey (eds), *Field Methods Casebook for Software Design*, New York: John Wiley & Sons.

28. See L.E. Wood (1996), 'The ethnographic interview in user-centred work/task analysis', in Wixon and Ramey, *Field Methods Casebook*.

29. J. Tso, 'Dinosaur bones', p. 72.

30. B. Johnson and D. Masten (1998), 'Understand what others don't', *Design Management Journal*, **9** (4).

31. http://www.cheskin.com/what/concept/digitalethno.html, accessed 16 August 2000.

32. http://www.brandnew.com/gettingcloser/gcfaq.htm, accessed 16 August 2000.

33. K. Hafner (1999), 'Coming of age in Palo Alto: anthropologists find a niche studying consumers for companies in Silicon Valley', *The New York Times*, 10 June.

34. R.B. Leiber (1997), 'Storytelling: a new way to get close to your customers', *Fortune*, 135 (2), 2 March, 102.

35. Cited in Kupfer, 'Designing products'.

36. J. Morrow (1999), 'Using anthropology in product development', Proceedings of the third international conference, European Academy of Design, Sheffield, 30 March – 1 April, vol. 2, pp. 135–60.

37. Cited in Kupfer, 'Designing products'.

38. W.B. Carlson (1992), 'Artifacts and frames of meaning: the cultural construction of motion pictures', in W.E. Bijker and J. Law (eds), *Shaping Technology/Building Society Studies in Socio-technical Change*, Cambridge, MA: MIT Press.

39. R.J. Logan (1997), 'Research, design and business strategy', *Design Management Journal*, **8** (2), 34–9, p. 35.

40. Ibid.

41. J. Pine and J.H. Gilmore (1999), *The Experience Economy: work is theatre and every business a stage*, Boston: Harvard Business School Books. See Chapter 1 of this book for our summary.

42. D. Norman (1990), *The Design of Everyday Things*, New York: Doubleday.

43. Ibid., p. 188.

44. D. Norman (1999), *The Invisible Computer: why good products can fail, the personal computer is so complex, and information appliances are the solution*, Cambridge, MA: The MIT Press.

45. Ibid., p. 185.

46. Ibid., p. 40.

47. Ibid., pp. 189–93 detail his definition of UE.

48. See M. Bruce and R. Cooper, *Marketing and Design Management*.

49. D. Rhea (1992), 'A new perspective on design: focusing on customer experience', *Design Management Journal*, Fall, pp. 40–48.

50. D. Ashcraft and L. Slattery (1996), 'Experiential design strategy and market share', *Design Management Journal*, **7** (4).

51. T. Swack (1997), 'Web design analysis: creating intentional user experiences', *Design Management Journal*, **8** (3).

52. D. Juhl (1996), 'Using field-oriented design techniques to develop consumer software products', in Wixon and Ramey, *Field Methods Casebook*, pp. 215–28.

53. S.M. Dray and D. Mrazek (1996), 'A day in the life of a family: an international ethnographic study', in Wixon and Ramey, *Field Methods Casebook*, pp. 145–56.

54. H. Beyer and K. Holtzblatt (1999), 'Contextual design', *Interactions*, Jan/Feb, pp. 32–42, p. 34.

55. K. Holtzblatt and H. Beyer (1996), 'Contextual design: principles and practice', in Wixon and Ramey, *Field Methods Casebook*, pp. 301–33, p. 309.

56. See especially: H. Beyer. and K. Holtzblatt, K. (1998), *Contextual Design: defining customer-centered systems*. San Francisco: Morgan Kaufmann Publishers.

57. Swedish Center for Working Life (1985), The UTOPIA project, Stockholm: Swedish Center for Working Life, Royal Institute of Technology.

58. See M. Cooley (1980), *Architect or Bee: the human/technology relationship*, Slough: Langley Technical Services, and H. Wainwright and D. Elliott (1982), *The Lucas Plan: a new trade unionism in the making*, London: Allison and Busby.

59. Tech-Ed Inc. (2000), Participatory design, http://www.teced.com/ue-pd.html, accessed 21 August 2000.

60. M. Good (1992), 'Participatory design of a portable torque-feedback device', *Proceedings of CHI '92 Human Factors in Computing Systems* (Monterey, CA, 3–7 May 1992), pp. 439–46.

61. Ibid.

62. This aspect of practice-centred research is beyond the scope of this book and has been the subject of considerable debate within the design academic community.

63. K. McCullagh (2000), 'Design praxis: towards a design context rooted in practice', in E. Dudley and S. Mealing (eds), *Becoming Designers: education & influence*, Exeter: Intellect Books, pp. 39–52, p. 47.

64. M. Press (1995), 'It's research, Jim', *co-design journal*, issue 2, pp. 34–41.

65. McCullaugh, 'Design praxis', p. 50.

66. K. Friedman and A. Ainamo (1999),'The problem comes first: establishing design as a science-based profession', *Proceedings of the Third International Conference,*

European Academy of Design, Sheffield, 30 March – 1 April, vol. 1, pp. 294–316, p. 310.

67. C. Rust, A. Wilson and G. Whiteley (1998), 'Artificial Arms – A Fresh Approach to a very Old Problem', *Design Research Society Conference*, Birmingham, UK, September.

68. C. Rust, G. Whiteley (1998), 'Analogy, Complexity and Holism – Drawing as 3-D Modelling', *POINT – Art and Design Research Journal*, **1** (6).

69. C. Rust, A. Wilson and G. Whiteley (1997), 'The Development of Upper Limb Prostheses Directly Analogous to Real Limbs', *Medical and Biological Engineering and Computing*, vol. 35 Supplement – Proceedings of World Congress on Medical Physics and Biomedical Engineering, Nice, France, September.

70. C. Rust, A. Wilson and G. Whiteley (1998), 'Using Practice-Led Design Research to Develop an Articulated Mechanical Analogy of the Human Hand', *Journal of Medical Engineering and Technology*, **22** (5) 226–32.

71. K. Bauersfeld and S. Halgren (1996), '"You've got three days!" Case studies in field techniques for the time-challenged', in Wixon and Ramey, *Field Methods Casebook*, pp. 177–95.

72. D. Cortright (2000), 'Brief: Microsoft', *Interactions*, March/April, pp. 39–40.

73. D. Norman (1999), *The Invisible Computer*, p. 194.

5   Communicating design

DESIGN – IT'S A PEOPLE THING

In the previous chapter we explained how understanding consumers, appreciating how they live and the experiences that are meaningful to them and involving them in the processes of design, are essential. We have also seen how designers need to work with other specialists in marketing, ethnographic research and engineering to gain and apply this understanding. So, if people are fundamental to design, then communication becomes an integral part of the design process, and a key skill for designers.

To understand the vital role played by language and communication in design we need to look at two aspects of design – first, the design process itself which is commonly perceived solely as the domain of visual/creative thinking, and second at the trends that are rapidly reshaping the professional context of design. Both will reveal the social and linguistic dynamics that lie at the heart of design and define its very nature. Our central argument is that design is itself a social negotiated process that demands an understanding of communications equivalent to any other profession. As we will also argue, this view of design contradicts the view that designers have of themselves and the skills that they require to do their jobs.[1]

COMMUNICATION AND THE DESIGN PROCESS

The design process demands engagement with a multiplicity of personnel, as illustrated in Figure 5.1. At the outset, in the design formulation stage, the designer is preoccupied with research, relating to the consumers, clients and users of the designed product, and searching for understanding of the context in which they operate, their needs and their responses to the design idea. They are also often working in a team of both designers and other professionals. The language for this engagement is both verbal and visual. However, at this stage verbal interaction is often dominant, with visual stimuli used to create consensus and general understanding of the problem, issues, ideas and contextual assessment.

During the evolution-design refinement stage, the designer is also searching for understanding and knowledge, sometimes related to the technologies involved in developing the product, whether they are materials and processes or systems and information technology. They are also establishing reactions to concepts and plans with the clients, users, consumers or the manufacturers/producers, or other general stakeholders with whom the 'product' will interact. It is in this phase that communication activity is dominated or driven visually, supported by the other senses, such as tactile and olfactory, with verbal support for consensus and confirmation of understanding.

During the production, manufacture and implementation phase the design communication embraces the co-developers, the manufacturers, technologists, distributors and all stakeholders in the design supply chain. The communication often includes the specification for manufacture and delivery of the product to the customer and user. Here specifications and instructions (verbal and written) are balanced alongside the visual aspects of the model, or design, concept.

In the evaluation phase of the design process, designers are studying and researching reactions to the product and its context. This may involve both verbal and visual analysis, verbal in terms of consumer stakeholder response to inquiries through market research, sales reports and so on, and visual in terms of behavioural anaslysis including ethnographic studies of the product in use or in context.

We must conclude therefore that the design process is reliant on communication methods, and where once we believed the dominant communication realm of the designer was visual, we must consider all methods of communication. This chapter goes on to discuss the two dominant means of communication, visual and verbal, and the trends in design that are driving the communication forces and the changing communication methods for the designer.

VISUALISING DESIGN

Creating 'visions of possible worlds' Enzio Manzini wrote: 'The existing skill designers have, is to make the intangible, tangible, to conceive of an idea for a product; a piece of jewelry, set for a play, a web page, and to use visual techniques to share that idea with others.'[2]

One of the original skills for such visual communication is the ability to draw: everyone can draw; however, designers are trained to develop this as an advanced form of communication. Drawing does not just use pencil and paper to create an image; it can be undertaken using a computer, a camera, or found imagery; it is a form of visual sense making, combining visual elements in various media to create an image of a 'possible world'. Clive Ashwin discusses drawing as a system of signs, in relation to the theory of semiotics.[3] Drawing for design is deeply involved with the creation and interpretation of signs as symbols. For example, the design of logograms for corporate identity is often symbolic in two senses: they employ alphabetic motifs such as company initials; and they attempt to symbolise the company's supposed

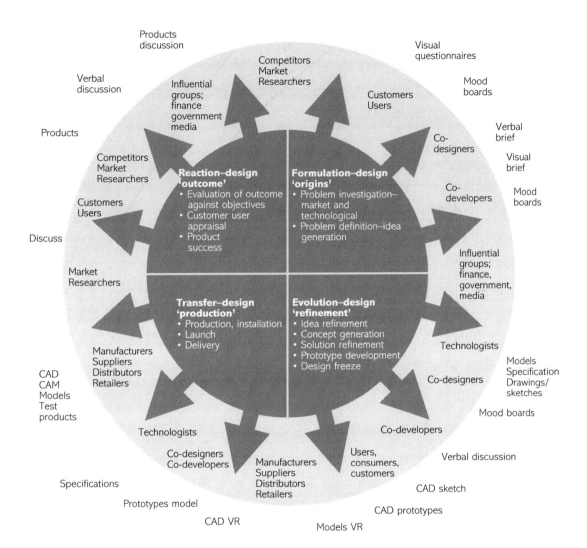

Figure 5.1 Design process and communication interaction

character by means of appropriately devised forms, be they 'robust', 'refined' or 'sophisticated'. Ashwin goes on to provide three levels of drawing specificity and six communication functions:

Levels of drawing specifications

- Monosemic – where there is only one correct interpretation, such as cartographical and engineering drawings

- Polysemic – where more than one interpretation is possible, such as a drawing of a car for which there may be interpretations of speed, power, and so on
- Pansemic – where there are unlimited interpretations of the drawing, such as in abstract or non-figurative drawing.

Six communication functions

- Referential – where a drawing tries to describe something in as objective and dispassionate a manner as possible. Examples here are architectural or engineering drawings where the transmitter tries to avoid any ambiguity, using standard coding and signs to communicate the meaning in the drawing.
- Emotive – communicates certain subjective responses such as excitement, attraction, repulsion. Here the use of drawing is intentionally emotive, in fields such as advertising and fashion, where the transmitter is determining what they wish to convey and using styling, drawing so as to create that through colour, pattern and so on.
- Conative – that persuades or exhorts the receiver to respond and behave in a certain way. Again, drawing tries to persuade the receiver to undertake a course of action, for example a client to accept a proposal or, in advertising, a consumer to buy a product.
- Poetic – to communicate an intrinsically admirable self-justifying form.
- Phatic – a communication that does not attempt to record or communicate facts or information but serves as a means of initiating, maintaining, or concluding communication, equivalent to the expression 'Hello'.
- Metalinguistic – created for the purpose of explaining other signs, such as the key to a map.

Most drawing for design is a combination of each of these functions that may occur in relation to the level of the drawing. Indeed, as Ashwin suggests, throughout the range of communicative modes the semiotic concepts of denotation and conation occur, that is, denotation is the commonsense and obvious interpretation. However, used in a poster or advertising, it may evoke other ideas or associations. For example, a sign for a ladies toilet means that that is what you are likely to encounter; connotation is the associations or ideas that may be evoked by a 'ladies' toilet sign.

This approach to the interpretation of drawing may provide us with techniques to understand further the messages transmitted by designer through visualisation. Design, however, does not always remain two-dimensional. In the process of creating products the designer often turns to the three-dimensional form, via 'scale' and 'full-scale' models, from clay cars, to fashion maquettes, to rapid prototype products.

It is with three-dimensional design, and in particular industrial or product design, that the aspect of connotation moves into the domain of product semantics. The theory of product semantics originates with the belief that people surround themselves with objects that make sense to them, that they can identify as to what they are, when, how, for what, and in which context they may be used. And that designers are professional sense makers. Form and meaning are intricately related and it is this relationship that is the principal concern of product semantics. As Krippendorff describes in his essay 'On the essential contexts of artifacts,

> Something must have form to be seen, but must make sense to be understood and used. Form entails a description (of something) without reference to an observer or user (for example geometry, physics and objectivist esthetics, which need no reference to the person applying them). In contrast, meaning always requires reference to someone's (self or other) cognitive processes. Accordingly, the designer's form is the designer's way of objectifying and hence, disowning their own meaning in the process of making sense for others.[4]

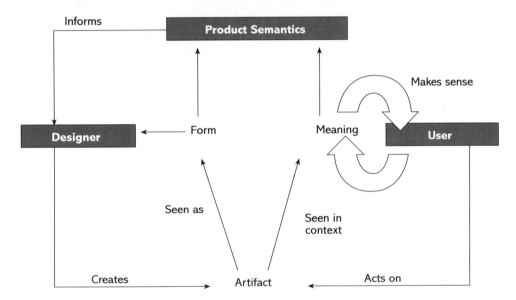

Figure 5.2   The relationship between the designer and the user in making sense for others
Source: K. Krippendorff (1998), 'On the Essential Contexts of Artifacts or on the Proposition that "Design is Making Sense (of Things)"' in The Idea of Design, A Design Issues Reader, Third Edition, Cambridge, MA: The MIT Press.

One might argue that the designer never disowns their own meaning yet makes sense to others. Products semantics, then, leads us back to the knowledge that designing is a process of understanding and communicating the product and its context. Lannoch and Lannoch describe a set of semantic dimensions, which describe most operational meanings of objects:[5]

- Identities: shape, pattern, identifying features
- Qualities: attributes described usually by adjectives, e.g. high-tech, fast, five-star
- Orientations: usually related to the personal interaction with object, e.g. front, back, left and right side, inside, outside

- Locations: for example, on the floor, on a shelf, detached, mounted, usually in relation to the user's space
- Affordances, states, dispositions, and logic: in simple terms this may be related to states such as full, empty, open or closed; however, there are numerous and intricate states affordances which can be applied to products, for example, happy, sad, angry. The user will bring all types of cognitive models and interpretations to such states and it is here that anthropomorphisms and metaphors are frequently used.
- Motivations: related to both tangible and intangible motivations, the product will have a function but also a value; for example a car will offer a means of transport but also enhance the user's feeling of self-worth.
- Redundancies: products cannot provide uniform understanding and meaning to the entire population – 'People have different cultural histories that emphasize reliance on some clues over others or favour different paths of exploration. Unless designed for very homogeneous populations, industrial products must afford these differences, allowing visual, tactile, acoustical and verbal indicators or clues to different interpretations of form to exist side by side.'[6] There is always a level of redundancy in the meanings of products.

Both semiotic and product semantic theory provide us with frameworks to deconstruct the images and the products designers create. They also illustrate the complex nature of the communication process and in particular when that communication relies on nonverbal means such as drawings and models. Designers use a number of media through which to communicate design during design process.

Briefing and requirements capture

Although this part of the process frequently involves verbal engagement (as discussed later in the chapter) with the client, user and other stakeholders, even here there are opportunities to establish understanding via visual means. Research has been undertaken by the University of Dundee to develop a visual questionnaire for interior designers using computer-generated images of offices to establish response on several variables related to physical and psychological aspects of interior design.[7] The research concluded that such visuals could play an important role in the design of questionnaires for research activity in design disciplines, since they can clarify the nature of the questions and enhance communication between respondent and researcher. In addition, they would enhance the validity of the data, and can be effectively used for product evaluation in consumer research where visuals can serve the purpose of giving information on manufacturing details used, interior parts that are not visible otherwise and so on. For living design (architecture, town planning, interior design and the like) pictures can help respondents visualise a specific situation. However, the Dundee study emphasised the need to design, pre-test and pilot carefully on a sample population to ensure effective communication. Another means of visual communication used frequently between the designer and client at briefing is the mood board. This can be a collective imagery which represents interpretations of the customer, the context and connotations of the type of product, using found imagery of people, products, places, colours, shapes, textures and so on. This enables both the designer and the client to debate the meanings expressed by the images and their relative appropriateness to the problem under consideration.

Concept design

Mood boards are also used as the designer moves from defining the brief, problem or opportunity to developing the concept and using visual means to communicate ideas.

Initially the designer uses drawings/sketches, which often mean very little to any one else but themselves. However, when working in a team they tend to develop a common language for the other designers and team participants. In the car industry, for example, stylists work at the front end of the design process in concept design and design development;, they have a particular responsibility for accommodating user and market requirements, and their representations of design proposals function holistically as a visualisation of the overall design. This is necessary in determining the appearance of the vehicle, but also so that design proposals can be communicated within the design team and to management. Concept design depends upon the quick production of a number of illustrations or sketches, which can be loose or informal or dimensionally rigorous.

For the car design and manufacturer, Tovey describes

> the concept phase as the time when management has been able to consider a wide range of alternative designs, represented as sketches and sometimes in the context of influence boards displaying lifestyle or mood images. Often 50 or more sketches will be presented both to establish the theme of the design, its feel and impact, and to relate the aesthetics to the dimensional requirements for areas such as engineering, ergonomics and product legislation.[8]

Tovey and his team at Coventry University have been developing a CAD-based sketch mapping technique (Figure 5.3) because in such a three-dimensional environment it is impossible for management to commit to a design until it has been converted into a three-dimensional product. Until recently it has been a complex and time-consuming activity to transfer the design from concept to detailed design.

> Such Cad tools offer advantages to both the stylists and managers by enhancing three-dimensional understanding of concept sketches, thus contributing to both the quality of the designer's visual thinking and to the facility with which management judgements can be made in determining which designs should be developed further.[9]

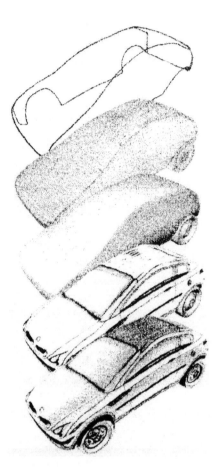

Figure 5.3   CAD sketch mapping for automotive styling
Source: M. Tovey and G. Harris (1999), 'Concept design
and sketch mapping', *The Design Journal*, vol. 2, no. 2.

Detailed design and product introduction

The communication of design information becomes increasingly important as the design becomes more detailed and closer to manufacturer and product introduction. Communication between members of a design team and co-developers has always been a problem at this phase, as illustrated by Claudia Eckert for design in the knitwear industry.

> Designers who design the visual and tactile appearance of the product often fail to communicate effectively with the knitwear technicians, who do much of the detailed design in interpreting the design specification to program knitting machines. The problems are exacerbated by the differences between designers and technicians who have different cognitive styles and very little overlapping expertise.[10]

Part of Eckert's recommendations to overcome such communication problems is again the use of CAD through which a common language can be developed, translating concept design into detailed design specifications.

Indeed, in many industries the use of CAD is adopted at the detailed design phase. One of the benefits at this stage is its ability to test for realism. As Loosschilder confirms, CAD offers the possibility of creating highly realistic concepts, particularly important for consumer testing products; in this sense 'realism pertains to the portrayal of a product as it is, in an actual purchase or usage situation'.[11] CAD data can be used to portray material characteristics and graphic detail. They enable the production of models through rapid prototyping systems and can also be combined with animation and simulation techniques to illustrate the product from a number of angles and undertaking certain actions.

The use of CAD varies across design disciplines and industries: the automotive, the architectural, and the interior product design industry are certainly moving forward into very sophisticated techniques, from 2D and 3D CAD to virtual reality and totally immersive virtual environments. The fashion and textile industry has been slower to take up 3D CAD, although the technology is available. Frequently the resistance is related to the cost of the software, the skills and knowledge of the designers, or the level of integration between software systems for design and manufacture.

The future in visualising design is certain to be dominated by digital technology, whether 2D, 3D or virtual environments. Developments in the technology will enable all the tools and media used by the designer to become digital, from the collection of lifestyle and visual imagery on screen to the creation of a living moodboard to CAD concept sketches, to virtual reality models set in virtual environments, to a digital data set for manufacturing. This digital visual communication, will mean not only the development and enhancement of visualisation, but also distributed and global design at a simultaneous and faster pace, providing a totally digital experience from the first mark to final product. This will put increasing communication and interpretation demands on the designer and the necessary development of accompanying skills and competencies.

There is one question which must continue to be addressed by designers using such technology: the relationship between realism and validity, in the sense of predictive validity, that is, does the virtual concept relate to the actual concept? The problem for the designer is that if design decisions are determined through digital media, how can the designer use this method of communication to convey all attributes and dimensions of the product? For example, a sense of space in a room, a retail environment or a car, a sense of texture of a fabric or a product, or a notion of auditory or olfactory aspects of a theatre or a retail environment. These questions mean the designer must consider more than the visual, and develop skills to provide the total sensory experience through digital media in order to communicate with all stakeholders in the design process.

Visual versus verbal communication

We can see, therefore, that technology is enabling faster, perhaps easier more consistent and yet more sophisticated ways for visualising design, but there is frequently the need for verbal discussion and description. Ashwin comments that

> many characteristics of verbal language are not easily transferable to pictorial or other systems of communication. In verbal language, individual signs (verbs) are combined in a linear sequence that permits analysis in terms of both the meaning of each sign and its position with the syntax of the sequence. For this reason verbal communication has been described as a discursive system. Pictorial communication usually presents interpreters with manifold ensembles of signs rather than sequences, and the interpreters must make their own order of the presentation, perhaps attending first to the whole and then its parts or vice versa. For this reason pictorial systems have been described as presentational, as opposed to discursive systems.[12]

It is for this very reason that the designer has to develop both controlled and calculated drawing/visualisation skills alongside excellent verbal communication to both extract and communicate understanding during design process interaction. This chapter goes on to discuss the other aspects of communicating design and the trends that are influencing design communication.

TALKING DESIGN

'Talking design' is the title of a recent detailed case study of graphic design that highlights the social interaction and complex verbal-visual communications that lie at the heart of the design process. The study, by Anne Tomes, Caroline Oates and Peter Armstrong of Sheffield Hallam, Sheffield and Keele Universities, argues that design may be considered as a negotiative process, and not purely an act of genius which marginalises verbal critique.[13] It is worth noting that this finding has been echoed in analyses of other design disciplines including architecture,[14] engineering[15] and product design.[16]

In their study, Tomes, Oates and Armstrong suggest that if the aim of design is the negotiation of a solution acceptable to both client and designer, then its practitioners must be both fluent and confident in undertaking translation between verbal and visual modes of communication. Only through practising a form of verbal–visual ping-pong can the concepts encapsulated in the written brief be incorporated into visual design thinking, ideas in progress relayed back to the client, verbal discussion undertaken, and its outcomes assimilated into further design development.

It is worth considering in some detail the process of design revealed by 'talking design'. Representing an 'ethnographic' study of a graphic design team working for a finance sector client, the study is based on the analysis of meetings with clients, study of the design team's methods and interviews with all parties involved. The process that emerges is summarised in Figure 5.4.

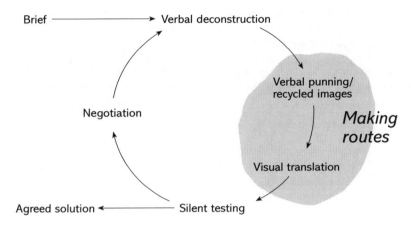

Figure 5.4   The 'talking design' design process

After the initial design brief, expressed by the client verbally and in written form, the designer begins with a process of 'verbal deconstruction' – verbally reworking the brief, that is, 'getting it down to a little nugget' that encapsulates the essential requirement of the brief. The next phase in the process is described by the team in terms of 'making routes' during which word-play and verbal punning are used to find an interpretation. These are then turned into a visual translation of the word-play, which can draw upon recycled imagery that the client is familiar with. There is evidence of the existence of a 'verbal–visual dictionary' between designer and client which is developed through their continuing relationship over time. In this particular case the two parties had worked together over eight years.

The visual translation is presented to the client through 'silent testing', in other words without any initial verbal explanation. This mute display can be brief with the team waiting for a reaction. The client articulates their reaction – a verbal translation of the visual – and the mismatch between interpretation and intention sets the agenda of the next stage in the process – detailed negotiation.

Despite the views of many clients, a designer's belief in the design may be based on their experience of what works and how designs are received: 'When designers speak of something that "works" they are not simply articulating a preference, but claiming knowledge of the public (asserting their professional knowledge)'.[17] The negotiation concerns resolving disagreement over the visual translation of the verbal in the mind of the public. The outcome of this is a further reworking of the brief and continuing around the design cycle until a solution is agreed.

What is clear from the evidence of 'talking design' is that verbal work is an integral part of all phases of design. Much of this takes the form of a search for commonalties between designer and client in terms of verbal-visual translation, and the development of mutual understanding. But the critical finding from this study is in terms of designers' self-identity:

'The major implication of this study is that the self-image of designers is in some respects at odds with the manner in which they actually work ... The graphic designers in our case study tended to regard the verbal culture of their clients as alien to their own, predominantly visual practice ... As against this, it is clear from our interviews, that verbal work is an integral part of all phases of the design process ... It is as if young designers view design as primarily a matter of individual self-expression, which just happens to take place in an employment context which involves relationships with the client and with other designers. If, on the other hand, these relationships are regarded as integral to design ... the skills of verbal–visual translation must also be recognised as integral to the design process. From this point of view, 'Talking design' is design.[18]

None of this is to deny that visual skills are any less important to design. The central point is that the visual and the verbal act in tandem throughout design. The role of language as an intrinsic element of design is summarised as follows by Fleming:

[Language] is used in the communication of constraints and requirements; in group problem-solving and decision making; in designer–client dialogue and negotiation; in inquiry, research, and testing; in naming, specifying, representing, and elaboration; and in evaluation, application, and interpretation.[19]

Other studies have traced the use and importance of language and communication in all of these stages. According to Byrne, the definition and understanding of a design problem's connotative aspects is most effectively achieved through verbal expression in the form of carefully considered adjectives.[20] Communication across the verbal–visual divide is essential in explicating the client's hidden requirements which, concerned with such qualitative concepts as 'feel' and 'mood', may be excluded from the formal language of the brief. The use of evocative words or phrases as creative triggers is likely to increase coherence between client requirements and design solution, in effect constituting a half-way point between language-based and visual forms of cognition. Clarke and Fujimoto explain how this technique was successfully employed in the design of the Honda Accord, where the encapsulation of the product's emotive qualities in the phrase, 'a rugby player in a business suit', increased coherence between the various development functions' understanding.[21]

In addition to increasing the potential for a design solution to reconcile various stakeholders' objectives, the process of translation between visual and verbal forms of expression can in itself constitute a catalyst for creativity. This is at its most obvious in graphic design, where a process of 'verbal punning' is frequently employed to generate solutions with both verbal and visual resonance. Verbal description of work in progress can however indicate new creative potential in other disciplines by liberating design from the grammar imposed by its practitioner's chosen media, whether charcoal stick or CorelDraw. Lawson's observations show that design solutions derive in part from their form of representation, for example tending to exclude considerations of vertical space when plans are the sole method employed.[22] In this context, verbal articulation and discussion have the potential to broaden creative outlook.

It has been asserted that human perception and memory are stored in language mode and are therefore most effectively accessed through verbal discussion.[23] Fielding's observations suggest that verbal questioning and discussion are a naturally occurring and essential facilitator to problem solving and planning activities, which should be fostered in design activity:

> Words, because they stand for objects and events, are an appropriate vehicle for stabilising conceptual issues in the mind while they are being attended to in physical activity, and for constructing future situations which can be given reality in later activity.[24]

It appears that complementing the essentially visual process of design with verbal discussion stimulates creativity by accessing memory and provoking thoughts that may otherwise be obscured by concentration on the physical activity of drawing. Such verbal articulation may therefore be considered essential in generating a solution that draws upon the full spectrum of the designer's experience and cognitive abilities.

It should, however, be recognised that this argument is countered in some accounts by the assertion that language imposes its own cognitive constraints, restricting creativity to concepts that may be verbally encoded. Koestler, for example, believes that true creativity can only begin when language-based forms of cognition are suspended by entering a state of trance or kinesthetic experience.[25] Even within a critique of the design process which emphasises its negotiative aspects, Lawson warns that words and verbal phrases harbour associations which can equal visual representation in their capacity to 'blind' both designer and client.[26]

What emerges from a variety of studies into the design process is the central role played by language and communications, not merely as a presentational aid, but as a part of the thinking and exchange that redefines problems, develops creative solutions and evaluates outcomes. However, when we consider some of the key trends in design, we discover that overlying the issue of communications within the design process are fast-changing social dynamics which place changing demands on designers in terms of communications, teamworking, developing long-term professional relationships or 'alliances' and taking a leadership role. It is to these that we now turn.

KEY TRENDS IN DESIGN

1. Teamworking

> We have a 'village of specialists', a group of good people with whom we work. This is the modern way: brilliant people coming together to create fantastic products.
>
> Paul Priestman of Priestman-Goode, designer of the Tamagochi babysitter

As we explained in our previous book, the role of design in product development has changed from being part of a relay race, in which the product 'baton' was passed from one department to the next, to being part of a rugby team, in which the 'ball' is passed freely from one team member to another until it reaches the 'touchline' of a product launch.[27] In the former model, product development was a linear process with marketing, design and engineering in turn contributing their specialist knowledge. Communication between departments was minimal, with each being consulted separately by the project manager.

The 'rugby approach' characterises cross-functional integration, in which a team of specialists from each department involved in the project is brought together, working as a team from start to finish. Design becomes a cyclical process of individual work and group discussion, where solutions evolve through developing and refining a series of increasingly informed proposals. The use of cross-functional teams is now standard practice in companies worldwide, and is set to increase in response to developments in communications technology. Its key benefits include:

The creative dynamic generated between people with diverse perspectives, knowledge and experience

As one of the UK's leading design consultancies explains;

> At Elmwood we have amongst others a former dancer, a connoisseur of fine wines, a highly vocal roller hockey player and an enthusiastic rock climber. Very different people, very different life experiences, very different goals. Yet when such diverse characters combine, the results will always be different and exciting.
>
> Elmwood Design Limited (1996), *There is No Finish Line ...*,
> Leeds: Who Shares The Barber? Limited, p. 11

Harnessing this creative synergy to the project's goals generates highly innovative solutions, which, because of the uniqueness of the team behind them, are resistant to imitation by competitors. Within design management, new emphasis is being placed on design resulting from unique combinations of expertise, rather than from technological breakthrough.[28]

Closer communication between design and other key functions

Closer communication produces designs which draw on expertise from marketing and technical functions, and are therefore inherently better suited to both consumers and manufacturing capabilities. Jonathan Ive, who heads the industrial design team at Apple Computers, talks about its application in developing the iMac:

> When you are doing something that is so radically new, you can't work in (single) functional groups. The design team worked closely with the engineering team because for one thing, the iMac footprint is very, very small. You have to integrate and miniaturize, and when you do that you have thermal considerations. You have to think about noise and fans.

Reduced product development times

Reduced product development times result from better-informed design and the capacity to address problems as they occur; they afford significant commercial gain in the context of shortening product life cycles and increasing development costs. One study of cross-functional interactions in the product development process concluded: 'Interactions actually speed up the development process, perhaps by avoiding costly mistakes early in the process, which take valuable time to correct as the process moves toward commercialisation'.[29]

Learning from others *and* from working together, resulting in a broader knowledge of other specialisms, improved creativity and problem-solving capabilities

The product development manager of a pewter manufacturer in Sheffield explains this in terms of his design team, and the experience of working with design students on live projects:

> 'You learn something new every day in this job, you never stop learning about new techniques, new tools, new ways of doing things. One of our designers is very good on tooling and making the piece easier to manufacture, and another is very good on what sells in Japan. I've learnt a lot from both of them, and from the two colleges that we work with. Seeing how the lecturers get the students to think about what they're doing and develop their ideas has shown me how to question designers and make sure they've thought everything through.[30]

A high degree of personal involvement and motivation, increasing cooperation and encouraging solving problem

Jane Beebe is a design consultant who adopts a very 'hands-on' approach to working with manufacturers in the glass and metal industries. She considers it essential to work closely with employees on the shopfloor, working with them to develop and implement design solutions. As she explains, 'Involving everyone and letting them have their say makes them feel that they've made a valid contribution. The ownership of the product shifts onto them, so then they'll take pride in it whereas otherwise they won't put that effort in'.[31]

Coherence in complex products such as interiors and cars, which incorporate several design disciplines in a single product

Working in teams allows a product's core values or characteristics to be embodied in all aspects of its design, from function and physical form to brand identity, user interface and product packaging. The scope for this integrated approach to design is increasing still further as communication technologies are developed to address its specific requirements.

Web-based systems incorporating interactive sketchpads and videoconferencing facilities are allowing collaboration between team members located across the globe. Combined with secure intranets, these tools bring a rich diversity of resources to the meeting situation: instant digital images of models, sketches and other images, realistic 3D CAD renderings of product proposals, and web-based technical data and market intelligence information. Team members can discuss ideas, sketch and brainstorm together, and refer to and manipulate images, text and numerical data. Intranets can then become a powerful project resource, as a gateway to web-based information, as a place for storing and ordering information, and as a record of ideas and rationale.

At the specifications stage, e-mail is supplementing expensive face-to-face meetings as a quick and effective means of finding information and clarifying details. In addition, improved user interfaces are allowing designer and manufacturer to work from the same data, transferring specifications directly from CAD software to rapid prototyping or manufacturing systems. Bill Evans, founder of California-based Bridge Design, is a strong advocate of using new communications media in such ways. He says: 'Digitally enhanced communication is a booster to successful product design ... Digital design is eroding the boundaries between disciplines and dissolving geographic borders'.[32]

West Midlands design consultant John Yair echoes this view:

> Being connected to manufacturers by e-mail has totally transformed the way that we work. There's often no need for paper drawings, because toolmakers can generate toolpaths for CNC machining directly from my 3D CAD models. When you think that I can zip down a 10 megabyte solid model and transfer it to China for the cost of a 10 minute local call ...[33]

2. Diversity

Product development teams are drawing on increasingly diverse forms of specialist expertise, as it is recognised that innovative product ideas and solutions to design problems can be found in unexpected sources.

As we saw in the previous chapter, designers increasingly work with users, anthropologists, technologists and marketers, and may even find themselves in discussion with a chemist, craftsperson or colour therapist. Purple Moon's software designers, for example, were only successful in developing a female-oriented computer game after extensive collaboration with child psychologists.[34]

Returning to the Apple iMac, Jonathan Ive describes how a problem defeating Apple's own engineers was resolved through consultation with an unexpected source of expertise:

> The translucent resin [used for the coloured casing] presented a problem because of the high volume of products we needed to produce. We had to make sure that the color and level of translucency were exactly the same in the first computer and every one thereafter. This led us to finding a partner who does a lot of work in the candy industry, because a lot of candies are translucent. These guys have so much experience in how you control the compounding and a great understanding of the science of color control'.[35]

Again, this is a trend set to increase with the development of new computer technologies that assist the communication of ideas and problems to outsiders. It is becoming increasingly cost-effective to produce photo-realistic renderings, realistic prototypes, and animated simulation of products functioning in their intended environments. This has particular advantages in involving consumers, as the accuracy of pre-launch product testing increases with the prototype or simulation's accuracy. With digital products, designers can observe consumers actually engaging with fully functioning prototype user interfaces, providing a clear picture of user behaviour and indicating design faults.

In a broader sense, new technologies are bringing a previously inconceivable diversity of information and expertise directly into the design studio, via the World Wide Web. Designers now have immediate access to resources and specialists across the globe, and are using the Internet's capacity for producing the unexpected to find novel ways of tackling problems. Research has shown that they are increasingly using list-servers and news groups as yet another means of integrating a diversity of expertise into their work.

By combining new insight with existing expertise, companies are creating products with built-in competitive advantage. They are applying their new knowledge to meeting new consumer needs and new technologies (Box 5.1). They are catering for the increasing demand for intelligent, integrated product solutions from consumers who are increasingly well informed and discriminating. Moreover, by creating knowledge through a unique combination of expertise, they are increasing resistance to imitation by competitors.

3. Design alliances

The 1980s saw the expansion of the design consultancy industry in the UK, as in-house design departments closed in response to corporate downsizing. Whilst this outsourcing of design cut clients' costs and improved flexibility – allowing consultants to be chosen to match the demands of individual projects – it also created new problems. Designers' lack of contact with in-house departments meant that their work became less well informed by the company's existing knowledge. Design's goals were typically short-term and project-specific, rather than long-term and strategic. This has been described in terms of 'the distancing of design' in some research.[38] The late 1990s have seen the emergence of a new model – the design alliance – which in many ways combines the best features of in-house and consultancy models. The alliance is an ongoing arrangement with a high level of involvement and commitment, which can be formalised by contract or ownership.

For example, independent consultancy Therefore has spent a proportion of its time on Psion hand-held computer projects, while working simultaneously for other clients. Kenwood has employed a similar 'time-share' approach, its design team working off-site but with in-house status. In packaging design, a consultancy is often

---

Box 5.1   Renaissance Man

Malcolm Garrett is one of the world's leading new media designers. His highly innovative approach to typography first gained prominence in his design work for The Buzzcocks in the late 1970s, following which his Assorted iMaGes company gave a graphic identity to the music of Duran Duran, Simple Minds and other 1980s music. In 1986 Malcolm Garrett bought his first Apple Macintosh, and less than a decade later folded Assorted iMaGes, to establish AMXstudios, dedicated to the design and development of interactive media (www.amxstudios.com).

Operating from its offices in London's Soho, AMXstudios is regarded as a cutting-edge consultancy, working for clients across all new media to generate business worth over £2 million in 1999. A webcast pioneer for the music industry, AMX is behind websites for Oasis and the Spice Girls, but its broad portfolio also includes interactive TV banking for the Woolwich Building Society. As the technologies of computing and television collide in an explosion of diverse media, AMX has maintained its lead in the creative exploitation of new technologies.

Garrett has built a reputation for innovative applications that aim 'to hide technology, to make the design transparent and make it do the right job for the user in an effortless manner'.[36] A recent example of this is a collaborative project with former fashion designer Helen Storey, whose 'Women in mind' exhibition, touring internationally until 2004, bridges art, science and technology. AMX is providing the interactive systems for installations that explore female identity and sexuality, enabling the audience to engage with the formation of thinking processes.

Creating such applications draws on a highly diverse range of expertise. AMX employs computer programmers, authoring designers, animators, graphic designers, video specialists, film makers and illustrators. According to Garrett, 'This range of technical and creative skills promises to cut through the last vestiges of the science-technology/art-design divide that characterised our culture a few decades ago. New media creative teams will integrate the technical and the creative in a marriage of art and science not seen since the Renaissance'.[37]

An author, worldwide conference presenter and visiting professor, Malcolm Garrett demonstrates how designers in new media can play a crucial role in shaping the future of interactive communications. He is a model design entrepreneur who has relished change, taken commercial risks, and exhibited a broad, flexible approach to developing a client base and integrating the practice and theory of design.

---

allied with a particular brand, as in the example of Graphique's work on Unilever's 'Daz' detergent.

Samsung, the Korean electronics giant, like all major Korean and Japanese corporations maintains a large in-house design department. However, in 1994 it established a joint venture design studio in California with the IDEO consultancy, called iS. This studio specialises in design for the US market – taking a group of designers on rotation from Korea, alongside the American team. This provides some key advantages for Samsung in terms of access to lifestyle research, knowledge of the local market, and exposure to new ways of thinking.[39]

Even within more conventional designer–client relationships, the attitudes underpinning these formal alliances are changing the way that people work together. Designers are developing long-term, in-depth relationships with a smaller number of clients, as described by Leeds-based consultancy Elmwood:

> Design is a process that should inspire both designers and clients if they are to lead the running. For this reason we prefer to seek out like-minded clients – individuals and organisations who think like we do, who design as much as we do, who get excited like we do. Both parties benefit. We get a kick out of our work. Our clients get to share in a unique way of working that introduces them to a new range of possibilities. Such an approach naturally encourages long-term partnerships with our clients.[40]

Recent research has also shown the emergence of a new form of alliance in which manufacturers use craftmakers to contribute to the design and new product development process. Industries including furniture, ceramics, glass and metalware have all developed such forms of 'craft alliances'. However, the advantage to the manufacturer goes beyond simply a design input, bringing new knowledge into the enterprise: 'The potential has been demonstrated for such knowledge to create new skills and learning capabilities, generating knowledge-based competencies, and products which derive competitiveness from their uniqueness and inimitability'.[41] This research has opened up possibilities for long-established material based industries to transform themselves into knowledge-based learning organisations that can compete internationally. It also underlines the crucial need for craft-based designers to be expert communicators if they are to fulfil their role.

Research into design management has identified other benefits of such alliances over one-off or occasional consultancy jobs. Margaret Bruce and Birgit Jevnaker have written a definitive text that explores the whole issue of design alliances.[42] From their analysis, and other evidence, we can draw the following conclusions:

- Alliances provide the low overheads and staffing costs characteristic of the consultancy model, without its costly learning curve: designers' familiarity with the company saves time and money at the briefing stage.
- Alliances benefit from external consultants' ability to challenging assumptions and established methods, from their experience of working with other clients, and from their network of contacts beyond the company. As designers develop a deep understanding of company culture, strategy and capabilities, so this fresh approach can be used to inform design with a close strategic fit.
- Alliances allow design integration beyond project boundaries, in defining the brief as well as responding to it, and in evaluating and learning from its long-term impact.
- Alliances allow interpersonal relationships to develop which bring the advantages of familiarity in terms of trust, mutual respect and understanding, without the

inhibitions often imposed by company hierarchies and functional divisions. Communication between designer and client or other colleagues can be more open, honest and objective than in either in-house or standard consultancy models.

4. Designer–entrepreneurs

The trends detailed above challenge outdated stereotypes of designers as solitary visionaries behind a drawing board (or screen), or as product stylists kept at arm's length by their corporate clients, or as craftmakers at odds with the interests of manufacturing industry. Finally we must consider the growing significance of the designer as an entrepreneur – acting as the hub and driving force of the production process.

The design consultancy sector itself, which in the UK employs over 20,000 people and generates an income of over £12 billion, is evidence itself of the entrepreneurial spirit within professional design.[43] However, many designers go beyond the conventional role of the designer as consultant and become more directly involved in the business of delivering products and services to consumers. Bruce and Jevnaker have described this as an emerging form of design alliance – entrepreneurial mobilisation – in which the designer is a 'dialectical, knowledge-intensive, source of innovation' who can take on an entrepreneurial role in the new product development process.[44]

In the history of twentieth-century British design, one particular example stands out of an entrepreneurial mobiliser – a designer whose approach to innovative design was rejected by established manufacturers, and for whom the only way of getting these designs to the market involved setting up a factory from scratch. Winning the support of retailers such as Selfridges and John Lewis, this designer succeeded in bringing modern design into the UK's homes.

As a woman designer, working in the highly conservative North Staffordshire pottery industry, Susie Cooper's only chance of tackling shape design was to establish her own manufacturing company, as women were restricted to designing pattern. In 1929, at the age of 27, Susie Cooper set up her business which, after an uncertain start due to the Great Depression, was to employ up to one hundred pottery workers. The practical, stylish designs were a success at trade fairs and did much to innovate the otherwise staid tabletop of UK homes. Her ware was popular up to the early 1960s, when the Wedgwood Group bought up her company.[45] Susie Cooper demonstrated that a strong design vision, wedded to business skills and determination, was the only way of modernising UK's traditional industries. Her example is particularly inspiring given the additional huge challenges that she was confronted with as a woman seeking to establish her own factory in the man's world of inter-war Britain.

Sir Terence Conran came to prominence just after Susie Cooper's firm was absorbed into Wedgwood. Again, here we have a case of a designer with a mission – not just to change the face of Britain's tabletop, but the house around it, and the stores where household goods were bought. With the established retailers unwilling to take on his modern furniture designs, Conran's only option was to establish Habitat. This developed into the Storehouse Group, which at its peak controlled Mothercare, Richard Shops and British Home Stores. Storehouse's eventual demise led Sir Terence to reinvent his business around restaurants and the Conran Shop, while IKEA took charge of Habitat.

James Dyson shared with Susie Cooper and Terence Conran the rejection of industry for his new design – in this case the dual cyclone 'bagless' vacuum cleaner. Again, determination and an entrepreneurial vision led to the establishment of his own factory and the marketing of a product that has become a market leader.

Despite the high profile examples of designer–entrepreneurs, such as Sir Terence Conran or James Dyson, there are few analytical case studies available. Elsewhere we have written of the case of New York designer Eric Chan, who subcontracted manufacture for his own telephone design to factories in the Far East, while co-ordinating the marketing in the USA.[46] There is also the partnership between Smart Design and Oxo, leading to the Good Grips kitchen tool range.[47] One recent journalistic account examined furniture designer Martin Ryan's success as a manufacturer.[48] It is regrettable that examples of design-led industry are more readily found in the Sunday papers than in the literature on design management.

However, what is clear is that the opportunities for designer–entrepreneurs have never been greater, for the following reasons:

- Diversifying lifestyles increase the demand for niche products.
- Online retailing provides direct access to consumers.
- New communications systems allow UK-based designers to directly access lower-cost manufacturers elsewhere in the world.
- Business support and advice are widespread.

For many decades, designers have done it for themselves. In the twenty-first century we can expect to see the designer–entrepreneur become far more widespread as a professional model, and as this happens it changes the roles and responsibilities of designers even more.

THE DESIGNER AS COMMUNICATOR

Adopting a team-based approach to design, building alliances with clients and taking entrepreneurial initiative have put new emphasis on the designer's ability to work with others, transforming design into a communication-led activity. Interaction and discussion have become integral to the design process itself, and fundamental to building positive working relationships. In this context, designers have a responsibility to communicate their thinking in a language which can be easily understood by colleagues more used to interpreting words than images.

The increasingly team-based approach to product development has led to a broadening of roles: individuals are no longer seen as specialists with narrowly defined responsibilities, but as generalists with a particular area of expertise. Professional competence is seen as the ability to relate function-specific knowledge to a broad contextual understanding, to apply it with creativity and to work effectively towards project goals.

Designers have begun to seek new skills and knowledge, and to undertake a broader, more strategic role in product development. No longer seen as primarily concerned with aesthetics or function, as stylists or as 'visual people', they are becoming a fully integrated resource. Designers are developing in-depth understanding of the relationship between design and company strategy, products and consumers, their work and those affected by it. New technologies are allowing them to diversify into market research, rapid prototyping, typesetting and manufacture. In the course of a project they may assist in devising strategy, in formulating briefs and designing market research projects, in resolving technical problems and in devising advertising campaigns. Jeffry Corbin, president of a US-based design consultancy, has described the way in which design activity has diversified from being solely concerned with aesthetics and function to encompassing concerns including market definition and positioning, and strategy definition and implementation.[49]

This new breadth of approach applies equally to other contributors to product development, who are becoming knowledgeable about design and capable of relating it to their own specialisms. Designers in challenging assumptions, testing ideas, stimulating creativity and resolving problems welcome their contributions.

This approach is illustrated by design researcher Birgit Jevnaker's description of the design process she observed in three Scandinavian manufacturing companies:

> Selected design choices were delineated, vividly discussed and explained by more than one party. Critical information as well as lively rhetoric was exchanged, while people in the firm's network were exposed to drawings, models or finished products and communication material designs. This finding is in sharp contrast to the myth of the individualistic designer working in his / her design studio and communicating only through his/her designs.[50]

This broadening of roles and blurring of boundaries between them is complemented by recognition of the value of skills, knowledge and insight specific to each function. Designers need to recognise their particular strengths in:

- translating the group's collective knowledge into actual product attributes
- visualising product concepts and communicating them visually
- combining rational, intuitive and creative thinking
- capturing group discussion as it occurs through sketches and diagrams
- handling and transforming complex information
- working with incomplete information: testing and refining potential solutions.

Designers are communicating differently, researching differently, trying to reach under the surface of society, pushing boundaries and developing theories – the scientists of the 21st century, builders of experiences. We are not just talking about designers, but 'design' – the activity that is undertaken by many and facilitated by a few very skilled people.

All of this has profound implications for the professional definition of design and its future development. It is this question that the following chapter addresses.

NOTES

1. This chapter draws upon some material co-authored by Mike Press and Karen Yair at Sheffield Hallam University developed for a one-year research project commissioned by the Design Council to develop a teaching tool on communication studies for design students.
2. E. Manzini (1995), 'The Ecology of the Artificial and the Designer's Responsibility' in R. Buchanan and V. Margolin (eds), *Discovering Design*, Chicago: The University of Chicago Press.
3. C. Ashwin (1989), 'Drawing Design Semiotics', in V. Margolin, *Design Discourse*, Chicago: The University of Chicago Press.
4. K. Krippendorff (1998), 'On the essential contexts of artifacts or on the Proposition that "Design is Making Sense (of Things)"', in V. Margolin, R. Buchanan (eds), *The Idea of Design, A Design Issues Reader*, Third Edition, Cambridge, MA: The MIT Press.
5. Helga Lannoch and Hans-Jurgen Lannoch (1987), 'Vom geometrischen zum sematischen Raum', in K. Krippendorff, 'On the essential contexts of artifacts'.
6. K. Krippendorff, 'On the essential contexts of artifacts'.
7. N. Anjum, R. Ashcroft and J. Paul (1998), *The Design Journal*, **1** (2).
8. M. Tovey and G. Harris (1999), 'Concept Design and Sketch Mapping', *The Design Journal*, **2** (2).
9. Ibid.
10. C. Eckert (1999), 'Managing Effective Communication in Knitwear Design', *The Design Journal*, **2** (3).
11. G. Loosschilder (1997), 'A picture tells a thousand words. Testing product design concepts using computer-aided design', *The Design Journal*, (1).
12. Ashwin, 'Drawing Design Semiotics'.
13. A. Tomes, C. Oates and P. Armstrong (1998), 'Talking Design: Negotiating the Verbal–Visual Translation, *Design Studies*, **19** (2) 127 – 42.
14. B. Lawson (1990), *How Designers Think*, Oxford: Butterworth-Heinemann.
15. L. Bucciarelli (1994), 'Reflective Practice in Engineering Design', *Design Studies*, **5** (3) 185–90.
16. M. Bruce and B. Morris (1998), 'In-House, Outsourced or a Mixed Approach to Design', in M. Bruce and B. Jevnaker (eds), *Managing Design Alliances*, Chichester: John Wiley & Sons.
17. Tomes et al., 'Talking Design'.

18. Ibid., p. 140.
19. D. Fleming (1998), 'Design Talk: Constructing the Object in Studio Conversations', *Design Issues*, **14** (2).
20. K. Byrne (1990), 'A "Semantics" of Visual Design: the Care and Feeding of Studio Projects Within a Communication Theory Context', *Design Studies*, **11** (3) 141–163.
21. K. Clark and T. Fujimoto (1990), 'The Pewter of Product Integrity', *Harvard Business Review*, November/December.
22. Lawson, *How Designers Think*.
23. L.S. Vysgotsky (1978), *Mind in Society* (eds M. Cole, A.R. Luria, M. Lopez-Morillas and J.V. Wertsch), Harvard University Press.
24. R. Fielding (1994), 'Human Language and Drawing Development: Their Productive Iterations', *Journal of Art and Design Education*, **13** (2) 145–50.
25. A. Koestler (1964), *The Act of Creation*, London: Hutchinson, p. 173.
26. Lawson, *How Designers Think*.
27. See R. Cooper and M. Press (1995), *The Design Agenda*, Chichester: John Wiley and Sons, p. 126.
28. R.W. Ruekert (1995), 'Cross Functional Interactions in Product Development and Their Impact on Project Performance', *Design Management Journal*, **6** (3), 50–4.
29. See ibid., p. 54, and E. Rhodes and R. Carter (1995), 'Emerging Corporate Strategies', *Co-Design*, no. 3.
30. Interview: Richard Abdy, Product Development Manager, A.R. Wentworth Ltd.
31. Interview: Jane Beebe, freelance design consultant.
32. B. Evans (1998), 'Stevenson's Rocket: design in the digital steam age, *Design Management Journal*, 9 (3) 29–34, p. 34.
33. Interview: John Yair, design consultant.
34. C. Ireland (1998), 'The story of purple moon', *Design Management Journal*, 9 (4), 42–6.
35. D. Hirasuna (2000), 'Sorry, no beige', Apple Media Arts, http:/www.apple.com/creative/collateral/ama/0102/imac.html, accessed 23 January 2001.
36. http://www.amxstudios.com/news/features/garrett.html, accessed 14 August 2000.
37. B. Cotton and M. Garrett (1999), *You Ain't Seen Nothing Yet: The Future of Media and the Global Expert System*, London: Institute of Contemporary Arts, p. 23.
38. J. Lewis (1988), 'The distancing of design', Open University/UMIST Design Innovation Group, working paper WP-11.
39. For further details on these and other examples see H. Aldersey-Williams (1996), 'Design at a distance: the new hybrids', *Design Management Journal*, **7** (2) 43–7.
40. Elmwood (1996), *There is no finish line*, Leeds: Who Shares the Barber? Ltd, 14.
41. K. Yair, M. Press and A. Tomes (1999), 'Design through making: crafts knowledge as facilitator to collaborative new product development', *Design Studies*, **20** (6), 495–515.
42. Bruce and Jevnaker, *Management of Design Alliances*.

43. See: Creative Industries Task Force (1998), *Creative Industries Mapping Document*, London: Department of Culture, Media and Sport.
44. Bruce and Jevnaker, *Management of Design Alliances*, p. 120.
45. For further details on Susie Cooper see J. Attfield and P. Kirkham (eds), *A View from the Interior: feminism, women and design*, London: The Women's Press, chapter 6.
46. M. Press (1995), 'Buddy, can you spare a paradigm?', *co-design journal*, **1** (3).
47. D. Formosa (1996), 'The design of Good Grips kitchen tool', *Design Management Journal*, Fall.
48. H. Aldersey-Williams (1998), 'The DIY designer–manufacturers', *Independent on Sunday*, Business Section, 22 February.
49. J. Corbin, 'The Design Consultant as Strategic Resource', *Design Management Journal*, **7** (2), 38–42.
50. Bruce and Jevanaker, *Management of Design Alliances*, p. 120.

6 The design professions

Every human being is a designer ... many also earn their living by design ... a professional minority ... whose work carries a strong visual motivation and whose decisions help give form and order to the amenities of life ...

Norman Potter[1]

When designers talk about themselves, they seem to undergo a terrible transformation. The moment we open our mouths we're seized by an overwhelming urge to try to pass ourselves off as accountants. We talk a great deal about cost-effectiveness and the vital contribution of totally integrated design programmes to the client's bottom line. We use a lot of phrases like 'strategic planning' and 'market analysis'. We often end up denying all interests in creativity, so anxious are we to establish our credentials as serious business people ... but at the end of the day, our work will stand or fall – as it always has – on the strength of our ideas and the skill with which we express them.

Ben Casey and Lionel Hatch,[2] The Chase Creative Consultants (1993)

The origin of the word 'profession' is based on a 'declaration or vow of religious faith entry into religious order, or vocation or calling especially of learned or scientific or artistic kind'.[3] As you progress through this book or indeed many publications in or about design you will indeed find that design is a religion and most of those who practise it are devoted to it. They are professionals in the true sense of the word. However, like any profession there are sub-divisions or specialisms. This chapter will discuss the design profession, its origins and the specialisms which arise from it, and goes on to consider the future of this profession.

When beginning to discuss the design profession one cannot fail to consider the early work by Norman Potter, who in 1969 alluded to the difficulty of using the word 'design' 'to denote a wide range of quite different experiences – both in the outcome of design decisions and the activity of designing.'[4] Potter took a broad view of design and simply grouped the work into three categories: product design (things); environmental design (places); and communications design (messages), making the proviso that the 'distinctions are in no way absolute'.

Maintaining this broad view is probably the most useful way of considering design in an environment of continual technological and market change. However, in order to locate design skills and competencies and to consider their value, one must analyse further the breadth of the profession of design. Indeed differing design 'professions' have evolved by educational push and by corporate and consumer pull, which means that there are various perspectives from which to assess the profession and its future.

THE DESIGN PROFESSION FROM A PRACTITIONER PERSPECTIVE

Design as an activity has played a major role in society, ever since the pattern books of the Industrial Revolution; indeed, design skills were used by the Arts and Crafts Movement and the modernist and the post-modernist movements. However, many commentators believe that design as an independent profession began in the early part of the twentieth century. In the UK the Design and Industries Association began in 1915, Stanley Morison, the great typographer, worked as a designer for the Monotype Corporation in the 1920s, while Susie Cooper was operating as a ceramic designer. At the same time in the USA, consumer demand for durables such as fridges, vacuum cleaners and cars meant that the work of Raymond Loewy, Walter Dorwin Teague and Norman Bel Geddes, all of whom formed independent design consultancies, became well known. It is interesting to note that all three did not train specifically as industrial designers but came from backgrounds of advertising, typography, theatre and window display, engineering and illustration. During World War II the Ministry of Information set up the Design Research Unit. This was chaired by Herbert Read and included a panel of architects, designers and engineers. The aim was to network designers and engineers in order to provide industry with practical advice although most of its work was based on its members' backgrounds, such as graphic design and interior design. It was intended to be the UK's first design consultancy.[3] After World War II design became more important as part of the route to building up economies. In the UK the Council for Industrial Design was set up, in Japan, the Japanese Industrial Designers Association. In the USA Walter Paepcke set up the Aspen International Design Conference. Designers began to see the vital role they could play in boosting industry both nationally and internationally.

During the 1950s and early 1960s much of the training of designers still resided in the arts and crafts tradition, or perhaps commercial art and industrial design. Professional designers used their skills to tackle most design problems, ranging from product design, graphic design, interior design and so on. During the 1960s and early 1970s the major UK design consultancies began to appear, such as Minale Tattesfield and Pentagram. The design schools offered courses covering a wider range of disciplines such as graphic design, product design, surface pattern design and interior design.

Graphic design perhaps had specific origins in the area of advertising and sales. Most designers working in this area until the mid-1960s were called commercial artists, and spanned the boundaries between corporate identity, packaging and advertising. But as the design consultancies developed their competencies in graphic design, specialising in corporate identity, typography and packaging, so the advertising industry split off, developing marketing and commercial acumen and different organisational structures. Today in the UK those working in advertising rarely class themselves as design consultants. As Myerson suggests,

Ad agency folk often regard the design of packaging, brochures and logotypes as small beer compared with the glamour of the big-budget, high profile press and TV work. Designers for their part tend to regard much of advertising as inelegant hard-sell at the dirty end of the business, no matter how commercially effective it is.[4]

This schism is not necessarily as great outside the UK. For instance Carl Sherriff, a creative director in Australia, suggests that in Australia there is more one-stop shopping, probably because it is a smaller market.[5]

Up to the 1980s then, professional design skills were being developed by particular disciplines aimed at specific industries, looking to satisfy their customer needs and differentiate themselves by offering innovation and quality as well as the other attributes which designers built into the products and services, such as aesthetics, styling, functionality semantics, durability and the like.

During the 'designer decade' of the 1980s, design became consumed by the media, and was often seen by business as a panacea for all ills. The cult object prevailed, often associated with design and the designer label dictating every sphere of life, for example, the origins of Alessi or the development of the brand label, of Gucci, Ralph Lauren and so on. It was at this point that the UK design consultancies boomed, having been fed by the plethora of young designers from the growth in UK design education. Many consultancies offered a multidisciplinary approach to a company's design problems, which included graphic design, product design, interiors and even management consultancy. The consultancies were able to sell their services around the world. Indeed in 1987 Beryl McAlone reported on a study for the Design Council in which it was claimed that the UK had the strongest design consultancy industry in the world.[7]

This design bubble burst with the 1990s recession. There was a reduction in demand for what was seen by many companies as 'the icing on the cake', and as a result a reduction in the use of the large multidisciplinary design consultancies. Design consultancies suffered more than industry and commerce as a whole.[9] Many businesses failed because they had grown too large too quickly. They were offering services beyond their own competency, for instance, management consultancy, and as a result of their size and costs, were not able to respond flexibly to the needs of the market. Since the early 1990s the design consultancy industry has reconstructed itself. Those companies that have survived have downsized, have focused on their core skill, design, and have been able to communicate the value of their specific design skills. We are now in a world where it is generally agreed that design is a critical part of business success and that the design profession encompasses individuals with a wide range of skills and competencies.

This development of the design professional is only part of what Findeli defines as the physiognomy of design.[10] He believes this can be presented as a result of the meeting and complex interaction of various lineages. The main ones include:

1. The decorative arts tradition that goes back to the beginnings of human culture
2. The theoretical or discursive/normative tradition in design, originating in the

---

Box 6.1   Examples of the developers of the design profession

Susie Cooper (b. 1902)

A ceramic designer who designed distinctive earthenware (trademark of a leaping deer) in the 1930s; later she designed tableware for the Royal Pavilion at the Festival of Britain. Her company became part of the Wedgwood Group in 1956. There was a revival of popularity for her lively ceramic designs in the 1970s.

Source: Julier Guy (1993), *The Thames and Hudson Encyclopaedia of 20th Century Design and Designers*, Thames and Hudson, London.

Stanley Morison (1889–1967)

Stanley Morison was a typographer who worked as typographical adviser to The British Monotype Corporation. In 1932 he made Times New Roman for the *London Times*. This has become one of the most widely used typefaces of the twentieth century.

Source: *The Art of the Printed Book 1455–1955* (1973), The Pierpont Morgan Library, New York.

Raymond Loewy (1893–1986)

Loewy studied engineering, yet he worked as a fashion illustrator for *Vogue* and *Harper's Bazaar* and as a window display artist for Macys when he went to New York after World War I. In the late 1920s, after working as an industrial designer, he formed his own company. His early work was for Gestener on copying machines, then he became known for the cold spot refrigerator, the scenicruiser coach for Greyhound, the logotypes for Exxon Oil Company and Shell Oil Company as well as the interiors of Skylab for NASA. Loewy is cited as being responsible for positioning the role of design at the service of the corporation and consumerism.[11]

Walter Dorwin Teague (1883–1960)

Teague studied at the Arts Students League and worked briefly in an advertising agency. He then set up his own office and became involved in packaging design, which developed into complete product design for companies like Kodak. He is famous for the baby Brownie camera, which included the use of plastics. Teague worked for other US companies: he designed the Ford and the US Steel pavilions for New York's World's Fair in 1939. In 1944 he became the first president of the American Society of Industrial Designers.

---

nineteenth century; including Henry Cole, Gottfied Semper, the Bauhaus, the HfG in Ulm, and post-modern discourse

3. The professional tradition born in the United States in the late 1920s and its pioneers (Loewey, Teague, Geddes, and so on)

4. The technological and managerial furrow, only some fifteen years old and not yet a tradition (computerisation of products and management design)

The design profession from a practice perspective does indeed present a complex physiognomy, which is much more than Findeli's four lineages and which is being influenced by technology, markets, culture and education.

Box 6.1 (concluded)

Norman Bel Geddes (1893–1958)
Bel Geddes studied at the Art Institute of Chicago, worked in theatre design and shop window display in the early 1920s, beginning his industrial design work in 1927. His company went into liquidation after World War II due to his lack of commercial acumen, but he is noted for his theories in industrial design, namely streamlining.

Design Research Unit
Founded in 1943, a UK design consultancy set up by the Ministry of Information during World War II. It was chaired by Herbert Read with a panel of architects, designers and engineers, including Misha Black and Milner Gray. Its work was predominantly in house styles and interiors during the 1950s. It never undertook product design.

Minale Tattersfield (founded 1964)
Founded by Marcello Minale and Brian Tattersfield in 1964, 'noted for bringing to mainstream commercial design highly creative and often witty design solutions using the minimum means necessary.'[12]

Aspen International Design Conference (founded 1951)
This is an annual conference, bringing together international designers and architects to discuss a different design-related theme each year.

Pentagram (founded 1972)
This design consultancy was formed as a multidisciplinary design studio in London, comprising graphic designers Alan Fletcher, Colin Forbes, architect Theo Crosby and industrial designer Kenneth Grange. Its notable work includes the corporate identity of Reuters, British Rail, products for Kenwood, Ronson and the Parker Pen Company.
Source: Julier Guy (1993), *The Thames and Hudson Encyclopaedia of 20th Century Design and Designers*, Thames and Hudson, London.

THE PROFESSION FROM AN EDUCATIONAL PERSPECTIVE

The evolution of design education followed to a degree the development of the profession in industry. In the UK, until the mid-1960s and early 1970s, most design skills were developed in art schools and then colleges of art and design. The education was very much vocational training, with an emphasis on developing skills in the studio, the learning being derived from the atelier teaching method, whereby a small group of students working on design tasks were tutored by a designer or artist. Frequently the tutors were part-time and therefore practising as artists and designers in their own right. This practice continued when the colleges were subsumed into polytechnics in the late 1960s. During the 1980s there was a growth in higher education numbers and a reduction in higher education funding. In order to respond to this new situation, a change in teaching and learning methods was required. These changes not only demanded a reduction in part-time teaching by professional designers to save costs, but with class sizes growing, another approach to the education of designers was needed. This approach involved more emphasis on the theoretical and historical perspectives of design. For the first time, perhaps, there were design academics looking for a body of knowledge. There wasn't one, of course, or if there was, it was difficult to bring together. The theory and knowledge of design had been in the tradition and in the heads of practising designers.

The profession of designer has not been accredited with the professional status which has been attributed to architects or engineers. Academically, therefore, there had been no impetus to develop a body of knowledge, as was the case with architects and engineers. This lack of professional status may be a result of the disparate manner in which the profession has represented itself. Designers have been characterised not only by their discipline-specific skills, for example interior design, but also the area of operation, kitchens and bathrooms.

Viewing the way the *design disciplines* have been categorised (Table 6.1) from an educational perspective provides us with general classification for the profession, which is still pre-eminent in the UK education system and is reflected in the professional orientations in industry.

The design courses offered today have some different orientations, however. There are the studio-based craft courses, where the emphasis is on designing and making; such courses include glass and ceramics, jewellery and silversmithing. There are courses whose predominant orientation is design from an industry and professional stance; these focus on developing design skills and relating them to industry that is, solving product or graphic design problems. The theoretical courses tend to consider the history and contextual aspects of design as well as provide an understanding of the subject itself. This book focuses on the type of information covered by many such courses. Because of the changes in UK design education as described above, there has been much discussion on the relative merits of moving undergraduate education from a vocational skill development and training emphasis to one of intellectual discourse, leaving the skill generation to vocational pre-degree education. This is probably more of a discussion about the percentage of theory and practice rather than a choice of either practice or theory, and will be an ongoing debate, particularly while the profession is struggling to define itself.

Design education in other European countries had various origins. In Italy even today most designers come from an education in architecture. In the US the broadly based tertiary education system has meant that students of design rarely do have the concentrated studio and atelier system of mentoring which the UK system adopted. They study a smaller number of design modules combining them with broader arts and humanities subjects.

Table 6.1   Art and design course categories
Source: Art and Design Courses 1997/98, Design Council 1996, Trotman and Co., Richmond, Surrey, UK.

Graphics – graphic design (general), book/magazine design, illustration, media/multimedia, packaging, photography, printing, typography

Fashion/clothing – fashion/clothing design (general), theatre costume, footwear, combined fashion/textile

Textiles – textile design (general), carpet/rug embroidery, knitted textiles, printed textiles, surface pattern /decoration, textile technology, weaving

3D – products – product design (general), ceramics, furniture, glass engineering design, industrial design, jewellery/silver

Spatial design – spatial design (general), architecture, building exhibition display, interior, landscape, theatre/stage

Multidisciplinary

Other

In the US since World War II the Bachelor of Fine Arts has been the degree for students wishing for a professional education in art or design. The National Association of Schools of Art and Design is the nationally recognised accrediting agency for programmes in art and design and it distinguishes between BFAs and BAs. BFA are 'professional' programmes, usually granting the BFA, while the BA is a liberal arts program. In the US all undergraduate programmes must include a liberal arts component. As the Association of Independent Colleges of Art and Design (AICAD) describes it,

> the difference between a BFA and a BA is in the ratio between art and design and general studies. In a BFA approximately two thirds of the course work is in the 'creation of the visual arts', with the remainder in general studies (literature, history, sociology etc). In a BA approximately two thirds of the course work is in general studies, with the remainder in visual arts.[13]

This is replicated at postgraduate level with the MFA and the MA. The AICAD state that 'the BFA is the most appropriate degree for serious, motivated students seeking to become professional artists and designers'.[14]

However, because the students in the US follow a modular structure and take up various majors, the courses do not necessarily follow the industrial demands and mirror the direction of the professions as much as the UK's system attempts to do.

The development of industrial design education in the US is very well described by Arthur J. Pulos. In *The American Design Adventure* 1940–1975, he states that the first undergraduate degree in industrial design was launched at Carnegie Tech by Alexander Kostellow and Donald Dohnerin in 1935.[15] Pulos then describes the 40 years in which there was continual definition and refinement of what was industrial design education, whether it was training or education and whether it bore any relationship to the practising designers. For instance, in 1946 after a Conference of Schools of Design, Walter Dorwin Teague summarised his impressions of the academic world in a letter to Richard Bach, dean of education at the Metropolitan Museum:

> 'It was a great pleasure for us to meet the educators and exhibit ourselves to them. I hope the meeting was in some measure enlightening. I think however that none of us gives a damn about whether or not they "liked the group picture".
>
> We feel that they need us a lot more than we need them. We have created a profession, and some of them are delighted to teach it, with only the vaguest idea of what it is all about.
>
> If nothing more, I hope it gave them some idea of the difficulty of an adequate academic training for industrial design. By our practice we will create a definition of industrial design and I trust the conference committee will be acute enough to discern it.

Pulos goes on to suggest, however, that education for Teague had been an important factor in defining his professional status in that five years earlier, he had called attention to existing academic industrial design programmes in support of his own claim to be a professional. In a case heard by the New York Supreme Court, he had succeeded in being exempted from paying taxes levied on non-professionals.

In 1944 John Vassos and Kostelow and other designers proposed an amendment to the New York State Education Law (Article 84-A) that would have established educational requirements and licensing regulations for industrial designers. The amendment was not passed. Many designers lobbied against it, 'jealous of their independence and unwilling to submit to the scrutiny of their peers and suspicious of the growing academic design establishment'.[16]

The debate between practising design and industrial design education continued for many years through many forums such as the Industrial Design Education Association (which tried to build a network of design educators and a communication link to practising designers) and The Industrial Designers Society of America (IDSA). IDSA indeed recommended academic minimums for industrial design education built around Information (the acquisition of knowledge) 'formation' (the solution of problems related to products and systems), and communication (the development of skills for exploring, storing and transmitting ideas). These minimums were used as a basis for many schools around the US and the world to develop their own personalised curriculum.[17]

After World War II most schools in the US taught a combination of design, including advertising design, industrial design, interior design, fashion design, and illustration or commercial photography. Rob Roy Kelly, a practising graphic designer and teacher for 35 years, described two-dimensional programmes of that period as either advertising design in the better schools and commercial art in the lesser ones.[18] Graphic design as an educational programme began at Yale in 1950. During the 1950s US corporations started to develop an identity which 'gave enormous impetus to Graphic Design'. It was during this period that the profession was established. In the

Table 6.2 US undergraduate majors offered at 34 AICAD (Association of Independent Colleges of Art and Design) member colleges

Advertising	Animation	Architecture
Architectural Studies	Art Direction	Art Education
Art History	Art Therapy	Cartooning
Ceramics	Clay	Communication Design
Computer Animation	Computer Graphics	Design Marketing
Drawing	Enamelling	Environmental Design
Fashion Design	Fibers	Film
Filmmaking	Fine Arts	Furniture Design
Glass	Graphic Design	Illustration
Industrial Design	Interior Architecture	Interior Design
Jewellery	Landscape Architecture	Medical Illustration
Medical Photography	Metals	New Genres
Package Design	Painting	Papermaking
Performance	Photography	Printmaking
Sculpture	Textiles	Transportation Design
Video	Weaving	Wood

1980s the American Institute of Graphic Arts became a national organisation. However, as in the UK the distinction between graphic design and advertising is now beginning to blur, and marketing and technology are influencing graphic design education, suggesting that this professional discipline is about to redefine itself once again.

What do we learn, therefore, about the design profession from the pattern of education? It is not a profession comparable to law or medicine; there are still no specific subjects or statutory aspects in which the professional designer must have qualifications. On examination of the topics or subjects offered both in the US and UK, there is a plethora of subjects covered in both breadth and depth, some of which are very vocationally and practically oriented, some more theoretical. The design curriculum is influenced by professional practice, market demands and changes in the educational system.

The 'profession' has not been defined categorically by either the practitioners or the educators. Despite attempts in both the US and the UK to licence or regulate designers and identify statutory knowledge and skills, this has never been achieved. Perhaps therefore it would be wiser to consider the profession as a set of disciplines, identifying the context in which they operate and the skills required to practise in those contexts.

DESIGN DISCIPLINES AND SKILLS

If one tries to identify the core skills which designers have, one can follow how these have been developed into professions. Walker alluded to the craft roots of design, which included perception, imagination, visualisation, dexterity and manipulation.[19] The skill to perceive a need or the imagination to develop an idea and then visualise a solution either two- or three-dimensionally has always been a central theme of design.

Taking Potter's original definition of design areas, one can differentiate particular skills related to their particular design orientation, as follows.

Messages

Messages includes graphic design, illustration, multimedia design, interface design, information design, photographic design, fashion editorial design and advertising design

Primarily this area of design activity is concerned with representation and communication in a two-dimensional environment. The emphasis is on line, pattern, colour, space, the form of both an image or a letterform, and the communication of content, both of image and text. As Maurice de Sausmarez described it in 1964, 'it is dependent upon the expressive and constructive use of the specific phenomena of vision.'[20] The more recent change which has occurred in this field has been the move from the printed medium to the digital medium. Designers who are now working with computer graphics, CD-ROM technology and the World Wide Web, that is, interactive media, have to take into consideration the added dimensions of space and time:

> Time for instance expands the formal vocabulary an author can use to express a message. For example tone of voice can be communicated through timing and rhythm as well as through traditional dimensions such as size, colour and transparency. New design issues will need to be addressed. For example if type presented in sequence appears on different parts of the screen, the designer needs to alert the reader of an upcoming change in order for the reader to move her eyes to the proper location. Otherwise reading all these words is missed and communication fails.[21]

Some commentators believe that 'the distinction between text and images is disappearing. In its place we will see the emergence of a new vocabulary consisting of typographic images and pictorial images. Animated dynamic typography will extend the expressive qualities of text to a level that can reach beyond the impact of images.'[22]

The technology is also merging professionals in this field with other media-related professions such as people in advertising, music, film and TV. This has been described as the 'missing industry', using copywriters, directors, musicians and designers to communicate through digital media. The question arises as to how education can develop to embrace this missing industry. The potential for designers to work with, or as, media professionals is now great. The technology has enabled the merging of media such as drawing, photography and film, resulting in the graphic designer/artist, commentator on culture, creating messages using complex imagery, or the merging of graphic design/information design with three dimensional forms

Box 6.2   The Parthenon Sculptures at the British Museum

In Greek mythology Tiresias, the blind seer of ancient Thebes, was blinded by Hera but compensated by Zeus with the gift of second sight. As a metaphor for the Museum's project, the name Tiresias is fitting, for not only is the intention to introduce visually impaired people to the Parthenon frieze, but also to show sighted visitors something that they might otherwise not have seen. The tactile displays in the new galleries are centred on a selection of plaster casts of the west frieze, which is explained by another sound guide and supplementary graphics. The graphics are raised in relief in the new technique of 'touch art'. Using similar methods, opportunities are also offered to learn about the Parthenon itself and its setting on the Acropolis at Athens, and to explore by touch some original pieces of ancient architecture.

Although developed initially for visually impaired people, the Tiresias Project is an important new resource for all those who wish to learn about the Parthenon and its sculptures by directly communicating an understanding of the Parthenon frieze to a broad audience. One of the most important monuments to survive from classical antiquity, the frieze is also one of the most complex and perhaps puzzling to some Museum visitors. With the insight of Tiresias, many more people will be able to understand the subject than ever before.

The accompanying book, complete with its own five-hour commentary on cassette, *Second Sight of the Parthenon Frieze*, published by British Museum Press, is available from the Museum shops price £40. It includes a series of tactile images representing a selection of key passages from the frieze interpreted and drawn so as to make them accessible to a new audience. This process has involved a number of specialist advisers including the Royal National Institute for the Blind.

Source: www.thebritishmuseum.ac.uk Reproduced courtesy of the Trustees of the British Museum.

such as the gallery at the British Museum for the visually impaired, where they have used relief, sound and 3D books to describe the Parthenon Sculptures.(see Box 6.2).

It is particularly ironic that advertising and design may be moving closer together again. Before the 1960s and the growth of design consultancies, the ad agency was usually the first opportunity for work for the graphic designer. Now 'New technology is giving graphic designers the ability to produce and edit moving image and sound, dimensions that were once the exclusive right of advertising creatives.' Mike Dempsey of CDT Design suggests that 'what is likely to emerge is a new set of people outside the conventional agency and design structures, equipped with hybrid communications skills'.[23] This argument is further supported by the increasing demands of new media, with the advent of digital TV, online shopping and the fact that we have two million plus Internet users. There is a demand for user-friendly interactive design, and therefore design consultancies and design groups are emerging with specialists in creative technology or interactive design (see Box 6.3).

Box 6.3   *SmartMoney*

Source: SmartMoney/*ID Magazine*, Vol. 46, No. 4, June 1999.

Interactive Media Design Review Winners 1999, *The International Design Magazine*, June 99

SmartMoney magazine, a *Wall Street Journal* publication set up in 1992, became the leading personal finance publication. Its web site, connected to the *Wall Street Journal* mega-site, was described as expansive and, like the magazine, deeply informative.

The site represents stock market gains and losses with innovative graphs showing both changes at once and adapting as the market moves up and down. It allows for those with red–green colour blindness to opt for blue–yellow colours to show changes; provides investors with the option of a more traditional view of stock market statistics via a suite of trading and analysis applications; and links into additional company information through drop-down menus.

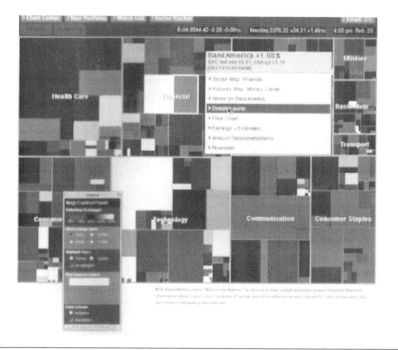

Designers working with messages must be equipped with the capability to understand the communication needs of both the sender and the receiver, the ability to manipulate images, letterforms, colour, sound in space and time and communicate the results through visualisation and creation abilities. For example, messages are an important medium in the competitive environment of marketing, in particular brand image development. The skill here for the designer is the translation of brand values using colour and image to create the brand identity and brand atmosphere that work in both print and digital form (see Box 6.4).

Box 6.4 Indesit by Wolff Olins
Source: *Design Week*, vol. 15, no. 7, February 2000.

Italian white goods manufacturer Merloni wanted to reposition its tired old Indesit brand as a company that would appeal to young consumers across Europe. Wolff Olins created a brand concept which could be applied to all communication material including the Web, corporate and technical literature, advertising and promotion. This focuses on Indesit's core values – simple, reliable, strong, involving, value for money rather than cheap. The client wanted consumers to have an emotional response to the products – it had to be about more than just function. 'The new Indesit identity had allowed us to give a new personality to a dormant brand through a bottom-up process, which generated a strong commitment by everyone in the company,' says Luca Manuelli, marketing director. He adds that the identity 'represents a unique example in the white goods industry of empowerment of the brand values. It has the merit of having created a clear, but at the same time flexible, format with the opportunity of capitalising on and sharing good ideas generated by our different markets.'

One of the reasons that Indesit chose to work with Wolff Olins was because it provided strategic and creative support and took into account the limited financial resources available to invest in the brand.

Doug Hamilton, Wolff Olins creative director, says that the repositioning 'is helping the chief executive officer to make fundamental changes to the Merloni business, helping the organisation to change the way it thinks about itself (an Italian domestic appliance manufacturer), and change the way it behaves and communicates.'

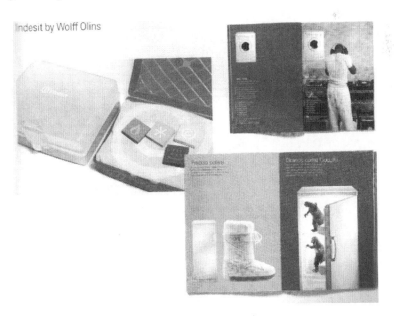

Things

Things includes packaging design, product design, industrial design, shoe design, fashion design, ceramic design, jewellery design, glass design and automotive design.

Designers concerned with 'things' are predominantly designing in a three-dimensional environment. In this category there is a spectrum of professionals from the pure artist craftsmen, ('making' in this sense is often related more to artistic expression and creation) and to the commercially oriented designer who is designing for a market and an end user. There are also designers who work in between these extremes, those who design and produce on a small-batch basis. All these designers are concerned with three dimensional form, line, shape, texture, properties and materials, and depending on their specialism the functional and user qualities of the 'thing'.

One of the most recent issues for 'thing' designers is the impact of new technologies. These can be in relation to: the act of designing, that is, the use of computer aided design and virtual reality; the manufacture, such as rapid prototyping and robotic manufacture; and the materials, for example the advent of smart materials or the use of new textiles.

Figure 6.1   'A flexible, wearable computer developed by Speck'
Source: Speck Product Design

As with the 'messages' category, some design disciplines in this area are merging with professions outside their specific field. This is particularly evident in product design. Product designers are involved with the entire innovation process, interfacing or merging competencies in electrical engineering, mechanical engineering and software development. Such an example might be Speck Product Design in California, whose principal, Craig Janek, not only designed but also developed and sold a flexible wearable computer to Via Inc (Figure 6.1).[24]

Designers of 'things' therefore must be equipped with the skill to understand the requirements of the many stakeholders concerned with the creation and use of the 'thing'. They must be able to extract these requirements, interpret and synthesise them; use problem-solving abilities to isolate the key issues; use knowledge of manufacturing techniques, of materials, of functions and design elements such as shape, texture and colour to produce a 'thing' which solves the design need or problem. They must also use visualisation skills to illustrate and communicate the concept for effective manufacture and user adoption.

Places

This includes interior design, theatre design, retail design, exhibition design and set design. Designers of 'places' work in two- and three-dimensional environments. They are concerned with the interaction between the human and the environment – the scale, shapes, images, colours which all affect the senses. Work in this area goes from the simple shop window to the multi-sensory 'insane' exhibition, such as the winner of the ID Annual Design Review 1996 in the category 'environments'. This was housed in the headquarters of a small German electric company:

> the designers used sophisticated electronic circuitry and light weight aerospace materials, they used glass tubes as part of a helio-organ which played cacophonous music when sunlight – bounced by means of mirrors and prisms, is interrupted. There was a solar timepiece, a large rotating disk where sunlight burns a continuous trail. Each disk lasts a season and, in the end, contains a three-month record of the sun's intensity. Every piece of apparatus has a remarkably logical explanation.

The designers (Hodgetts & Fung) intended each element to provoke visitors into meditating on the idea of solar power – and imagining what the earth might be like without the sun's rays. The jurors described the work to be not the work of contemporary designers but of mad scientists.[25]

This example illustrates well the trend in this area of the design profession towards the increased influence of technology as a medium of expression and therefore designers again are developing technological-based skills or are working in an environment with other disciplines, being less reliant on craft-based making skills.

Designers of 'places' must once again have the skills to understand a comprehensive set of design requirements, to extract them from the 'place' stakeholders, that is, client, customer/user and manufacturing/construction teams. They must use visualisation skills to manipulate colour, texture, shape, light, sound and odour to create the environment, the 'place'. They also require communication skills, both verbal and visual, to explain the concepts to the stakeholder audience.

Designers play a pivotal role in the creation of the material world. For designers working within the realm of places, messages and things, there are common influencing factors – technological change, environmental change and market change. These are not only changing the nature of the profession, but also making demands on it. It has now been recognised by the design profession that design skills are an important part of their services, but in conjunction with a combination of management and business skills. The trend is towards design being part of the multifunctional team armoury to enable them to integrate with scientists, organisationists and psychologists etc. and use their combined knowledge to create the most appropriate and effective design solution.

SPHERES OF DESIGN

The trend toward the designer working in a multifunctional team has in another sense driven them to further specialisation. The design professional and the skills they need are being defined further by the sphere in which designers now operate. For instance, product/industrial designers operate in manufacturing industry but are further specialised into consumer products, industrial products, medical products, equipment and transport design. As competition in this environment increases, so does the demand to add something extra. The design must not only answer the design brief but also translate design values. Designers must therefore be in tune with the product environment and its stakeholders. For instance, Tim Parsley, a leading US-based designer, believes that humour and soulfulness are important in consumer product design (Box 6.5):

> I see a greater understanding of how designers can help connect objects to people as we all get bored of tidy plastic boxes and well thought out but ultimately non expressive objects … It's as if industrial design is growing up and we're learning how to become more sculptural and inspire emotion in people.[26]

In the equipment arena, concern for the user is paramount. It is related to what Edie Adams, manager of hardware ergonomics and usability at Microsoft, calls 'the two poles' of equipment design: 'One is the problem-solving and humanising aspect; the other is bringing beauty to what might otherwise be very staid'. The Midwest Dental Airtouch by IDEO team Chicago, led by John Brassil, demonstrates these kinds of concerns. The aim was to create a friendly design, non-threatening to patients and attractive to dentists, and easy to integrate into their offices.

This immersion into the needs of the customer and sphere of design is further

Box 6.5 Humour in product development
Source: Rexite SpA

Hannibal Tape Dispenser by Julian Brown, crafted of translucent or opaque ABS plastic for the Italian housewares firm Rexite.

Julian Brown studied industrial design and designs for international manufacturers such as Sony, Haworth, Johnson & Johnson, Apple, 3M, Zonotta, Lemnos and Acco.
This product was best of category in the 1998 ID Annual Design Review 1998.

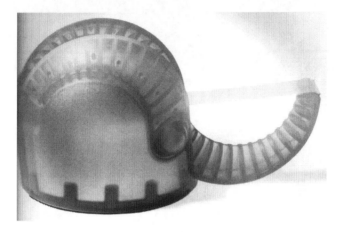

illustrated in the transport arena. Design has always been a core skill for the automotive industry in differentiating both its exterior styling and its interior details. An enormous amount of effort is concentrated on ergonomics and styling through comprehensive user and market testing. In the aircraft industry BA has used user-centred design effectively to achieve commercial success by introducing 'beds in the sky' (Figure 6.2) using Consultancy Design Acumen and BA's project team to design a totally new first-class environment from a user perspective.

Such specialisation has occurred in other industrial sectors; retailing, for instance, uses specialist retail designers for interiors and branding. The leisure industry uses design to create its interior experiences. Companies such as Cadburys, for instance, used Imagination (an international design consultancy) to create a 'fun' chocolate experience (Figure 6.3).

These examples illustrate that the sphere in which the designer operates has become so demanding that the profession is therefore further defined and specialised. The skills and attributes needed by a designer operating in these spheres remain very similar. They are, however, applied in a highly focused and sensitive manner, where the professional designers understand thoroughly the context in which they are operating.

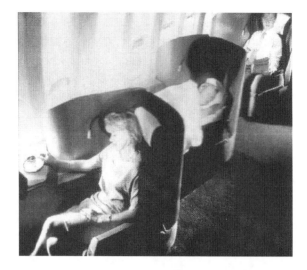

Figure 6.2   'Beds in the sky', British Airways first-class seat
Source: British Airways

Figure 6.3   'Cadabra – A fun chocolate experience'
Source: Imagination Ltd

ATTRIBUTES NEEDED BY A DESIGN PROFESSIONAL

To operate as a design professional in any discipline an individual must have certain attributes/skills. These can be sub-divided into the following two groups:

The act of designing
Manipulation of – colour, texture, shape, sound, space, odour and so on.
Visualisation of concepts using context-specific materials and media.

The process of designing
Research, question, integrate, isolate
Be intuitive, sensitive, holistic, divergent, convergent
Deconstruct, synthesise, reconstruct, innovate, and create
Communicate – verbally, non-verbally, in words, images and forms.

The 1994 Lanre *Professional and Business Guide to Design Services* lists twelve categories in its contents page, which include Architecture, Fine Art and Engineering. All three involve design-related activities, yet traditionally there has been a history of the three being separate from the other design disciplines.[27] Architecture, for instance, has developed as a discrete discipline and profession with a large body of knowledge behind it, and a strong lobbying professional grouping. Engineering has also developed in a similar manner.

Both these professions are taught in most cases in independent faculties within universities. The other design disciplines have to a certain extent failed to develop as a united force either by discipline or as a broad group. The profession of designer cannot be defined simply by the subjects taught or the orientation of the courses, because of the demands of the university sector. It is changing as a discipline, struggling between a vocational skill and an intellectual discipline. Industry is demanding specialist industry-related knowledge, further segmenting the profession. Individual designers are therefore building on their own innate abilities, and developing their own professional portfolio.

THE PROFESSIONAL BODIES AND WHAT THEY DO

Currently design is represented by no single or predominant international professional body. Most countries have their own professional associations which are subject-specific, for example the Interior Decorators and Designers Association based in London. This association was formed by a group of leading interior decorators and designers who are described as a commercially professional, to uphold standards and have views on educational and training requirements in the profession. Other organisations are more general, such as the UK Chartered Society of Designers (CSD). The

CSD has around 7,000 members practising in the areas of product, interior, graphic fashion and textile design as well as design management and education. Members have access to:

- advice on copyright, design protection, contractual and legal matters, an information and library service
- business services such as debt collection, credit checking and professional indemnity insurance at reduced rates
- a range of publications offering guidance on business practice and conditions of engagement
- a programme of training seminars designed to help members update their skills in areas such as marketing, new business, project management and presentations skills, evening talks and social events
- a bi-monthly newsletter

The International Council of Societies of Industrial Design (ICSID) is an umbrella body established in 1957 to advance the discipline of industrial design at the international level. Describing itself as 'a non-profit, non-government organisation, ICSID facilitates co-operation and interaction between its members worldwide, providing a global force through which independent organisations can combine resources and efforts'. ICSID's membership comprises education, professional, corporate organisations and societies. Its activities are focused on communication through conferences, exhibitions, and congresses about design. The ICSID website lists the membership, which indicates the number of associate bodies and professional organisations throughout the world.[28]

Any trip around the Internet will link one to numerous design-related associations; however, there are few professional organisations for accrediting designers as in the other professions, such as the RIBA in architecture, or the BMA in medicine. In the UK the Chartered Society of Designers does have a Royal Charter to offer chartered status to its members but this has rarely achieved the credibility it desires. Very little merit is awarded to a chartered designer. Designers can practise whether they are chartered or not, and losing such status is rarely detrimental to the individual designer. A chartered designer has little more professional status than an unchartered designer.

There has been debate over the value of the professional bodies; indeed in 1997 Liz Farrely, design journalist, reporting on the careers of 1989 design graduates believed indications were that 'through the recession design continued to grow and develop, with no thanks to professional bodies or government stepping in to help a profession in crisis, but by the way of people aiming to be creative, to survive and to succeed'.[29] The group on which she reported survived by 'developing new skills: starting a business; learning how to work for someone else; teaching; diversifying; venturing beyond their chosen sphere to reinvent themselves, their strategies were as diverse as their imaginations'.

This underscores yet again the importance of a professional portfolio which designers develop throughout their professional career. An example of the migration of designers into other areas is shown by the development of design management.

THE RISE OF DESIGN MANAGEMENT

The 1980s gave us a number of fashionable ideas claiming to get the UK back on its feet, get innovation straight in our heads, and get more and better products into our eager hands. These ideas included design management. A key part of this strategy was the encouragement to use design, through grants and through the exemplars and evangelising of the Design Council. It was the 1980s that saw the emergence of 'design management': research and prescriptive measures to encourage firms to make use of design as a competitive weapon.

The term itself dates to the 1960s with the establishment of the RSA Design Management Award in 1965 and the publication of Michael Farr's book *Design management* the following year. These developments reflected efforts within the consultancy sector to raise the professional status of design by offering services that addressed a wider range of product development and corporate strategy issues. An increasing concern with systematic design methods, as developed by Bruce Archer and John Chris Jones, was linked to efforts by the profession to distance themselves from the 'romantic hero' model of the designer.

But it was in the 1980s that design management became a political project. The Society of Industrial Artists and Designers' (SIAD) Design Management Group was formed in 1981, and the London Business School championed the subject academically through its MBA programme and a series of seminars that were published by the Design Council.[30] Design management was soon embraced by design education, and courses were established within design faculties at DeMontfort, Middlesex, Staffordshire and other universities, together with the Royal College of Art. Design management symbolised the hegemony of business management in the new political economy of education.

Design management had a number of key objectives:

- Through research it sought to demonstrate the commercial value of investment in design to industry and commerce.[31, 32] The recently restructured Design Council took on the commissioning of such research as its main mission.
- Management practices and strategies were identified in exemplar companies from which approaches to policy development in corporate design management were elaborated.[33, 34]
- New means of discussing and disseminating the design management message were developed, including the Design Management Institute, *Design Management Journal* in 1989, *Co-design journal* in 1994, the European Academy of Design in 1995, the *Design Journal* in 1998.

- Through new course development at undergraduate and postgraduate levels to educate students in the skills, knowledge and understanding relevant to design management.

However, today, design management is in need of far more critical reflection on its purpose and direction. The term could be seen as unhelpful and a catch-all for a number of very distinctive and separate practices and issues. In design education it is vital to empower students to be proactive in business and culture, but design management, as it has defined itself in a number of institutions, does not constitute a body of knowledge or set of critical aspirations that makes this possible.

Various 'design managements' are revealed when you examine what 'design managers' actually do, suggesting the need for discrete areas of research, education, training and professional recognition. As Nick Hornby observed in his novel *High Fidelity*, Bill Wyman and Keith Richards both play the guitar, but you wouldn't say that they do the same job.

The following case studies illustrate how designers develop unique skills, which could be classified as Design Management.

Case study 1: Alison Fitch, Reebok UK (1997)[35]

Background

Alison trained as a fashion and textile designer with a BA (Hons) degree from Manchester Metropolitan University, UK, between 1987 and 1990. As a graduate, her first job was with a fashion and textile importer. Although she began work here purely as a designer, over the four years she was with the company she was promoted to a position where she took on many more responsibilities, including design, sourcing and procurement, and manufacturing management roles. Before leaving to join the team at Reebok, Alison found herself in sole charge of certain accounts and managing the entire design process from initial concept stages through to manufacture and production. It was during these years that she first learnt about the fashion design industry as a business, learnt to cope with people – both customers and suppliers – and learnt about project management.

Alison began work for Reebok in 1994, when she was appointed as 'design manager'. She was in fact Reebok's first design manager, and the role was crerated as a result of restructuring. Previously such concerns had been the domain of the senior designer and the product development manager; now this work has been divided between the design manager and the sourcing manager. It is the task of the sourcing manager to oversee the production and manufacturing side of the design development: visiting factories currently in operation; establishing possible new sites for production; dealing with the human resource problems related to the factories and their staff and so on, whereas the design manager is entirely concerned with the design and production of the garments themselves.

Although Alison is constantly liaising with the senior brand manager, the decisions remain very much led by the design department, and future directions and briefs are devised by Alison and her team of designers. This is a key role for Alison as design manager.

The role and responsibility

Alison's full job description and title is 'Design Manager of Apparel'. She is in charge of all design work that is carried out in-house in the UK. Alison defined her role and responsibility as follows:

- **Design**
  'My core role as Design Manager is being responsible for the ranges themselves and making design decisions ... Understanding the structure of the range and coordinating it.'
  – Developing a vision for new ranges
  – Working with the designers on trends and predictions
- **Management** – Managing the design and development of the ranges
- **Planning** – Production schedules – managing the design process to production hand over
  – Working with the sourcing manager to procure the samples and apparel production
- **Communication** – Presenting to the sales force
  – Working with marketing to develop the product support in the form of promotion and fashion graphics
  – Working as 'An Ambassador for design throughout the company'
- **Personnel** – Managing a team of eight designers
  – Dealing with human resource issues which occur, such as performance appraisal, job specification, and designer training and development.

Human Resource management has become a major element of her work:

> Since I started it has changed and a great deal of my job was involved in designing my own ranges whereas as the teams have been built up this has shifted and now I am basically in charge of keeping them motivated and ensuring they are doing what is required of them.

Skills required

Alison believes that a main reason why she has taken so well to this particular role has been her own family background and instinctive love of being with and working with people. 'I was brought up in a pub and learnt to mix with an awful lot of different people from a very early age. This has helped a great deal as you have to deal with so many different types of people in this job'. Further she says:

> Instinctively I love to be with people and as a result I don't find it a trauma to manage a design team and this is essential. You cannot ever feel insecure. You are handing design responsibility to a team of people and you need to have the confidence in them in order to make it work.

- **Design skills**: Within this particular role as design manager a background of practical design has proved to be essential – enabling Alison to fully appreciate the task in hand, to plan accordingly, to design and to step in whenever necessary.
- **Design awareness**: Ability to visualise how a design on paper will look three-dimensionally.
- **Interest in design**: A keen interest and aim to keep the ranges forever new and different is essential – especially as the very nature and structure of the ranges would make it easy to lapse into a situation where little is ever altered.
- **Design vision**: It is essential to be both creative and practical in the sense that the design manager must fit the design ideas into a commercial and realistic context.
- **Commercial awareness**: It is imperative to understand design work within its business and market context.
- **Personal skills and attributes**: Just as important as academic and practical design skills are initiative and instinctive personal skills.
- **Patience**: Alison rated this as one of the most important skills for a design manager, as she often finds herself incredibly frustrated when trying to get her own ideas and design suggestions recognised by others in the firm.
- **Persuasion**: Ultimately it is Alison's job to present the design teams' ranges of work to the sales force, and this involves constant persuasion both visually and verbally. The design manager needs both vision and persuasion. In the past the sales division has had a great deal of sway over the designs chosen for production. 'Constantly battling to gain respect from a design aspect' … Alison has spent her years at Reebok trying to convince others that design is far more than arts and crafts and very highly directional and persuasive as a 'selling tool'.
- **Confidence**: in both yourself and the design team: It is essential to personally believe that the work you are presenting is a good proposition: 'There is nothing worse than presenting work that you yourself do not believe in'.
- **Adaptability**: The nature of this job entails a character that 'can wear many different "hats"'. In addition to this Alison has had to adapt her own skills in line with the company; Reebok have a very strong culture, and Alison has been on a number of courses to develop a Reebok approach to such activities as interviews and presentations.
- **Polyphasic**: An essential skill of design management for Alison is to keep a number of balls in the air at any given time – being able to juggle ideas and worries simultaneously and with relative ease.

'You have got to be able to have 20 million things going on in your head at once – you have to be able to juggle'
- **Imagination**: 'Not only in terms of design but also in terms of how to use people to their best advantage'.

What is design management?

For Alison, design management involves

> Range building in a commercial market place; building into ranges; the correct and most appropriate use of colour and interesting fabric; creating the right silhouettes; devising price pointers; creating a range that is commercial enough to appeal to a wide range of customers. The design manager is employed in order to ensure that each range incorporates each of these elements regardless of who actually designed it.'

Case Study 2: Karin Ward, Prudential

Background

After A Levels, Karin received direct entry into a degree course in graphic design at Hornsey. As a graduate, her first job was working for Waltham Forest as an in-house designer; this role taught her to be independent as she was working alone with all design elements. Having decided she needed commercial experience, Karin set up her own business with a college friend. On leaving this business, she went to work for MGM Cinemas as a graphic designer for their video literature and again was in sole charge – 'There were ten people in the States doing what I alone was doing'. From this job she then joined 'Crown House plc' where she implemented a new corporate identity. After one year working there she joined the in-house design team at the Stock Exchange until finally joining Prudential in 1989, completing her transition from designer to manager of design.

When Karin first joined Prudential she worked within a separate design division. She headed this team, turning them into a unit that could service the company professionally, mainly working towards producing the marketing literature in response to the various divisions requirements: 'Competing against all other design agencies and fighting against the prejudice that out-house was better than in-house'.

After a period of intensive restructuring in the company as a whole, the decision was made to outsource all design work; the design team therefore disbanded and Karin took on the role of head of design – a post she has now held for over a year.

Since January of 1996 the company has centralised into what is known as Prudential UK. Since this time the company has created a bank, and for various legal reasons this needs to be a separate operating arm. It is the strategic team which oversees the work of each of these 'arms', and this is where Karin's role as design manager fits. Much of her responsibility lies in the look of Prudential Assurance and that of the Bank.

The role of design manager

Karin's role entails a number of diverse, yet closely linked activities:

- **Design policy definition** – Considering the corporate identity of the company:

> Clearly we have to use the identity correctly but what we are trying to do is to put the Prudential brand into a tangible form. A brand is often not a tangible thing, it is more of an emotive feeling about what you think of a company. What we are trying to do is put this down on paper and into our literature.

   – Coordinating the company sales literature
   – Producing a report and communications strategy.
   Part of Karin's role has been to work with the results of commissioned market research to produce a communications strategy for Prudential, within which she has clearly defined what the brand values are, what it is they are trying to achieve, and a plan.

- **Managing the**   – Selecting a preferred list of design consultancies appropriate for Prudential.
  design process

  –   Ideally we will get agencies together like a family where they know each
            other and work together upon projects. Creating a feeling that they them-
            selves are an extension of Prudential staff.

  – Devising a design brief and implementing a design process:

            In effect what I have done is create a design management process which is
            very much tailored to this company specifically and operates in a company
            which is to some degree resistant to using a central resource – they much
            prefer to do it themselves and it is taking that into consideration.

  – Selecting an appropriate design solution:

            If we were a company only selling a new product it would be a much
            easier proposition. People often hold up BMW as an excellent example of
            brand management – though, with respect to BMW, they are selling cars
            which are a luxury purchase and a desirable purchase and which operate
            in one or two markets – they can sell the smallest to the largest BMW in
            the same way.

  – Overseeing the rolling-out of the new design work – Karin's role ends in the
    actual production of the design work.

- **Communication –**   – Establishing the role of design in the company's success. Karin believes
  selling design   part of her role lies in convincing others within the company of the
                                   importance of design and the 'added values' that it can offer:

            The drive for design comes from the need to service your customer better
            and add value and to differentiate. Because there is nothing else in finan-
            cial services to differentiate as they are all very much of a muchness.

  Karin believes that her main battle is getting her role in design management
  seen as necessary by the other members of staff at Prudential

            It is because it is design management and the company has never had
            design management and to them anything that comes out of this area
            they find hard to understand because they have never had to go through
            this process.

Skills required

- **Design awareness**: 'I do not necessarily think that you need to be a designer but you do need to
  have an appreciation. I think more than anything else it is communication and understanding what
  the company is trying to do with its literature and to ensure that it does that to the best of its
  ability.'
- **Management skills**: 'An ability to instigate and manage process in a sympathetic way.'
- **Persuasion**: 'Working within large organisations and working with people generally who do not have
  a real understanding of design and who actually see it as that unnecessary bit of frippery – you need
  to be able to help them to understand the value of it.'

- **People management**: 'It is about handling people and delivering the message in a way that people do not feel threatened or patronised ... A relationship with people is very important and an appreciation of where they are coming from; the skills are working with the major stakeholders and the ability to bring them all together.'
- **Interpersonal skills**: 'Possibly one of the most necessary elements of the job and this is where I feel designers often fall down. Some good designers find it hard to talk to those who do not understand what it is that they are trying to say – they get both frustrated and irritated and this comes across.'
- **Patience**: 'Because it is a very frustrating job – certainly in my experience. Mainly because my role has not been in place before and there is an awful lot of resistance to "another process". The only way you can prove to them is to do it and this takes patience as the results are not immediate.'
- **Flexible yet prepared to be firm**: 'Must be able to give when it is appropriate to give and be hard line when you need to be hard line, it is being able to identify where you need to put your foot down and where you need to stand back.'
- **An eye for design**: 'I have an assistant working for me who is not a designer but she has a very good eye for design, so I can see how an individual can do the job without being a designer ... although she does not possess practical design skills she has an appreciation of the process and an understanding of where creativity starts and stops and where pragmatism and logic comes in.'
- **Natural ability**: 'There are elements of natural ability which are essential and you cannot create – and these would be an eye for creativity and an eye for design; if you haven't got that, any amount of understanding processes and all that sort of thing is just not going to get anywhere' ... Clearly, when interviewing – you need to see something that gives you that comfort factor that they have an eye for design.'

Definition of design management

For me design is communication and as design manager you are the custodian of the visual communication to the customer ... Basically you are responsible for maintaining the consistency of the communication output to the customer ... It is not just paper based – it is the entire question of how we communicate to our customer.

Case Study 3: Clare Newton, The Chase

Background

Clare began work as a design manager for The Chase in 1996 and she is one of four design managers within the consultancy, having originally studied for a degree in design and technology which involved a quite practical approach to design, focusing on graphic and furniture design, with additional elements such as silversmithing.

As a graduate, Clare began work in a very small publishing company as a Macoperator and type setter. Although she was involved in page layout, it was 'very crafted typesetting, rather than graphic design'. Within this same company she was promoted to the role of studio manager where her role lay in over-seeing the work on the printing press, along with the activities of the designers. She was responsible for the work of four designers, two of whom were juniors, and a copywriter – making sure schedules were devised, and work was completed on time and to a high standard.

From this role she then joined a company called ADS which specialised in telemarketing but which had an artwork division. Clare worked as 'account handler', although she relied on her own skills, as this post was the first of its kind within the company. A far more sound grounding in this role was gained when she began work at U. A. Simmons – an advertising agency. Working within a far more structured design studio she was taught a number of skills, from handling clients effectively to general administration and paperwork. Clare then moved to The Chase as design manager.

A total of 27 people work at The Chase, divided into three teams each comprising one or two senior designers, a creative director, junior designers, a team leader and a design manager (of which there are four in total).

The teams themselves are client-based and work with specific clients; Clare's team is primarily responsible for the Co-op Bank, along with a few very much smaller clients.

The role and responsibility of the design manager

'Everything but design' Clare describes her role as 'the friendly role as well as the financial role ... the management side of the designer/client relationship'.

As a design manager, Clare's main responsibilities include:

- **Planning**   Devising production schedules and also a weekly production management structure
- **Finance**   'A main responsibility lies in the invoicing and the chasing, particularly if an account is in trouble in any way'
- **Communication** With the client, the designers, and also suppliers. A large amount of time as design manager is spent liaising and communicating with the client – 'taking them out to lunch and ensuring everyone is happy with how the design work is progressing and dealing with any problems'.

Skills required

- **Communication**: 'Definitely communication, definitely getting on with people.'
- **Persuasion and sales ability**: To be a successful design manager Clare believes it is essential that you have such abilities – 'You are, in effect, selling the company.'
- **Interpersonal skills**: 'Need someone who can talk on many different levels. Build up relationships – clients need to feel they can approach you, rather than the director when they are not happy.' Intuitive skills are also essential, and Clare believes that, 'You either have these skills or you haven't.' She thought it essential to be a people's person and to fit into the team. 'If the design team disliked you it would prove incredibly hard.'
- **Articulate – 'The strong arm of the designer'**: In many ways Clare believes that the design manager's role is to represent the strong side of the designer who is not afraid to talk about schedules and costings and 'all of the practical and realistic elements that designers are often loath to talk about'.
- **Organisation**: Clare believes this to be imperative in her role as design manager: 'I tend to have a to-do list two pages long which I draw up every night to ensure everything that should be done is.... because when you are working with creatives they have little desire to be organised.'
- **Visual awareness**: Clare believes that more important than practical design skills are visual awareness skills: 'They need to be aware. It is a real asset if the design manager is very aware of design and actually has done it in the past.' However, she also stressed that there is a danger in being too confident in your own design skills: 'It can be difficult if you are actually a designer going into design management because you cannot help but get quite involved and have your own personal opinion on something – and this can cause some anxiety.'
- **Business negotiation skills/commercial awareness**: 'Business ideas are important as it gives you credence and makes people listen to you.'
- **Financial awareness**: Clare stressed the importance of the design manager being financially aware and willing to work with figures.

Definition of design management

Clare's own definition of design management was short and simple: 'Everything but design'. Within The Chase, design management is very concerned with issues of PR and personnel, and constant liaising and communication with the client is a core part of Clare's role as design manager. Whereas the design itself is the concern of the designers, the design manager only tends to intervene to ensure that the designs are realistic in terms of cost and appropriate in terms of the client's aims.

Case Study 4: Peter Hampell, Imagination

Background

Peter holds a degree in modern languages; he spent the first twelve years of his career in advertising. Working first on the account-handling side in the London office of an American advertising agency, then joining Saatchi and Saatchi as an account director working for clients such as Kellogg's, *The Sunday Express*, *The Sunday Telegraph*, Castlemain XXXX, Holsten Pils and Cadburys. From this Peter then joined Imagination as client services director.

Over two years Imagination was repositioned under the broad concept and heading of the 'brand experience'. This was partly because senior management believed that they could no longer operate profitably in the long term within their specialist marketplace and needed to devise a form of positioning which would allow them to compete in a marketplace beyond their core businesses of exhibitions, product launches and conferences.

The main aim of Imagination is to persuade others that they need far more than just advertising strategy. They must form a far wider picture which encompasses a complementary brand experience strategy with a brand strategy: 'encouraging a consistency in corporate voice and corporate communication across all that they do', whereas most view design as a linear and narrow sphere: 'It is all about the entirety of the designed elements; what the salesman says, what colour the van is, what type the van is, the receptionist, what things look like etc. All these elements are essential and this holistic approach is our overriding aim.'

'Moving into the strategic formulation rather than staying at the product end and what that meant was strategic relationships and not project-based execution – devising long-term partnerships.' With this shift in emphasis came a realisation that a different type of project manager was needed:

> People who could not only manage and coordinate a process, handle a client, understand a brief and translate it into something the creative could get excited about and work with and then coordinate a production process – on time and on budget. We needed people who could do all of this plus understand a brand, understand a brand strategy, and understand how to develop a partnership and long-term relationship.

To facilitate this approach they developed three major prongs to the client-facing unit:

- The design director, responsible for the artwork and design work itself – ensuring that the work produced is in line with the client's initial aims and specification.
- The account director, with overall responsibility for the design process and relationship with the client.
- The planning director, responsible for strategic input, marketing context and consumer context, along with information about the brand; basically all marketing and strategic issues,

> Such a role is in fact unique in design work. The aim is to establish the clients' whole operating strategy and operating environment and learn from the client where they should position themselves etc. ... It is quite a creative role in a sense and one which hopefully provides some insight, and helps in defining the crucial elements such as target audience, competitive context, what the brand itself is about and what the product can achieve ... Because they provide direct planning input they are fairly fundamental to the creative product.

Peter's roles and responsibility

Peter is the client services director and as such sees this as design management; his roles and responsibilities were described as follows:

• **Client interface**	'I am responsible for the client relations, co-ordinating the Imagination resource to deliver the design work against the set objectives'. It is Peter and the marketing director who initially meet with the client ... The marketing director sells the company and I explain how the company can deliver such promises in terms of design; describing the processes involved, how they will be handled, who will be responsible for them and their relationship with the consultancy, along with discussing the more practical issues of contracts, numeration deals etc. but most importantly determining with the client their actual design aims and current problem'.
	'Interfacing with the client at a senior level'. As client services director Peter is responsible for building the client–consultancy relationship and identifying the projects – depending upon the client's communication requirements.
• **Client marketing strategy formulation**	'With the client's marketing strategy in mind I then advise them on how this 'design tool box' can help to deliver and meet those marketing objectives.' When dealing with clients, it is Peter's role to assess their situation and to determine what issues are facing them, and how they interact with other agencies.
	However, although this role is carried out externally in terms of contracting clients and making them 'understand what is brand and why brand experience is important.' This also has to be done within the company to all staff: 'my job is internal monitoring and external monitoring and both are equally important.'
• **Management and communication**	With the changes in company structure Peter's current role has become 'clarifying these new roles both internally and externally, clarifying the processes that are involved and making sure they are all doing it properly – implementing processes and skills.'

Skills required

- **Design understanding**: 'Although someone need not be a designer they would still require an intuitive understanding of design and an excitement by creativity ... An interest in creativity and its effect on other people – this is what should excite anybody who works in the creative business ... The skill is in accessing the specialist resources and not necessarily having specialist knowledge. Knowing when to draw people in and how to use people is essential.'
- **Commercial awareness**: 'An interest and understanding of the ways in which business works, marketing strategies are put together, and how brands operate.' An understanding of the general issues and challenges that confront marketers in whatever industry they are working in – on a general but also a specific level: 'You have got to understand the marketing business context within which you are working.'
- **People management**: 'It is a general interest in the psychology aspect: you have got to be interested in people, and not just from a consumer perspective. Your job needs you to be excited by as well as excite a whole lot of different people within the whole process. If this comes across as anything but genuine you are rumbled fairly quickly. You have got to be skilled in motivating people.'
- **Client-facing skills**: 'The client needs to feel absolutely confident that you are in control of a process.'

- **Intuition**: 'You need to be naturally able to spot and draw out the issues when meeting the client; you also must know which questions to ask and when to challenge a client and how to rationalise your ideas and arguments.'
- **Interpersonal skills**: 'You have got to be able to listen, and have a good antenna to recognise sensitivities and politics etc. You cannot bulldoze your way through and need to be very sensitive to certain issues. A great deal of marketing is common sense – the intuitive and clever bits are knowing how to manage people because this is where the satisfaction comes from.'
- **Adaptability and flexibility**: 'There is a need to be infinitely flexible in the creative media you work within because you should be interested in it – a jack of all trades ... You need enough understanding of all of the creative disciplines to be able to talk sensibly and with authority to a client who knows less than you do.'

Peter's own belief is that ideally design managers should be recruited and their abilities built up gradually. He maintained very strongly that a great many of the skills needed involve personality, personal skills and intuition.

Definition of design management

I see design management as more of a client role. I see it more as someone who is trying to co-ordinate what traditionally falls into design areas and different design disciplines from the client's perspective and ideally working very closely with the marketing director, as design should be as much about marketing and communication as it is about physical structure and two-dimensional graphics.

Case study data collection by Kate Shepherd.

While only based on four case studies, we can propose a typology of 'design managers' that define very different and distinctive activities:

- **Creative team manager**

  Based on the Reebok case, the emphasis is on providing design direction and focus, managing a team of designers, and providing an interface with other corporate activities such as marketing and sales. Key skills are design, design leadership and personnel management.

- **Design procurement manager**

  Based on the Prudential case, the emphasis is on managing the relationship with external design consultants, defining corporate design policy and negotiating solutions with consultants. Key skills are design awareness, process management and general management.

- **Account manager**

  Based on The Chase case, this is characterised as 'everything but design', with a focus on financial control and, appropriately, chasing. Key skills are financial management and negotiation.

- **Marketing manager**

  Based on the Imagination case, design is seen as a sub-set of marketing with the emphasis on marketing strategy and project management. Key skills are marketing, strategic management and communications.

To these four categories, others could be added. Recent research by Chamberlain, Roddis and Press views design in terms of 'entrepreneurial mobilisation', as mentioned earlier, which we could characterise as 'process manager'.[36] In this case the designer manages and pieces together all parts of the NPD system.

These four case studies illustrate that the role of 'design manager' is multifaceted, and currently dependent on the individuals' own interpretation of their job. It is perhaps a term applied to them rather than a profession. These individuals are responding to the needs of their business and the contribution they can make to enable design to be used effectively.

This raises the issue of the vision that is propelling design education into the twenty-first century. While the 'romantic hero' narrative that justified design education for much of the twentieth century was in need of reform, is the 'manager' model the only alternative? Is 'design thinking' just a form of 'management thinking'? Self-identity has perhaps never been a strong point of designers and design educators. 'Design management' offered an identity appropriate to the culture of the 1980s, but today's culture, and the problems facing it, is different. The need for sustainable industry, the challenges of new technologies, issues of usability, the desperate need to rebuild our impoverished and ecologically scarred inner cities, to draw understandable maps of the crowded landscape of information – all these issues demand design thinking, design imagination and design in the service of citizens.

The contradictions identified earlier can be tackled if we explore the notion of design citizenship, and embed that within design courses. Existing design management courses, especially at postgraduate level, could then define themselves more in terms of the specialist fields of management that determine design processes – creative team management, design procurement management, and so on.

THE FUTURE OF THE DISCIPLINE AND THE PROFESSION

We are able, it would seem, to categorise the design professional by recognised disciplines; indeed the existing professional bodies do just that. However, to elevate design to professional status equivalent to that of law or medicine is not perhaps appropriate or indeed desired. With professional status often comes the constraints of codes of practice and ethical standards which, although entirely appropriate, often become rigid, difficult to change or question without the protagonist losing membership or professional recognition. Designers should be concerned with codes of practice and ethics, but should not be so restricted that they are unable to question boundaries in a manner which prevents their natural desire to change and innovate. The limitations of not having the baggage of legitimacy owned by other professions are a source of strength for design. This freedom enables the designers to redefine their role rapidly and contribute as the situation demands.

There still remains a need for discrete descriptions of design activity, that is, the design disciplines. These enable both the users of design and designers to place the design skill in context. We will no doubt always have a definition related to graphic design, although with the onset of the virtual and digital it may include digital design. We will always require these descriptors, but designers will use them as labels in their portfolio. They will change as soon as the commercial environment demands. It would therefore seem inappropriate to burden them with the constraints of professional status unless that remains flexible. If one considers designers as those people with the skills to innovate, to solve problems, to bring creativity to a situation, with an element of visualisation ability, and with the ability to deliver a product, then wherever there is a need to do this, designers can turn their hand to it.

We all know that the birth of our current design professions (in the restricted sense, industrial design; product design; graphic design; most modern architecture, i.e. the design of mass housing and commercial buildings, urban design, landscape design etc.) results from the conditions of production specific to the industrial economy. Most of these professions deal with material artefacts, since industrialisation first affected the mass production of objects (although graphic design is mainly concerned with material supports, its object, communication, is immaterial compared to other industrial products). But in the 20th century hardly any human activity and economic sector has escaped industrialisation: agriculture, healthcare, education, culture, leisure, justice, transportation, trade in short all the activities we call 'services'. As a consequence, the traditional professional practices have been considerably challenged.[37]

The situation succinctly described by Findeli leaves the educationalist with a problem. The intellectual aspect of design is still to a large degree ill defined. If designing is an activity that is constantly changing, how can we establish a body of knowledge about something that has no fixed identity? Instead of focusing on the problem of disciplinary boundaries, Professor Kats emphasised the definition of problems for study: 'we are not a discipline, nor should we be one, despite our prototheory, scholarly materials, or university courses. We need to be inclusive, not exclusive: we will need new skills and insights as our current inquiries change.'[38] Such suggestions indicate that as with the profession, design educationalists will need to consider carefully their role in the development of the designer of the future.

The industry into which design graduates enter is indeed changing and the disciplines are frequently segmented, for instance graphic design has been 'niched' into 'identity design, branding, print, packaging and multimedia'. The larger consultancies operate an outsourcing policy, that is, they act as design managers using freelancers or occupational groups to provide the craft skill. This emphasises that designers must develop a portfolio, that allows them to adapt to a flexible and fast-moving employment environment.

There are therefore conflicting definitions and descriptions of the profession of design, with some parties referring to the transferable skills – core competencies of communication and visualisation – others relying on 'craft' skills – graphic design, product design and technology, emphasising fragmentation; the Mac operator and digital designer, the strategic design profession; and the design manager and design researcher emphasising the ethnological role of designers. It is truly a profession in transition. The concluding section argues the case for the proactive practitioner – the designer's role for the future.

THE NEW DESIGNERS

The future is smart. So claim many designers and manufacturers who look forward to a future in which wastebins talk to refrigerators and order groceries automatically when the empty orange juice carton hits the bin. The Pervasive Computing 2000 Conference in the United States, was one recent forum held to discuss common standards for such devices. Throughout the conference, the question of why people will need toasters that talk to microwaves was not tackled. According to Jeffrey Senn, chief technologist for the Maya Design Group, this issue is an irrelevance. 'Creating the raw technology' is the engineers' objective, he said. 'The market will answer the question of whether it is needed or not.'[39]

Left to the market alone, the future will be dumb. Far from being a self-balancing mechanism that defines needs and allocates resources, its track record suggests that 'the market' ignores many real needs, emphasising marketability and profit above user requirements or long term sustainability. As Italian designer Ettore Sottsass says, 'When you talk about the market, it's not so much how good the potatoes are, but how good you are at selling potatoes'.[40] Market-led innovation can be seen as a 'dumbing down' of design and technology – divorcing issues of consumption from production, ignoring ethical considerations, and focusing on the brand experience rather than the real day-to-day user experience. In other words, dumb – and dangerous as well.

Into the twenty-first century it is likely that designers will increasingly consider their role and responsibilities in terms of the apparent contradictions of the market economy, and the positive action they can take to avoid the dumb and dangerous design fostered by globalisation.

One strategy is to work within or for the large corporations, recognising a potential to 'humanise' market mechanisms. This is the view of Tucker Viemeister, vice president of Razorfish Design:

> We as designers are the advocate for the end user – that's social responsibility right there. You don't need to work for the Body Shop or Ben & Jerry's to be socially responsible. We're the only people in the development process who are really that concerned with what people are going to do with our stuff. The whole idea of design is changing. In the future designers are going to be more like psychiatrists: people who help others do what they want rather than tell them what to do'.[41]

Such a role can go beyond just ensuring that issues of user need and experience are embedded in the product development process. There appears to be some scope at least for linking a more radical design vision to the corporate agenda. Designworks is a leading Californian design consultancy, and subsidiary of BMW. According to Greg Brew, its director of transportation design, 'Design is evil. It creates an intense desire in people for new stuff. We're responsible for making products that people feel a great need to own, maybe for just a short period of time. And then they pitch 'em. Let's face it: our standard of living is based on the demise of the planet'.[42] Greg Brew and Marc Tappeiner, director of product design, are proposing a bold new concept to deal with this problem – a desktop personal fabricator that uses a shareware bank of product designs to produce products to individual needs, thereby minimising packaging and waste.

Craftmakers can also work in alliance with large corporations to address issues of sustainable design. Anne Chick is one of the UK's leading researchers in the field of sustainable design. She argues that 'design plays a central role in the development of lifestyle models and can therefore be seen as a powerful vehicle for creating sustainable social practices'.[43] She has described the example of Jonas Tortensson, a Swedish craft-based designer, who works with IBM in developing glassware from old cathode-ray tubes. The significance of this example is perhaps more in terms of extending the role of the craftmaker, engaging them with the 'corporate economy' and encouraging sustainable lifestyle models, rather than the bottom line contribution to recycling.

Historically, the failure of the market to deliver those services we now take for granted – in education, healthcare and social welfare – has been overcome by the interventions of government, driven by a progressive social agenda. In the UK and other European nations, government has also seen a role for itself in terms of design. One recent development in the UK has been the Design Against Crime programme, initiated by the Home Office and Department of Trade and Industry through the Design Council.[44] This aims to influence those involved in the development of new products to design in crime-resistant features before products are launched on the market.

Design Against Crime should be viewed in the context of the UK Labour government's commitment to modernise the economy, institutions and image of the UK driven by a vision of a creative, knowledge-based economy. Design policy, co-ordinated through the Design Council, plays a critical role in this. According to the Design Council's chief executive, 'Design has, it appears, been suffused as far as the very top of the new government'.[45] Recent initiatives have included developing and implementing design management policies for key government departments. Design Against Crime represents a significant step, in that it shifts design policy from its former emphasis on issues of industrial competitiveness to a critical area of social policy. This suggests a further strategy for designers – to take initiatives in influencing design policy at regional, national and European levels, to connect design thinking and activity with social welfare and justice.

But for some designers, artists and cultural activists, such strategies are at best deluded and ineffective. There is a new form of activism emerging, decentralised and network-based, radical and media-focused, anti-corporate and anti-global. Reclaim The Streets, adbusters, campaigns against specific corporations, and G-8 summit demonstrations are 'sowing the seeds of a genuine alternative to corporate rule'.[46] This movement raises profound questions concerning cultural choice, corporate power, civil liberty, civic space and the nature of work. Some designers are already engaged with such activism, and we can expect this to increase in the future.

Some of tomorrow's designers will seek to improve the design experience by working within the corporate sector, or in alliance with it. Some may work with government, while others will take a more radical position. And in so doing, all those women and men will create the history of design in the twenty-first century.

Despite all this seemingly limitless diversity and reconstruction in terms of professional definition, skills and knowledge, there are some common characteristics of the new designer that emerge from all the themes we have considered in this book.

Fundamentally, the new designer (Figure 6.4) is an intelligent maker. Craft skills and knowledge lie at the heart of design practice, whether these skills concern physical materials or virtual spaces. Craft knowledge provides an understanding and appreciation of quality, detail and sensual experience. It also makes things work. Bound up with the craft of design is an approach to creative problem-solving and the exercising of judgement and awareness of relevance. Reflective thinking is also an essential component of craft practice.

Designers are also knowledge workers – they must understand, apply and create knowledge through their practice. Being an active learner throughout one's life is

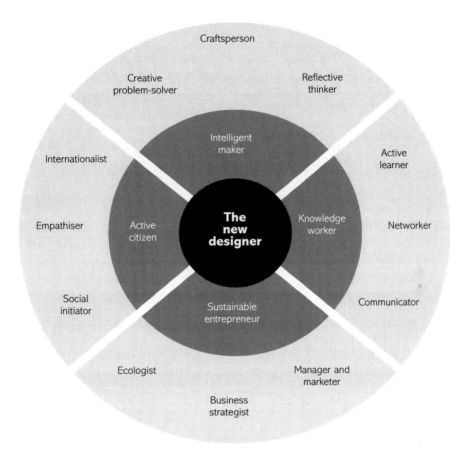

Figure 6.4   The new designer

essential, providing skills in research and reflexivity. As a social process, the creation and application of knowledge requires the designer to be a flexible networker, and an adept communicator.

The issue of sustainability should not be divorced from that of entrepreneurship. Designers are increasingly viewing themselves as sustainable entrepreneurs. Changing patterns of work already determine that we must increasingly view ourselves as 'individual enterprises'. Being a business strategist is thus essential for survival. Understanding business, management and marketing has always been essential in the practice of design, but even more so in today's (and tomorrow's) world of work. All of this is underpinned by an understanding of sustainable business practice.

And finally, the designer is an active citizen. As a principle that links each individual, through a set of rights and responsibilities, to the people in the world around them, citizenship involves empathy – and so too does design. The designer is also a social initiator and an internationalist. Some active citizens salute the flag, while others trash a McDonalds – we do not seek to impose one model of citizenship, but to highlight the need for the principle to be actively embraced.

Oh, and one more thing – above all, designers should be unreasonable. Yes, they should empathise, acknowledge the needs and aspirations of others, and recognise the imperative of sustainability. But after taking all this on board, they need the confidence and vision to make wholly unreasonable demands on a world that has neglected the needs and aspirations of most of its inhabitants. Our future depends on it.

> The reasonable man adapts himself to the world; the unreasonable one persists in trying to adapt the world to himself. Therefore all progress depends on the unreasonable man.
>
> George Bernard Shaw

NOTES

Thanks go the Susan Rolin for her knowledge of US design education, which she contributed to the authors for this chapter.

1. N. Potter (1980), *What is a Designer: things, places, messages*, Reading: Hyphen Press.
2. B. Casey and L. Hatch (1993), *The Chase Creative Consultants*, Manchester: Cheetah Books.
3. Oxford English Dictionary, 1934.
4. N. Potter (1974), *What is a Designer: Things. Places. Messages*, Reading: Hyphen Press.
5. Guy Julier (1993), *The Thames and Hudson Encyclopaedia of 20th Century Design and Designers*, London: Thames and Hudson.
6. J. Myerson (1997), 'Commercial Union', *Design Week*, 21 March, p. 26.
7. Ibid., p. 27.
8. B. McAlone (1987), *British Design Consultancy, Report*, London: The Design Council.
9. S. Potter, R. Roy, C. Capon, M. Bruce, V. Walsh and J. Lewis (1991), *The Benefits and Costs of Investment in Design*, Design Innovation Group, Open University, Milton Keynes.
10. Alain Findeli (1995), 'Design History and Design Studies: Methodological, Epistemological and Pedagogical Inquiry', *Design Issues*, **11** (1), p. 55.
11. Julier, *The Thames and Hudson Encyclopaedia*.
12. Ibid.
13. Association of Independent Colleges of Art and Design, website.
14. AICAD (Association of Independent Colleges of Art and Design), website.
15. A. Pulos (1988), *The American Design Adventure 1940–1975*, Cambridge, MA: p. 165–95.

16. Ibid.
17. Ibid.
18. Rob Roy Kelly (1993–94), 'Postwar *Graphic Design Education in America'*, *Graphic Design Education Association Bulletin*, ed. Kevin Bryne.
19. Walker.
20. M. de Sausmarez (1964), *Basic design: the dynamics of visual form*, London: van Nostrand Reinhold. Studio Vista.
21. T. White (1997), 'Belles lettres', *ID Magazine*, May, p. 82.
22. Ibid.
23. Myerson, Commercial Union.
24. Barry M. Katz, 'Speck Product Design', *ID Magazine*, Jan/Feb., p. 86.
25. Chee Pearlman (ed.) (1996), 'Sun Power: No more Daisy', *ID Annual Design Review*, p. 144.
26. *ID Magazine* (1998), *Annual Design Review*.
27. Lanre (1994), *The Professional and Business Guide to Design Services*, Bromley, Kent: Janvier Publishing.
28. ICSID URL: http://www.icsid.org.
29. L. Farrelly (1997), 'Rising by Degrees', *Design Week*, 31 January, p. 19.
30. P. Gorb (1988), *Design Talks*, London: The Design Council; P. Gorb (1990), *Design Management: papers from the London Business School*, London: Architecture, Design & Technology Press.
31. L.M. Service, S.J. Hart and M.J. Baker (1989), *Profit by design*, Scotland: The Design Council.
32. R. Roy and S. Potter (1993), 'The commercial impacts of investment in design', *Design Studies*, **14** (2), April, 171–95.
33. M. Oakley (1990), *Design Management: a handbook of issues and methods*, Oxford: Blackwell.
34. R. Cooper and M. Press (1995), *The Design Agenda: a guide to successful design management*, Chichester: J Wiley & Sons.
35. These case studies were originally published in R. Cooper and M. Press (1998), 'Heroes and Villains? The contradictory and Diverse Nature of Design Management', in *Managing New Product Innovation*, (eds), B. Jerrard, M. Truman and R. Newport. Acknowledgement is hereby given to Kate Shepard for undertaking the original research (Taylor & Francis, 1999).
36. P. Chamberlain, J. Roddis and M. Press (1998), 'Good vibrations', conference paper, DRS Conference, Birmingham, September.
37. Findeli (1995), 'Design History and Design Studies', p. 55.
38. Cited in V. Margolin (1995), 'Design History or Design Studies Subject Matter and Methods', *Design Issues*, **11** (1) Spring, pp.10 and 15.
39. L. Guernsey (2000), 'A chip in every pot', *New York Times*, 13 April, http://www.nytimes.com/library/tech/00/04/circuits/articles/13need.html, accessed 16 August 2000.

40. C. Pearlman (2001), 'A conversation about the good, the bad, and the ugly', *Wired*, January, p. 181.
41. Cited in M. Press (1995), 'Buddy, can you spare a paradigm?', *co-design Journal*, **1** (3).
42. J. Lewis (2001), 'Design is evil', *Wired*, January, p. 194.
43. A. Chick (2000), 'The environmental agenda: opportunities for craft makers and designers', in K. Bunnell (ed.), *A New Agenda for Creative Enterprise*, Falmouth College of Art, p. 37.
44. R. Erol, M. Press, R. Cooper and M. Thomas (2000), 'codesigning against crime', in *Collaborative Design* (eds) S.A.R. Scrivner, C.D. Chen and A. Woodcock, London: *Springer Verlag*; R. Erol, M. Press, R. Cooper and M. Thomas (2000), 'Design Against Crime': awareness in design education IDATER 2000 (Proceedings of the International Conference on Design and Technology Educational Research and Curriculum Development), eds P.H. Roberts and E.W.L. Norman, Loughborough University, August.
45. A. Summers (2000), 'Redesigning the UK', *Design Management Journal*, **11** (1), 18–21, p. 20.
46. N. Klein (2000), *No Logo*, London: Flamingo, p. xxi.

Glossary

aestheticisation • The process, also referred to as 'fashioning', by which goods and services become 'cultural' products as they are styled and marketed using **signs** to inscribe them with meanings and associations.

aesthetics • Principles of form and beauty, manifested in **styles** and definitions of taste. Often used to refer to the sculptural form of product design, or the 'artistic' qualities of graphic design.

appropriation • Describes how consumers make products meaningful, often creating a new register of meaning to that intended by the producer. An example of appropriation is the use by punks in the 1970s of safety pins as decorative body adornments.

brand experience • A holistic view of **branding** which views every connection between the consumer and the brand in terms of a direct connection with the brand's values – or a brand experience. These experiences reinforce the distinctive **identity** of the brand before, during and after purchase. Significantly, as a distinctive evolution of **branding** in the age of **consumerism**, consumers shift from being recipients of a brand to being brand messengers – **consumption** and interaction with the brand contributes to self-identity and the construction of meaning.

branding • The means of delivering **identity** to a **segmented** market. Following the definition of brand values (both emotive and functional), these are interpreted visually in the product design, graphics, packaging design and advertising strategy – all of which reinforce underlying brand values through **semiotics**.

casual dining • A shift towards eating habits and social interactions enabled by dining, that emphasise informality, social exchange and creative consumption. Has led to significant new trends in tableware and interior design.

consumer culture • A term which stresses the materialism of modern society and the dominance of consumption as a cultural activity.

consumerism • A characteristic of contemporary culture in which **consumption** becomes a source of pleasure and meaning, not just necessity. Key aspects include: commodities signifying meaning to communicate self-identity; cultural commodities are produced on an industrial scale; culture is characterised by many images and styles; consumption as a principle is extended to public services and citizenship.

consumption • In classical economics, consumption refers to the purchase of goods and services. The Frankfurt School of radical social theorists uses the term to describe how producers manipulate the market and dehumanise social life with commodities. In contemporary cultural studies and design studies it refers to the active process by which people create meaning and construct their identities through their use of goods and services.

consumption constellations • Sets of products that are related through their symbolic meaning and through association with a particular **lifestyle**.

corporate communications • The strategic integration of internal and external communications by an organisation to project a shared vision and **identity**, through management communications to employees, **branding**, public and investor relations and corporate advertising.

corporate culture • An important element of **cultural economy**, this describes how organisations define and communicate their meaning both to employees, shareholders and consumers. Driven by a belief that changing 'culture' is a way of improving performance, efficiency and motivation, new management practices include mission statements, training courses and an emphasis on consensus.

corporate image • see identity.

cradle-to-grave approach • Principles adopted in design and new product development that take into account the ecological impact of all stages in the product lifecycle.

creative industries • See **cultural industries**.

cultural capital • The knowledge of how to discriminate and apply **taste**. A concept developed by Pierre Bourdieu, this refers to an education and appreciation in art and culture, the capacity to produce culture and make cultural distinctions.

cultural economy • A term which recognises the importance of **culture** in all aspects of society and in particular the cultural dimension of economic activity. Includes a recognition of **corporate culture**, the increasing **aestheticization** of everyday life, the growing significance of **cultural industries** and the rise of **cultural intermediaries**.

cultural industries • Those industries responsible for the production of cultural goods and services such as film production and distribution, publishing, music production, fashion. In recent years there has been a marked shift towards integration whereby hardware and software are brought together, as in the case of Sony.

cultural intermediaries • A term derived from Bourdieu referring to those professionals involved in producing and promoting symbolic goods and services. They are found largely in the design, advertising, fashion and media industries.

cultural studies • A multidisciplinary area of inquiry that explores the relationship between social relations, meaning and identity. Part of its focus includes the analysis of popular culture and media.

culture • A wide ranging term with many definitions. A definition relevant for much of our discussion is: distinctive patterns of social life that reflect shared values, meanings and beliefs expressed in preferred material objects, services and activities.

decoding • The process by which the **encoded** symbolism of a designed product is read by the consumer, often leading to interpretations other than their **preferred reading**.

design audit • A method of analysing and deconstructing the delivery of **experience** by design through the identification of design process, policies, objectives and management structures at all levels of the organisation.

design experience model • A conceptual tool (Rhea) that views the entire cycle of **experience** surrounding a product or service.

design management • The implementation of design as a formal activity within an organisation, with a clearly defined relationship to corporate goals, and explicit systems of management, monitoring and resource allocation. Also, an academic discipline which investigates the commercial and organisational context of design.

design studies • A multidisciplinary field concerned with the social, cultural, philosophical investigation of design. A relatively new area of academic inquiry, design studies draws upon approaches from design history and cultural studies. There is also investigative territory shared with **design management**.

distinction • The process by which patterns of consumption reflect and contribute to membership of social groups whether differentiated by class, **sub-culture** or **lifestyle**.

ecodesign • An approach to design that applies the **cradle-to-grave approach** in a committed effort to enhance **sustainability**.

encoding • A term originating from media studies, but with application to design. Describes how design, through form, technology, styling and marketing can symbolically embed a **preferred reading** or interpretation within a product. See decoding.

engagement • A stage in the **design experience model** when consumers first become aware of a design. To succeed the design must make its presence known, attract and hold interest and communicate key attributes.

ethnography • The systematic study of a culture in a way that is inductive (without hypotheses or controls). By viewing an unfiltered stream of behaviour, the researcher aims to define the goals and values behind them. Ethnographic research methods (eg: video observation, contextual inquiry) have proved extremely useful in the **requirements capture process**.

experience • The totality of sensations, perceptions, knowledge and emotions gained through an event or interaction. In design terms, defining a product, service or brand in terms of multi-sensory and/or emotional needs. The term is also used to define packaged 'experience' gifts (eg: one hour helicopter flying or rally driving). In terms of the **design experience model**, it is the stage when a product or service becomes part of life experience.

experience-based design (EBD) • A methodology that reframes design problems in terms of the conditions of use and experience that give rise to a business problem that involves **ethnographic** methods used to understand user experience.

fashion • A term with many meanings, often used to refer to the apparel industry and related areas such as cosmetics, footwear, accessories and furnishings. Also describes the process by which many products today are chosen on the grounds of **style** and **semiotic** meaning. Related to an increasing rate of **product lifecycles** and the **aestheticisation** of consumption.

fashioning • See **aestheticisation**.

feminism • An intellectual and political movement seeking equal rights for women. Interprets economics, politics and culture through the concept of 'patriarchy' – the political and cultural domination of women by men. In the field of design, feminism has led to a reinterpretation of design history including: increasing the status of decorative and domestic arts, and reassessing women's role as 'passive' consumers.

focus groups • A technique of market research, which can also be applied to **usability** testing, in which a small group of consumers discusses a set of questions posed to them, and are encouraged to react to each other's comments.

Fordism • A system of production and consumption based on the mass manufacture and mass consumption of standardised products; a highly regulated system. See **post-Fordism**.

function • Considered as the operational requirements of a design. Design under **modernism** led to the aesthetic principle 'form follows function'. In the **post-modern** age of **experience** it has been suggested that 'form follows emotion'.

habitus • A concept developed by Pierre Bourdieu, referring to a set of classificatory dispositions and principles that mark out the **taste** of one social group from another.

hall tests • A long established market research technique in which consumers are shown a range of competing products and are asked to compare their qualities.

hegemony • A concept of Antonio Gramsci. It refers to the process by which the dominant class exercise power through social and cultural leadership rather than coersion. The boundaries of hegemony shift according to the ability of non-dominant classes to create cultural space of their own. The concept suggests how culture is the terrain for political struggle.

hyperreality • A concept developed by French sociologist Jean Baudrillard. Describes the condition of media culture in which signs take on a life of their own, and we can no longer discern the nature of the reality behind them. Surface appearance and signs are the new reality.

identity • (**corporate identity**) The character and values of an organisation, including its **corporate culture**, as presented through **corporate communications**, products, services, branding, property and behaviour of its staff. The rising importance of identity reflects the significance of emotional values in **consumer culture**.

innovation • Developing new products and services for the marketplace, new means of producing or delivering them, or new procedures and processes that contribute to organisational change. Innovation may follow from research that leads to an invention, a new set of design principles or new definition of market needs. **Incremental innovation** comprises evolutionary, gradual improvements in a design, while **radical innovation** involves a significant change in the product or service concept or design, as is the case following a new technological invention.

knowledge products • Those which impart knowledge or information to the user, thereby facilitating a range of **experiences**.

life context • The culture, ways of living, life practices and other products, services and innovations that exist in a particular **segment** of **consumer culture**, or **lifestyle** group. Understanding the characteristics and processes of life context is considered essential for designing meaningful **experience**, and is often studied using **ethnographic** methods. The first stage in the **design experience model**.

lifecycle analysis (LCA) • Techniques that draw on environmental impact data to analyse the ecological impact of design decisions at all stages of the product lifecycle. See **cradle-to-grave approach**.

lifestyle • The means by which individuals signal their identification with particular sub-cultures in society; shared values or tastes as reflected in consumption patterns; a super-product – a way of organising products and ideas.

material culture • The concern of a field of sociology that explores individual and social practices surrounding material objects, viewing products as social expressions, providing mediation between people, and a means of understanding the social world.

modernisation • The economic, social and tecnological transformations characteristic of capitalism in the nineteenth and early twentieth century – such as mass production.

modernism • The critical response of the arts, culture and politics to modernity, evidenced in art, literature, architecture, cinema and design.

modernity • The transformed character of life under capitalism.

personality • The character of an organisation, product or service as expressed through **identity**, **brand** and product **semiotics**.

post-Fordism • An historical shift from **Fordism**. New economic markets and consumer cultures are created through the application of new information technologies. Production can respond more responsively to changing and fragmented consumer markets.

post-modernism • A loose term to describe a variety of developments in the arts and intellectual culture. A move away from 'grand theory' to the embracing of fragmentation and discontinuity. An emphasis that meaning is subjective. Also refers to a stylistic approach in architecture, design and fashion towards playfulness and eclecticism, such as in the work of the Memphis movement.

preferred reading • The symbolic reading or interpretation that the process of **encoding** directs the consumer. However, the process of **decoding** may lead to other negotiated or oppositional readings.

product lifecycles • A marketing concept which describes the life of a product in the retail market. After its introduction, a product will gain market share, then reach a stage of maturity, after which sales decline as new competitors enter or the product becomes unfashionable. In most markets the rate of product lifecycles are increasing – in other words, the time between introduction and decline is becoming shorter.

psychographics • The use of psychological, sociological and anthropological factors to account for motivation in consumption, and construct market **segmentations**.

requirements capture process • A stage in the new product development process, following the definition of a problem or concept, by which information is methodically gathered and analysed leading to the definition of product or design requirements that provide specific detail to a design brief.

resolution • The final stage of the **design experience model** in which the consumer reflects on their overall **experience** and integrates the product or service into their **life context**.

segmentation • The process of identifying a group of consumers who have particular characteristics in common which determine their particular needs in a market.

semiotic systems • The interactive relationship between object, sign and meaning (or interpretant). This suggests that meaning is not fixed, but is determined by the viewer's own experience of the object. The word 'cat' holds different meanings for a person who has one as a pet, another person whose neighbour's cat has just eaten their budgie, and someone else whose granny has just been eaten by a lion. Meaning is thus subjective.

semiotics • The study of how meaning is interpreted from signs. It is applied especially to popular culture including advertising, photography and product design. Involves the analysis of **semiotic systems**.

sign • A physical image, word, object, message, gesture, etc. that refers to something other than itself. It comprises two parts: the signifier – the physical means enabling communication to take place (eg: the word 'cat') and the signified – the mental concept associated with the signifier (eg: small, soft-furred, carnivorous quadruped).

signification • The process by which **brand experience** leads to the **consumption** of a product or service as a signifier of **distinction**.

style • A dominant aesthetic within which objects and images are designed; the visible manifestation of mass **taste**.

sub-culture • A term used mainly in describing youth cultures and their ability to secure cultural space and distinctive identity.

sustainability • The principle of maintaining an ecological balance in social and economic systems to ensure that activities do not have a deleterious ecological impact.

taste • The application of aesthetic and social discrimination as defined by culture.

Third Age • Following the identification of life stages as a means of market **segmentation**, this refers to consumers aged over 50 who are entering an age of personal fulfilment through retirement on generous pensions, good health and active consumption.

trickle down theory of fashion • The view that fashions spread from the upper classes as status symbols that 'trickle down' to lower classes who aspire to their status. This seemed to work when class structures were stable, but appears to have less influence today.

universal design • An approach to design that aims to maximise the usability, inclusiveness and adaptability of products and services across all age ranges and levels of physical ability.

usability • Functional ease-of-use – the degree to which the **functions** of a product or service can be easily used or accessed by the user.

user experience • A term developed by Donald Norman, which refers to all aspects of a user's interactions with a product – how it is perceived, learned and used. It embraces technical, social and aesthetic concerns.

whole product model • A conceptual view of the whole environment on which design has an effect, integrating **product design**, **brand personality**, **identity** and **experience**.

Index